TURNING
— A —
BLIND EYE

Our Failure to See What Jesus Taught
Prevents Us from Living as He Walked

V O L U M E   1

BLIND EYE PUBLISHING, LLC

DEDICATION

To:
Kelley, my wife, the love of this life and the one to come;
Kristen and Hannah, my daughters who captured my heart;
Gregory, Joshua and Caleb, my sons who make me so proud;
Isabella, Bentley, Jaxon, Zoey, Elijah, Emma, Addi and Aden,
my grandchildren who bring me incredible joy...

For loving me in spite of all the blind eye faults in my own life.

But whoever habitually keeps His word and obeys His precepts [and treasures His message in its entirety], in him the love of God has truly been perfected [it is completed and has reached maturity]. By this we know [for certain] that we are in Him: whoever says he lives in Christ [that is, whoever says he has accepted Him as God and Savior] ought [as a moral obligation] to walk and conduct himself just as He walked and conducted Himself.

– 1 John 2:5-6

TABLE OF CONTENTS

FOREWORD

I DON'T THINK I've ever gone to see a movie twice within the same week of its release except on one occasion in 1999. That spring, I went to see the original *Matrix* movie twice in three days. The movie fascinated me because of all the spiritual principles I observed in the story and how it related to my Christian faith. The biggest principle I witnessed was the hero's pursuit of reality. What is real and what is true? The main character, Neo (played by Keanu Reeves), seeks to discover this truth, even at the risk of personal discomfort. In one famous scene, Agent Smith, the villain, meets with a disgruntled rebel named Cypher who desires to live a comfortable life in the matrix at the expense of his friends and what he knows to be true. He tips off the agents and the tactical police in exchange for a guarantee of personal comfort before communicating several of the more profound lines in movie history as he ate a fake steak. "I know this steak doesn't exist. I know that when I put it in my mouth, the Matrix is telling my brain that it is juicy and delicious. After nine years, you know what I realize? Ignorance is bliss."

Ouch! Unfortunately, this is where many of us live as well. In other words, it's so much easier to stick our heads in the sand and ignore uncomfortable truths than it is to face them, to do the hard work of applying them, and to let them transform our lives. Like the author, I too have lived significant parts of my life *turning a blind eye* to the teachings of Jesus out of ignorance, fear or apathy, always to my detriment. Because I failed to see what Jesus taught, I was not experiencing the life He bought.

All that changed in the summer of 1991 when "my truth" wasn't working anymore and I began to seek "the Truth" from those around me. In one life-changing conversation, a Houston Rockets teammate of mine said to me, "Dave, I've been watching you this entire year, and I think you know *about* Jesus, but I don't think you've ever committed your life to actually following Him."

The statement was absolutely true and stopped me in my tracks. A week later, I was meeting with a pastor friend of his who shared more truth with me. As he left my house that day, he asked me one final thing: "What are you going to do with these truths?"

I made a decision that day to commit myself to knowing and living the truths of Jesus to the best of my ability, and I've never regretted it! One section of Scripture the pastor shared with me that day is found in Luke 6:46-49:

> "*Why do you call Me, 'Lord, Lord,' and do not practice what I tell you? Everyone who comes to Me and listens to My words and obeys them, I will show you whom he is like: he is like a [far-sighted, practical, and sensible] man building a house, who dug deep and laid a foundation on the rock; and when a flood occurred, the torrent burst against that house and yet could not shake it, because it had been securely built and founded on the rock. But the one who has [merely] heard and has not practiced [what I say], is like a [foolish] man who built a house on the ground without any foundation, and the torrent burst against it; and it immediately collapsed, and the ruin of that house was great.*"

This passage was the first passage of Scripture that actually made sense to me. I remember thinking, *Wow, I think I've been building my life on a bunch of sand instead of something that will endure like God's Word.* Truly, I had built my life on my career, athletic ability, what other people thought of me, popularity, fame and fortune…all sand that ended up failing me. These verses, like the ones shared in this book, challenged me not only to hear Jesus' words, but to put them into practice.

Ironically, later that night I was introduced to Greg Feste at his home in Houston, Texas. Greg had given his life to Christ about six weeks earlier, and we lived only a few miles apart. Both of our lives had been radically transformed—Greg from a hard-charging, successful businessman, and me from an arrogant, self-sufficient NBA basketball player—into followers of Christ. We quickly became best friends and met four or five times a week for lunch for the next year to talk about our faith and encourage one another in our pursuit of Jesus and in our callings. At one point, Greg said, "Hey, man, I can't keep taking these three-hour lunches anymore because I actually have a real job, unlike you who only have to practice two hours a day."

Touché. Greg became like a big brother to me. For the last twenty-eight years, we have been in each other's lives for the highest of highs and the lowest of lows; and our passion for Jesus is still front and center. Greg hasn't walked out truth perfectly (and neither have I), but I do believe he has an incredibly important message for all of us. These truths are especially important for our current cultural context and this new generation that is growing increasingly confused and disillusioned. As a society we're not sure what to believe anymore, and so there's no better place to go than to actually read and study the red-letter words of Jesus!

One of the other things I have always appreciated about the Bible is how it doesn't sugarcoat people's lives. It gives it to us straight. It shows the good, the bad and the ugly. Even the great patriarchs of the faith were flawed and didn't live out their faith perfectly. Abraham lied about Sarah, Moses became angry and doubted, David fell into adultery, Elijah was depressed, Paul had a history, Peter denied Jesus, and John Mark deserted his leaders during persecution. But we can definitely glean life-changing truth from each of their stories. As Bill

Gates once famously said, "It's fine to celebrate success, but it is more important to heed the lessons of failure." They both speak powerfully!

Recently, the church I pastor in Austin, Texas, did a sermon series called "Living Life Backwards: How Ecclesiastes Teaches Us to Live in Light of the End." As I studied extensively for this series, I was reminded of one more flawed communicator named Solomon and the incredible truths we can learn from his journey. Solomon speaks from both wisdom and experience, as Greg does in *Turning a Blind Eye*. Greg knows the truth and has experienced both the power of living it and the pain of dismissing it. Solomon is imploring us to listen to what he did right and what he did wrong, but most importantly to listen to what God has to say and then do it. *Turning a Blind Eye* invites us similarly to reflect deeply on what Jesus actually said so we can then live the life He has called us to live.

It is my hope and desire that the truths in this book will be explored and embraced not only by new and seasoned believers but also by seekers and those who have maybe never even considered the claims of Christ as they have the power to radically transform lives! Ignorance, after all, is not bliss.

– Dave Jamerson
Former NBA player and
Leader Pastor, Renovate Church
Austin, Texas

INTRODUCTION

THE THOUGHT of writing a book can be overwhelming, and the task requires an immense amount of time and effort. I never intended to write this book, or any other for that matter, for these reasons as well as countless others. However, God made it clear to me that I needed to stop resisting and do just that so I could have the time and liberty to properly convey this message in hopes of helping my readers.

I am a purveyor of books and enjoy reading fiction, non-fiction, and Christian material in addition to the Bible, which is a daily staple for me. I don't consider myself an author and, in an earlier walk of life, I communicated messages God had put on my heart primarily through speaking. God put *Turning a Blind Eye* on my heart and mind several years ago, and though I did not know it at the time, God was preparing me to deliver this message. It was through my own personal experiences, shortcomings, failures and lessons learned the hard way that I began to take a deep look into my own heart and soul to try to understand why some of the chips in my life fell a certain way. I discovered through listening to the Holy Spirit that, although I could quote Scripture, and preach the Word I was *turning a blind eye* to so many topics Jesus Himself taught in the Bible. Because I failed to see what Jesus taught, I was not completely living like He walked. As a result of my own journey, I have written this book in total brokenness, humility and the fear of God with the sole intent of asking my readers to be open to the fact that, like me, you could be *turning a blind eye* to one or many of the core teachings of Jesus. This is not about me telling you that all or even some of the topics in the following chapters apply to your life, because that's not what God called me to do. My hope is that you, the reader, can see in this book exactly what our Lord said about each topic then determine if you need to make some change in your own life as a result.

Many of the topics covered are taken from teachings found in the Book of Matthew from Chapters 5 through 7. These chapters are widely known as the Sermon on the Mount. Other topics are taken from all four gospel accounts due to the fact that Jesus' teaching encompasses the entire four gospels. The common thread is that they all come straight from the mouth of Jesus and include some of His most crucial teachings as recorded by the authors. Some say His teachings were radical, but I prefer to say they were profound. Some say they were difficult if not impossible to follow, but I choose to say they can be quite easy if we're diligent in trying to follow them. The truth is that if we are depending on our own strength to follow the teachings of Jesus, then we will likely not succeed. Jesus said in Luke 12:12, *"For the Holy Spirit will teach you in that very hour what you ought to say."* If He can teach us what to say, then He can teach us how to live.

My story began on April 29, 1990, which was roughly four months before my thirtieth birthday. That was the day I truly acquired a *saving faith* in Jesus Christ and inherited eternal life. Prior to this miraculous day, I professed to be a Christian and believed I had inherited all the rights that came along with being part of a large denomination and attending church at least twice a year on Easter and Christmas Day. I owned a Bible with my name engraved on it but read it rarely. I attended college at a respectable institution that even had "Christian" as part of its name, but you can rest assured that my lifestyle and actions certainly didn't reflect a faith anyone would recognize. Jesus said in Matthew 15:7-9,

You hypocrites (play-actors, pretenders), rightly did Isaiah

*prophesy of you when he said, "THIS PEOPLE HONORS ME WITH
THEIR LIPS, BUT THEIR HEART IS FAR AWAY FROM ME, BUT IN
VAIN DO THEY WORSHIP ME, FOR THEY TEACH AS DOCTRINES
THE PRECEPTS OF MEN."*

I honored God with my lips but my heart or inner being was far away
from him. Upon graduating, I started a career in the securities bro-
kerage business back home in Houston, Texas. I was married shortly
thereafter to the love of my life, and two of our five children were born
prior to that life-changing day.

As I watched my first two children being born, I marveled each
time the doctor would deliver that baby from my wife's body and then
listen with joy to the high-pitched cries that many newborns make
when thrust from the warmth of the womb. Although I knew of Jesus
and the existence of God, the miraculous births of my children caused
me to privately reflect on the true meaning of life and what role God
played in it. I would think to myself that this child who had just been
born had started off as a very small embryo and turned into this perfect human being in just nine months! At that point in time, I knew if
there was a God that I wasn't Him!

The day I gave my entire life to the Lord has many similarities to
the birth of a child. I too was given a new life, born again this time in
the spirit versus the flesh. I was totally dependent upon God and the
people He put into my life to grow as a new Christian.

I've now been serving the Lord since 1990, which happens to be
half my lifetime as I am writing this book. I have been to the highest
mountaintops and the lowest valleys spiritually, professionally, personally, relationally and physically. There have been many instances
where I wish there could be a "do-over," especially as it relates to some
of my personal friendships and professional relationships. If I'm looking for someone who has *turned a blind eye* to the topics discussed in
this book, I don't need to look any further than in the mirror. I still

even to this day must ask myself what Jesus would do as I go about my day and interact with the world. Some days I'm successful, but there is significant room for growth on others. For those who read this book, my hope is to point out clearly and concisely the *blind eye* we are all capable of turning in our lives. The topics discussed chapter by chapter are by no means exhaustive, but I am confident that what is covered is enough to grab our attention.

As one of those "red-letter guys," I take to heart everything Jesus said in the New Testament, and I have written this book with that mindset. The entire Bible is the inspired Word of God, but I have always placed more of an emphasis on what Jesus taught as recorded in Matthew, Mark, Luke and John. God said it, Jesus repeated it, and we get to hear it. That's why every topic discussed herein is reflective of the Scripture noted at the beginning of each chapter with the intent of trying to view each topic from Jesus' perspective. Definitions are given so we can better understand each topic using today's terminology. Although I am a first-year post-graduate student striving to earn my master's degree in theology, I am neither an expert on the interpretation of Scripture nor a theologian. However, I have studied the Bible in depth for many years and believe that the core concept of each topic and the corresponding Scripture reference is indisputable. The Sermon on the Mount and the specific teachings are as relevant today as they were when Jesus taught them. Neither culture nor the time in history has any bearing on their significance or importance.

Some readers may disagree with my explanation of each topic or the suggestions for how to remove the *blind eye*, and that's okay. Everyone has a right to an opinion. All I ask is that you focus on each *blind eye* topic and ask yourself if it applies to you. If it doesn't, then move on to the next chapter; if it does, stop to reflect and allow the Holy Spirit to show you what you need to change. The first step in any process like this is to determine if it applies to you. If so, the second step is to ask God for forgiveness, which He will happily provide. The final step is to review the suggested solution(s) for removing the *blind eye* and apply it to your life.

Personally, I look at these *blind eye* topics from both an earthly and an eternal perspective, though heavily weighted toward the eternal. The reason is that it relates to my "life review" by God when I enter eternity. All of us will face the same process when we die. Our life and all the words we spoke, thoughts we had and actions we took—good, bad or indifferent—will be revealed. God has already seen the movie, but for us it will be the first showing! As born-again believers, we know that this has nothing to do with our salvation but everything to do with our accountability to God and the spiritual rewards that await us. My concern is two-fold—that I will have to bow my head in disappointment first when I see how differently I could have handled each topic in this book and second when every careless word that I spoke is revealed. Jesus said in Matthew 12:36-37,

> *But I tell you, on the day of judgment people will have to give an accounting for every careless or useless word they speak. For by your words [reflecting your spiritual condition] you will be justified and acquitted of the guilt of sin; and by your words [rejecting Me] you will be condemned and sentenced."*

Thank goodness for God's lovingkindness, forgiveness and mercy because I will certainly need it on that day. Until then, I will strive to do better by acknowledging my shortcomings as they relate to these *blind-eye* issues and working diligently to respond and act as Jesus commanded; and I hope you can do the same.

Turning a blind eye is an idiom describing "ignoring undesirable information."

THE phrase is attributed to an incident in the life of Admiral Horatio Nelson. Nelson was blinded in one eye early in his Royal Navy career. During the Battle of Copenhagen in 1801, the cautious Admiral Sir Hyde Parker, in overall command of the British forces, sent a signal to Nelson's forces ordering them to discontinue the action. Naval orders were transmitted via a system of signal flags at that time. When this order was brought to the more aggressive Nelson's attention, he lifted his telescope up to his *blind eye*, saying, "I have a right to be blind sometimes. I really do not see the signal," and most of his forces continued to press home the attack. The frigates supporting the line-of-battle ships did break off, in one case suffering severe losses in the retreat. Though a misconception exists that the order was to be obeyed at Nelson's discretion, this is contradicted by the fact that it was a general order to all the attacking ships (some of whom did break off), and that later that day Nelson openly stated that he had "fought contrary to orders." Sir Hyde Parker was recalled in disgrace and Nelson appointed Commander-in-Chief of the fleet following the battle. Admiral Nelson became one of the most famous admirals in the British Navy.[1]

The last battle he fought was on October 21, 1805, in the battle of Trafalgar when his ships were outnumbered thirty-one to forty-four against France and Spain. He won the battle in the Atlantic, but unfortunately was shot by a French musketeer and died after it was over.

I think it's important to draw a distinction between a *blind spot* and a *blind eye*. A blind spot describes areas of the road that cannot be seen by the driver while looking forward or through either the rearview or side mirrors. If you're driving in the countryside where there are a lot of hills, you will *not* be able to resolve that blind spot of the hill in front of you and pass a car until you get over it. It's the same in life when it comes to blind spots we can't see in our character or actions. The clear distinction is that a blind spot is when you are *prohibited* from seeing whereas a *blind eye* is when you *choose not* to see.

Someone once said to me that a certain issue in his life was a blind spot. My reaction was, "Do you not know it is there?" When he replied yes, I asked, "So, you can see the issue that's out in front of you?" He again replied in the affirmative, and I returned, "That's not a blind spot. Instead you are *turning a blind eye* to the issue that is affecting your life." In other words, this man was ignoring undesirable information. He was able see the issue in his life but chose not to address it at that time.

Jesus addressed three types of blindness: physical, where you *can't* see; spiritual, where you choose *not* to see; and mental, where you *think* you can't see.

PHYSICAL

As they were leaving Jericho, a large crowd followed Him. And two blind men were sitting by the road, and when they heard that Jesus was passing by, they cried out, "Lord, have mercy on us, Son of David (Messiah)!" The crowd sternly told them to be quiet, but they cried out all the more, "Lord, Son of David (Messiah) have mercy on us!" Jesus stopped and called them, and asked, "What do you want Me to do for you?" They answered Him, "Lord, we want our eyes to be opened." Moved with compassion, Jesus touched their eyes; and immediately they regained their sight and followed Him [as His disciples]. (Matthew 20:29-34)

SPIRITUAL

No one lights a lamp and then puts it in a cellar nor under a basket [hiding the light], but [instead it is put] on the lampstand, so that those who come in may see the light. The eye is the lamp of your body. When your eye is clear [spiritually perceptive, focused on God], your whole body also is full of light [benefiting from God's precepts]. But when it is bad [spiritually blind], your body also is full of darkness [devoid of God's word]. Be careful, therefore, that the light that is in you is not darkness. So if your whole body is illuminated, with no dark part, it will be entirely bright [with light], as when the lamp gives you light with its bright rays. (Luke 11:33-36)

MENTAL

> *Leave them alone; they are blind guides [leading blind follow-
> ers]. If a blind man leads a blind man, both will fall into a pit.*
> (Matthew 15:14)

The Scriptures in the physical blindness reference denote the word *compassion* as a noun that *Oxford Dictionaries* defines as "sympathetic pity
and concern for the sufferings or misfortunes of others."[2] Jesus Himself
felt compassion and took action for the physically blind men He healed
who were immediately able to see. He again used the term *compassion*
in the spiritual blindness reference and gave us an example of how to
take action through this Good Samaritan for all of us who *turn a blind
eye* in everyday life as the priest and Levite did to the man on the road.
The mental blindness references the religious people who think they
can see yet lead others away from the grace that God has to offer.

 We are going to focus on spiritual blindness throughout this book.
God clearly impressed on me that, before I can tell others what He
revealed to me, I must first look deep into my own heart and at my
own actions. As it relates to my shortcomings in *turning a blind eye* to
the things of God, I had to use my life as an example and walk out
the principles in my daily life. Praise and worship played a major role
in opening my heart to the issues important to God in my own life,
and breakthroughs came in a mighty way. The Holy Spirit took me
to Matthew 7:1-5 where Jesus said:

> *Do not judge and criticize and condemn [others unfairly with
> an attitude of self-righteous superiority as though assuming the
> office of a judge], so that you will not be judged [unfairly]. For
> just as you [hypocritically] judge others [when you are sinful
> and unrepentant], so will you be judged; and in accordance with
> your standard of measure [used to pass out judgment],
> judgment will be measured to you. Why do you look at the
> [insignificant] speck that is in your brother's eye, but do not
> notice and acknowledge*

the [egregious] log that is in your own eye? Or how can you say to your brother, "Let me get the speck out of your eye," When there is a log in your own eye? You hypocrite (play-actor, pretender), first get the log out of your own eye, and then you will see clearly to take the speck out of your brother's eye.

I certainly have not achieved perfect spiritual eyesight or anything even close to it in terms of God's standard and the "logs" in my own eyes. I do, however, strive through the power of the Holy Spirit to do the best I can, knowing that God sees my heart and the desire to change so His grace and mercy abounds.

It all starts and ends with Jesus. In Revelation 1:8, Jesus said,

"I am the Alpha and the Omega [the Beginning and the End]," says the Lord God, "Who is [existing forever] and Who was [continually existing in the past] and Who is to come, the Almighty [the Omnipotent, the Ruler of all]."

This is important. Jesus gave us all the roadmap to see clearly, if we choose that path. Everything Jesus said and every action He took came directly from the Father. When we act on what the Lord says, we are doing it unto God our Father. In John 12:49 Jesus said, *"For I have never spoken on My own initiative or authority, but the Father Himself who sent Me has given Me a commandment regarding what to say and what to speak."* In John 5:19, Jesus said,

So Jesus answered them by saying, "I assure you and most solemnly say to you, the Son can do nothing of Himself [of His own accord], unless it is something He sees the Father doing; for whatever things the Father does, the Son [in His turn] also does in the same way."

If Jesus said it, then I want to do my best to follow it.

JOHN 13:13-17 says, *"You call Me Teacher and Lord, and you are right in doing so, for that is who I am. So if I, the Lord and the*

Teacher, washed your feet, you ought to wash one another's feet as well. For I gave you [this as] an example, so that you should do [in turn] as I did to you. I assure you and most solemnly say to you, a slave is not greater than his master, nor is one who is sent greater than the one who sent him. If you know these things, you are blessed [happy and favored by God] if you put them into practice [and faithfully do them]."

Jesus serves as an example to follow in all areas of our life, and there is no better place to focus on what He has taught us than on the teachings He gave in the Sermon on the Mount as well as all four gospel accounts.

In this first volume of *Turning a Blind Eye*, we will explore what God does and says to understand how we all can turn a *blind eye* to many of these important topics. All chapters begin with a red-letter Scripture for each topic followed by the definition of that topic with the exception being chapter one, in order to get a clearer understanding of the subject matter. I will share what God has placed on my heart through my life experiences, then give my thoughts about how to remove that *blind eye* we can all have. I have purposely packed the entire book with Scripture, primarily from the New Testament. My intent is to make God's words the entire premise of this book. My words as the author take a back seat to the Word of God, and the last thing I wanted when I began this project was to write a philosophical book with a good story line. It's what Jesus said that changed my life, so He is the primary focus of *Turning a Blind Eye*.

Our goal after reading this book can be summarized in two words: "Imitate Me." 1 John 2:6 says it very well: "*Whoever says he lives in Christ [that is, whoever says he has accepted Him as God and Savior] ought [as a moral obligation] to walk and conduct himself just as He walked and conducted Himself.*" The apostle Paul encouraged the same in 1 Corinthians 11:1 when he said, "*Imitate me, just as I imitate Christ.*" Let's get started and learn what we must do to accomplish this vital task.

CHAPTER 1

RED LETTERS

But Jesus loudly declared, "The one who believes and trusts in Me does not believe [only] in Me but [also believes] in Him who sent Me. And whoever sees Me sees the One who sent Me. I have come as Light into the world, so that everyone who believes and trusts in Me [as Savior—all those who anchor their hope in Me and rely on the truth of My message] will not continue to live in darkness. If anyone hears My words and does not keep them, I do not judge him; for I did not come to judge and condemn the world [that is, to initiate the final judgment of the world], but to save the world. Whoever rejects Me and refuses to accept My teachings, has one who judges him; the very word that I spoke will judge and condemn him on the last day. For I have never spoken on My own initiative or authority, but the Father Himself who sent Me has given Me a commandment regarding what to say and what to speak. I know that His commandment is eternal life. So the things I speak, I speak [in accordance with His exact instruction,] just as the Father has told Me." (John 12:44-50)

THE TWELVE-step recovery program includes this saying, "If you want to hide a secret from an alcoholic, then put it in the Big Book." The Big Book is the worldwide text used in recovery and an essential tool for staying sober. The reasoning behind that statement is because many alcoholics or addicts simply do not read that book enough. The same is true of Christians and the Bible, and even more so when it comes to the 31,426 words Jesus spoke while on this earth. To put this in perspective, in the version used in this book, the entire New Testament is 184,600 words.[1] The four gospels, which include Matthew, Mark, Luke and John, total 83,680 words. If you eliminate all the duplications accounted for in all 4 gospels, the total is 65,493 words. The words Jesus spoke account for about 48 percent of all the recorded words in the first 4 books of the New Testament.[2] I believe that fact alone should compel us all to dig deeper into the words He spoke.

The entire Word of God was written by humans who were inspired by God but think about this: the words Jesus spoke came to us directly from the Father Himself through His only Son! This book's foundational purpose is to discover and understand exactly what Jesus said, so we can have our eyes opened and *not turn a blind eye* to these critical teachings found in the red-lettered text. Can there be anything more important in life than to know every recorded word that Jesus spoke? Absolutely not. Yet how often do we hear this subject preached from the pulpit? Many pastors today are pressured by leadership to deliver a sermon that is received well by the congregation and, by no fault of their own in many cases, it appears more like a pay-to-play or performance-based exercise. In reality, many sermons could have a greater impact on people's lives by just focusing on the red-lettered words of our Lord. Every topic discussed in this book can be resolved by just looking at what Jesus said about that particular issue. In fact, heeding those words would keep most of us out of trouble and keep us from stumbling, as Jesus said in John 16:1, *"I have told you these things so that you will not stumble or be caught off guard and fall away."* This means that we can find answers to all of life's questions in His Word, and then let the Holy Spirit set in motion how we can follow those words in order to better follow Christ.

So why is it so important for us to focus on the 31,426 words Jesus spoke while on this earth? Its boils down to two words: *hear* and *see*.

Jesus never did anything that He didn't hear or see from God the Father. John 12:49-50 tells us,

> *F or I have never **spoken** on My own initiative or authority, but the Father Himself who sent Me has given Me a commandment regarding what to say and what to **speak**. I know that His commandment is eternal life. So the things I speak, I speak [in accordance with His exact instruction,] just as the Father has told Me.*

We also see this in John 5:19:

> *S o Jesus answered them by saying: "I assure you and most solemnly say to you, the Son can do nothing of Himself [of His own accord], unless it is something He **sees** the Father doing; for whatever things the Father does, the Son [in His turn] also does in the same way."*

I am not a rocket scientist but if something is being seen or spoken from Heaven by the God who created me, then that is really important, right? Yet aside from John 3:16— *"For God so [greatly] loved and dearly prized the world, that He [even] gave His [One and] only begotten Son, so that whoever believes and trusts in Him [as Savior] shall not perish, but have eternal life"*—some Christians can't bring to remembrance the other 31,401 words Jesus spoke. I have heard believers try to quote a verse by saying something like "Jesus said you should not judge anyone," when Matthew 7:1-2, 5 actually says the following:

> *D o not judge and criticize and condemn [others unfairly with an attitude of self-righteous superiority as though assuming the office of a judge], so that you will not be judged [unfairly]. For just as you [hypocritically] judge others [when you are sinful and unrepentant], so will you be judged; and in accordance with your standard of measure [used to pass out judgment], judgment will be measured to you…You hypocrite (play-actor, pretender,) first*

get the log out of your own eye, and then you will see clearly to take the speck out of your brother's eye.

Jesus was not saying we should not judge our brothers but rather that we should first take care of our own shortcomings—which He described as logs—so we can then help another remove the speck in his eye. If we don't, then we will have that same measure of judgment returned to us. Have you considered that a log is much bigger than a speck? It implies that, most of the time, our own shortcomings are much larger than those we're trying to point out in others!

Look at Jesus' words in this light. Every word, parable, deed, action, reaction and declaration Jesus spoke came from God and was given to us to follow exactly as it was communicated. It's very common for many of us to purchase an autobiography of someone's life when we want to get to know that individual from the perspective of a firsthand experience. This is exactly what the red-letter text does for us as it relates to Jesus and His life. With that in mind, we should read and study those 31,426 words Jesus spoke in order to know Him on a deeper and more intimate level so we can do our best to live as He walked.

In my mind, the words of Christ (shown in red lettering in some Bibles) contain all the answers to my life issues and teach me how to become more like Christ. The remaining books in the New Testament (except for Revelation) reflect how others carried out and put into practice His teachings. Matthew and John recorded the actual eyewitness accounts of Jesus' life. Mark was not an eyewitness testimony but rather counted on the testimony of Peter. Luke was not an eyewitness; instead, he relied heavily on the testimony of eyewitnesses and written sources.

The apostle Paul had to rely on these same eyewitnesses when he was accepted in the early church and prior to his martyrdom in AD 64. These men had no choice but to live by what they heard and by what they had seen, then record it for us to learn from in the New

Testament. They didn't have a complete Bible for guidance like we do today.

What if Jesus Himself came down and sat at your kitchen table during your quiet time and spoke these exact words to you alone? Would you value the importance of His words more if He did that? I believe the answer would be yes, but ironically, we ignore that same opportunity through His written Word today. His very words came from God to Jesus to His disciples then to us through the written Bible, as we know it today—yet we seem to make little effort to know what He said. If the Bible were viewed as a sandwich, the Old and New Testaments could represent the two pieces of bread on the outside; but what Jesus said would be the true meat in the middle. Just as an entire sandwich fits together and is eaten to satisfy our physical hunger, the entire Bible, if eaten regularly, will satisfy our spiritual hunger.

Many of us probably remember the bracelets we wore that asked, "What Would Jesus Do?" I wore mine proudly for some time. My problem at the time was that, though I wore the bracelet with the right heart, I never really focused on what Jesus said so I could do what the bracelet asked. If I had done exactly what He said to do in response to the question on that bracelet, I would have saved myself a lot of heartache, broken relationships and hard-knock lessons. I heard my dear friend Shauna pray something one day that stuck in my mind: "Lord, let me learn something before You have to teach me." I can assure you that if I had known every word Jesus spoke and put it into practice, God would have needed to teach me fewer lessons. We should learn and practice the teachings of those 31,426 words that our Lord spoke for many reasons, including avoiding hard lessons, becoming more Christ-like, overcoming strongholds, becoming a more effective witness and being obedient to the Word regardless of the consequences.

As we consider the importance of the words of Christ in this chapter, I want to examine what I believe to be three of the most essential lessons that Jesus gave us in Scripture.

First, He tells us what a true disciple of Christ is: one who believes His doctrine, rests on His sacrifice, imbibes His spirit, and imitates His example. Jesus said in John 8:31-32, So Jesus was saying to the Jews who had believed Him,

> *If you abide in My word [continually obeying My teachings and living in accordance with them, then] you are truly My disciples. And you will know the truth [regarding salvation], and the truth will set you free [from the penalty of sin]."*

Essentially, if we believe what He said, accept His sacrifice on the cross, have the Holy Spirit within us and follow His example, then we are *truly* His disciples—but how does this take place? Jesus made it very simple: *"If you abide in My word."* He didn't say, "the Word," although we do aspire to follow the entire Bible now that it is written; but He specifically said, "My Word." If we abide in *His* Word, then we are not only His true disciples, but also the recipients of a promise! He promises that we shall know the truth, and the truth will set us free. What could be better than knowing the truth and being set free? It's the truth because Jesus said it, and it will set us free by giving us all the answers we need for how to live in this temporal world. If we knew the truth, then none of us would have needed to wear a WWJD bracelet in the first place.

Secondly, He teaches us that following His words reflects our love for Him. John 14:23-24 says the following,

> *Jesus answered, "If anyone [really] loves Me, he will keep My word (teaching); and My Father will love him, and We will come to him and make Our dwelling place with him. One who does not [really] love Me does not keep My words. And the word (teaching) which you hear is not Mine but is the Father's who sent Me."*

Jesus said if we keep His Word that He and the Father will make their abode within us. The word *abode* means "a place in which a person resides, a residence, a dwelling, a habitation or home."³ He reminds us again in this Scripture that these are not His words, but the Father who sent Him. When we get saved, we all receive the Holy Spirit; and when those who love Jesus keep His words, He and the Father come to live within us. The benefit of our obedience due to our love for Christ is that when we are so full of the Holy Spirit that there is no room for anyone or anything else, that enables our light to shine. Just like the early believers were labeled "Christians" in Antioch because of how they acted, our testimony will also affect those around us. That alone would have a big impact on reaching the lost.

Thirdly, following the words of Jesus would enable us to produce more fruit than we could possibly imagine. Jesus said in John 15:7, *"If you remain in Me and My words remain in you [that is, if we are vitally united and My message lives in your heart], ask whatever you wish, and it will be done for you."* Did I read that right? Jesus said that if I abide in Him and His words abide in me that I can ask for whatever I wish, and it shall be done for me? I did read it right, and He meant exactly what He said. If I follow His words, God will give me whatever I ask for so that *He* is glorified. He didn't say He would give us anything we ask for so we could be glorified, but rather so that He could be glorified by the fruit we produce. *Glorify* means "to praise or honor someone or something,"⁴ and the fruit that glorifies God always leads to those who are lost and in need of a Savior. This fruit is not manifested by the world's standards, which include big houses, nice cars, a large net worth, or a position in a company; it is instead eternal in nature as it reaches the lost for Christ. Acts 13:48 gives us a perfect example:

> *When the Gentiles heard this, they began rejoicing and glorifying [praising and giving thanks for] the word of the Lord; and all those who had been appointed (designated, ordained) to eternal life [by God] believed [in Jesus as the Christ and their Savior].*

How do we get unbelievers to glorify God and His Word and get saved? Jesus told us in Matthew 5:16, *"Let your light shine before men in such a way that they may see your good deeds and moral excellence, and [recognize and honor and] glorify your Father who is in heaven."* If we want to reach the lost while we live in this world, which is the most important task in God's eyes, we're going to have to learn and practice what Jesus Himself said. Otherwise, the right light will not shine before men, and the glory of God will not be recognized.

REMOVING THE BLIND EYE

This is a no-brainer in my opinion. We all must first give more attention to what Jesus said, then layer the balance of the Bible on top of it. We should all be committed to doing what Jesus said. The entire New Testament should be seen through the lens of Jesus' eyes since He spoke for God Himself. Once we're able to view it that way, the rest of the Scriptures will come into focus.

I purchased a publication titled, *The Red-Letter Gospel* by Daniel John. It's a NASB version containing all the words of Jesus Christ, and it merges the gospel accounts in a storyline sequence with corresponding references to each account in all four gospels. It's an additional tool along with the Bible itself that enables us to focus solely on what Jesus spoke throughout the gospels. Let me say again that the entire Bible is important to study because both the Old and New Testaments together provide the redemptive process communicated by God. My point is, we must clearly understand and know what Jesus said, because His ways and words are the key to eternal life. Following the red-lettered words of Christ serve as a practical matter that will determine the type of foundation we build, upon which everything else in our lives will rest. This is why Jesus made this abundantly clear in Matthew 7:24-27 when He said the following:

So everyone who hears these words of Mine and acts on them, will be like a wise man [a far-sighted, practical, and sensible man] who built his house on the rock. And the rain fell, and the floods and torrents came, and the winds blew and slammed against that house; yet it did not fall, because it had been founded on the rock. And everyone who hears these words of Mine and does not do them, will be like a foolish (stupid) man who built his house on the sand. And the rain fell, and the floods and torrents came, and the winds blew and slammed against that house; and it fell—and great and complete was its fall.

CHAPTER 2

THE HEART OF MAN

But whatever [word] comes out of the mouth comes from the heart, and this is what defiles and dishonors the man. For out of the heart come evil thoughts and plans, murders, adulteries, sexual immoralities, thefts, false testimonies, slanders (verbal abuse, irreverent speech, blaspheming). These are the things which defile and dishonor the man; but eating with [ceremonially] unwashed hands does not defile the man. (Matthew 15:18-20)

HEART

Greek: from *kardia*—the heart; mind, character, inner self, will, intention, center

Cambridge English: the center of a person's emotions, or the general character of someone

Dictionary.com: the center of the total personality, especially with reference to intuition, feeling, or emotion

Merriam-Webster: one's innermost character, feelings, or inclinations

BEFORE WE discuss what the heart is in spiritual terms, here is a quick recap of the body, soul and spirit.

The *body* is the material part of our existence where we use our five senses to experience everything in the physical world. Equally important, it is the temporary dwelling place for our soul and spirit. The word *body* comes from the Greek word *soma*, which means "the corporeal or physical aspect of a human being."[1] Once physical death occurs, the body is rendered useless and returns to dust. Genesis 3:19 says we were actually made out of dust: "*By the sweat of your face you will eat bread until you return to the ground, for from it you were taken; For you are dust, and to dust you shall return.*" If you have ever seen a cremated body, you understand the absolute truth in this Scripture.

The *soul* is part of our immaterial existence, which, unlike the body, cannot be seen. The word *soul* comes from the Greek word, *psuche*, which means "breath or breathing being."[2] In other words, the soul is the "whole" of a person that experiences physical life. The soul is made up of the mind, will and emotions. The mind allows us to reason, the will to make decisions and emotions to feel. The soul is the part of every human being that lasts eternally after the body experiences death. The Westminster Confession says, "The bodies of men, after death, return to dust, and see corruption: but their souls, which never die nor sleep, having immortal substance, immediately return to God, who gave them."[3]

The *spirit* is the inner part of all human beings that God designed for the purpose of communicating and fellowshipping with Him. *Spirit* comes from the Greek word *pneuma*, which means "air, wind or breath."[4] Salvation of the soul allows our spirit to live with God eternally.

Body, soul and spirit explains our material and immaterial makeup as individuals. But what about the heart? The word *heart* is mentioned 725 times in the Old Testament and 105 times in the New Testament.[5] It must be important due to the sheer number of times it's mentioned. The heart is the core of a human being, and its condition determines the way we live on this earth and ultimately how we receive eternal life. John 2:25 says, "*And He did not need anyone to testify concerning man [and human nature], for He Himself knew what was in man [in their hearts—in the very core of their being].*"

That's what is implied when we say, "We need to get to the heart of the matter." Jesus knew what was in the heart of man. We all understand that we require a physical heart in our bodies in order to pump our blood and generate air to survive. If our heart fails, then we are physically dead. The spiritual heart is very similar and, although you can't see it, it must be healthy or a person can die spiritually. Your physical heart's condition is determined by many factors, but none are more important than what you feed it. If you eat foods that damage the heart, you will likely have symptoms to tell you something is wrong. If you ignore those symptoms, death is a possibility. The spiritual heart's condition is also determined by what we feed it. We feed the heart through what we allow the mind component of the soul to see and process. This is exactly what Jesus said in Matthew 6:22-23:

> *The eye is the lamp of the body; so if your eye is clear [spiritually perceptive], your whole body will be full of light [benefiting from God's precepts]. But if your eye is bad [spiritually blind], your whole body will be full of darkness [devoid of God's precepts]. So if the [very] light inside you [your inner self, your heart, your conscience] is darkness, how great and terrible is that darkness!*

For example, if you feed your mind visually with pornography, lust will be ingested and enter your heart. Since sexual gratification is now the motive, you will produce actions to satisfy that need. Your spiritual heart becomes polluted and now your spirit, soul and even your body suffer the consequences. Look what Jesus said in Matthew 5:27-28 about when we allow lust into our life: *"You have heard that it was said, 'YOU SHALL NOT COMMIT ADULTERY'; but I say to you that everyone who [so much as] looks at a woman with lust for her has already committed adultery with her in his heart."* Did you notice He didn't say we commit adultery in our mind, body or spirit? He said we commit adultery in our heart or core being. He then shows us how lust entered our hearts in the first place. Verse 29 says, *"if your eye,"* which is the gateway into the heart. This is why Paul said in Philippians 4:7 that we must guard the heart: "*And the peace of God [that peace which reassures the heart, that peace] which transcends all understanding, [that peace which] stands guard over your hearts and your minds in Christ Jesus [is yours].*" When you feed your physical heart, the food goes into your mouth and is deposited in the stomach. Then nutrients are sent through the bloodstream and pumped directly through the heart and into your entire body. In the case of the spiritual heart, that food is what is seen through the eyes. What your eyes see goes directly into your mind. From the mind, thoughts carry it directly into the spiritual heart where the motive is formed, corresponding actions are manifested, and our behavior is determined.

You only need to go back to the garden of Eden for confirmation that our eyes are the gateway to our hearts. Genesis 3:6 reveals that Eve was deceived by the devil because of what she saw first with her eyes:

> *And when the woman saw that the tree was good for food.* [She saw the tree was good in her mind then immediately developed it into a thought] *and that it was delightful to look at,* [that thought went into her heart to form the motive] *and a tree to be desired in order to make one wise and insightful,* [then out of her heart she manifested the action] *she took some of its fruit and ate it.* [It then modified her behavior] *and she also gave some to her husband with her, and he ate.*

Heart motives seem very important to God. *Motive* is defined as "a reason for doing something."[6] God values heart motives when we commit a certain action. Acts 8:21 says, "*You have no part or share in this matter, because your heart (motive, purpose) is not right before God.*" Proverbs 16:2 says, "*All the ways of a man are clean and innocent in his own eyes [and he may see nothing wrong with his actions], But the* LORD *weighs and examines the motives and intents [of the heart and knows the truth].*"

This spiritual heart is the immaterial organ God is after in our lives. God won't take our heart; we have to give it to Him. How do we give God a healthy spiritual heart? By chasing His first. That's what was said about King David in Acts 13:22:

> *And when He had removed him, He raised up David to be their king: of him He testified and said, "I HAVE FOUND DAVID the son of Jesse, A MAN AFTER MY OWN HEART [conforming to My will and purposes], who will do all My will."*

If our hearts are full of materialism, greed, the love of money, hatred, false doctrine, selfish ambition, unforgiveness and the actions mentioned by Jesus in Matthew 15:19—*"evil thoughts and plans, murders, adulteries, sexual immoralities, thefts, false testimonies, slanders (verbal abuse, irreverent speech, blaspheming),"*—there will be little desire, much less reason, to chase God's. A heart doesn't have to be perfect because that's impossible; but it must be clean, healthy and willing.

Think of the spiritual heart like a gas station. When you pull up to refuel your car, you don't see the enormous containers below the ground that store the gasoline. When you activate the pump, you simply expect it to produce good, clean gas to fill your tank. If the container below the ground has poor quality gasoline, that bad fuel will generate bad effects in your car. The spiritual heart is the same. You can't see where everything is stored, though you know it's there. The heart stores every emotion, desire and motive deep inside your being. If those qualities in your heart are good, then you will pump out goodness from your heart that results in positive behaviors. If the heart stores wickedness, negativity and evil, those elements will come out and result in bad behaviors. So, a good way to test the condition of your spiritual heart is to see what behaviors it's producing.

When you hear someone say, "He has a good heart," the implication is that whatever positive action that person accomplished, the motive was formed in his heart then manifested in his behavior. You can't physically see the motive formed in that person, but you can certainly see the actions that follow. It's the same for a person who claims to love God with all their heart, soul, mind and strength (Mark 12:29-31). If they love God, then their actions or behavior will make that evident. Matthew 12:34 says, *"You brood of vipers, how can you speak good things when you are evil? For the mouth speaks out of that which fills the heart."* It's not only our words that reveal the condition of our spiritual heart but our actions as well.

We all have heard the expression that a person's "heart has become hardened." While the physical heart can become hardened by disease, this saying actually applies to the spiritual heart. We see throughout Scripture examples of what a person with a hardened spiritual heart looks like and the consequences of that condition. In the Old Testament we see several cases where God hardened certain people's hearts, as in Exodus 9:12: *"But the LORD hardened the heart of Pharaoh, and he did not listen or pay attention to them, just as the LORD had told Moses."* Deuteronomy 2:30 tells us, *"But Sihon king of Heshbon was not willing for us to travel through his land; for the LORD your God hardened his spirit and made his heart obstinate, in order to hand him over to you, as he is today."*

In both examples, we see the terrible consequences for Pharaoh and King Sihon. God did not give them a physical heart condition; instead, He influenced the spiritual heart through the eyes, mind and thoughts to get into the spiritual heart and form the motive that determined a response or behavior. In the New Testament, we see both God and man hardening the spiritual heart. The disciples' hearts were hardened. Mark 6:51-52 says the following:

Then He got into the boat with them, and the wind ceased [as if exhausted by its own activity]; and they were completely overwhelmed, because they had not understood [the miracle of] the loaves [how it revealed the power and deity of Jesus]; but [in fact] their heart was hardened [being oblivious and indifferent to His amazing works].

In John 12:40, we see that mankind's heart was hardened by God so they could not see the true Messiah. *"HE HAS BLINDED THEIR EYES AND HE HARDENED THEIR HEART, TO KEEP THEM FROM SEEING WITH THEIR EYES AND UNDERSTANDING WITH THEIR HEART AND BEING CONVERTED; OTHERWISE, I [their God] WOULD HEAL THEM."*

A spiritual heart must be pliable, willing to hear and teachable in order to be soft enough to receive salvation and strive for sanctification. In our world today and especially in the United States, people's spiritual hearts have become not only hard toward God, but hostile toward Him as well—full of what is detailed in 2 Timothy 3:1-5:

*But understand this, that in the last days dangerous times [of great stress and trouble] will come [difficult days that will be hard to bear]. For people will be lovers of self [narcissistic, self-focused], lovers of money [impelled by greed], boastful, arrogant, revilers, disobedient to parents, ungrateful, unholy and profane, [and they will be] unloving [devoid of natural human affection, calloused and inhumane], irreconcilable, malicious gossips, devoid of self-control [intemperate, immoral], brutal, haters of good, traitors, reckless, conceited, lovers of [sensual] pleasure rather than lovers of God, **holding to a form of [outward] godliness (religion), although they have denied its power [for their conduct nullifies their claim of faith]. Avoid such people and keep far away from them.***

Many Christians would be offended by this statement and *turn a blind eye* to this reality. All any of us has to do is follow the news to see this illustrated in our society on a daily basis. It's commonly believed that only murderers, rapists, child molesters and perpetrators of other vile crimes have evil spiritual hearts. That certainly applies to this group of people, but a hardened heart doesn't have to be pure evil as humans define evil. A hardened spiritual heart can be any of the things described in 2 Timothy 3:1-5, so in God's eyes, although certain kinds of evil might have a different level of accountability when a person faces God, it's evil nevertheless according to Scripture unless there is true repentance and a saving faith. We are all born with sin in our hearts and as Psalm 14:3 says, *"They have all turned aside, together they have become corrupt; There is no one who does good, not even one."* That is our untreatable condition during our earthly existence and, as such, it can be put into remission only by renewing our heart through the acceptance of the sacrifice of Jesus Christ on the cross. It is He and He only who can give us a new heart that is trained on God and not on ourselves. Many people who profess Jesus are, upon closer inspection, lovers of money, arrogant, lovers of themselves, profane, lovers of what the world offers and unholy. Many of these people fit the description in verse five to a tee, but due to the hardness of their heart, they will not recognize it, much less repent of it—*"holding to a form of [outward] godliness (religion), although they have denied its power [for their conduct nullifies their claim of faith]."* This type of person can be deceptive because they can mask their true heart in a form of religion that looks good to the outside world. When challenged, they play the judgment card and get on with their charade of living without godly conduct, godly fruit or any acknowledgement of Jesus as the Son of God. Life is all about themselves and the world they have constructed.

Many of us have literal physical spaces we rent to store all the extra stuff we don't need for our homes or just keepsakes we want to hang on to forever. That storeroom typically has belongings that we will always want to keep and use later, but it also has useless items that we will never use. If we don't clean out that storeroom, it will continue to fill up, making it impossible to determine or see what is good and what is useless. The same is true with the spiritual heart. It is a storehouse of sorts for all that we treasure in life, both earthly and eternal. It is a storeroom for everything in our core being. It can have some good elements in it, but it can also have useless or negative elements that we are unwilling to let go of as well. If we don't clean out our spiritual storeroom, it too will begin to fill up so that it becomes harder to determine what is good or what is useless. Though we often have no idea how all that stuff got into our physical storage areas, when it comes to our heart, we do know. It is filled with what we allow our mind to see.

If we want to empty our physical storeroom, we back a pickup truck right to the door and start removing specific items. Our spiritual hearts or storehouses use a different method—the Holy Spirit. We all share our spiritual storeroom with the Holy Spirit, and He is aware of what doesn't belong in there with him. He is always ready to make room for good and productive elements by getting rid of all the bad that we allow to overcrowd our heart space. This is why Ephesians 1:18-19 says the following:

> *And [I pray] that the **eyes of your heart** [the very center and core of your being] **may be enlightened** [flooded with light by the Holy Spirit], so that you will know and cherish the hope [the divine guarantee, the confident expectation] to which He has called you, the riches of His glorious inheritance in the saints (God's people), and [so that you will begin to know] what the immeasurable and unlimited and **surpassing greatness of His** [active, spiritual] **power is in us who believe.***

If the storage tanks under a gas station were leaking due to a puncture, the station must dig up the tanks and either repair or replace them. Sometimes with our spiritual hearts, what we have allowed in has damaged so much of our core being that we need to dig out those things and replace them with good things that glorify God. Paul tells us in 2 Corinthians 1:22 that the Holy Spirit lives in our hearts:

> *It is He who has also put His seal on us [that is, He has appropriated us and certified us as His] and has given us the [Holy] Spirit*

in our hearts as a pledge [like a security deposit to guarantee the fulfillment of His promise of eternal life].

Galatians 4:6 tells us Jesus lives there as well: *And because you [really] are [His] sons, God has sent the Spirit of His Son **into our hearts**, crying out, "Abba! Father!"*

Jesus said the heart stores treasures that reveal what's important to us:

*But store up for yourselves treasures in heaven, where neither moth nor rust destroys, and where thieves do not break in and steal; for where your treasure is, **there your heart [your wishes, your desires; that on which your life centers]** will be also.* (Matthew 6:20-21)

The heart can also be a storehouse for what keeps us from God. If your storehouse is pumping out materialism, greed, lust, bitterness, anger, idolatry, covetousness, foul language and the like, then it's likely producing "bad gasoline." It should be cleaned out or replaced to make more room for the Holy Spirit so it can produce a good product.

Take an unforgiving spirit as an example. Matthew 18:35 says, *"My heavenly Father will also do the same to [every one of] you, if each of you does not forgive his brother from your heart."* Jesus didn't say we must forgive others from our body, soul or spirit, but from the heart. If something changes in the heart, then everything else follows.

REMOVING THE BLIND EYE

The heart can be changed, which is evidenced by our salvation experience. Once people are saved, it's common for them to believe that their heart is then "right"—and in the matter of salvation, that is correct if it's true, saving faith. With that being said, salvation doesn't mean Christians live with pure motives and desires or godly emotions. Just as Paul encouraged us to examine our faith, we should do the same as it relates to the true condition of our heart to see if the Holy Spirit needs to do some house cleaning. That is the first step in removing a possible *blind eye* to the condition of our hearts.

In order to achieve this, we must have a teachable heart. Jesus said in Mark 4:25, *"For whoever has [a teachable heart], to him more [understanding] will be given; and whoever does not have [a yearning for truth], even what he has will be taken away from him."* If your heart is not soft enough to be taught, then it has become hardened; and that leads to a path of potential destruction. Mark 6:51-52 tells us:

> *Then He got into the boat with them, and the wind ceased [as if exhausted by its own activity]; and they were completely overwhelmed, because they had not understood [the miracle of] the loaves [how it revealed the power and deity of Jesus]; but [in fact] their heart was **hardened** [being oblivious and indifferent to His amazing works].*

If our hearts are teachable, they can be cleaned and then trained to manifest godly actions and behavior. How do we know this to be true? Peter discusses folks having their heart "trained" in greed, which is an evil desire. We see this in 2 Peter 2:14, which says, *"They have eyes full of adultery, constantly looking for sin, enticing and luring away unstable souls. Having hearts trained in greed, [they are] children of a curse."*

So, if the heart can be trained for evil, then conversely it can be trained for righteousness. We can train it by opening the eyes to our hearts to be enlightened. If a person is *enlightened*, which is defined as "freed from ignorance and misinformation,"[7] then change can take place. Our goal should be to have a heart that is pleasing to God. Jesus said in Matthew 5:5, *"Blessed [inwardly peaceful, spiritually secure, worthy of respect] are the gentle [the kind-hearted, the sweet-spirited, the self-controlled], for they will inherit the earth."* God loves a kind and sweet-spirited heart—a heart that looks to give instead of to receive. When He returns or we go home to be with the Lord, He doesn't want to see what He mentioned in Luke 21:34-35:

But be on guard, so that your hearts are not weighed down and depressed with the giddiness of debauchery and the nausea of self-indulgence and the worldly worries of life, and then that day **[when the Messiah returns]** *will not come on you suddenly like a trap; for it will come upon all those who live on the face of all the earth.*

Our goal should be a pure heart, as stated in 1 Timothy 1:5: *But the goal of our instruction is love [which springs] from a pure heart and a good conscience and a sincere faith.*

When we change the heart, then we must guard it at all times. Proverbs 4:23 commands us, "*Watch over your heart with all diligence, for from it flow the springs of life.*" Guarding the heart means being careful what we allow into it. This could include movies, video games, TV shows, podcasts and even the people with whom we associate on a daily basis. We can't sit back and expect to maintain a pure, kind and loving heart if we allow the world to creep into it when it's within our power to stop it. If we can keep our spiritual hearts from getting stained from the world's ways to begin with, the less work we have to do to clean them.

CHAPTER 3

THE GREATEST COMMANDMENT

Jesus answered, "The first and most important one is: 'HEAR, O ISRAEL, THE LORD OUR GOD IS ONE LORD; AND YOU SHALL LOVE THE LORD YOUR GOD WITH ALL YOUR HEART, AND WITH ALL YOUR SOUL (life), AND WITH ALL YOUR MIND (thought, understanding), AND WITH ALL YOUR STRENGTH.' This is the second: 'YOU SHALL [unselfishly] LOVE YOUR NEIGHBOR AS YOURSELF.' There is no other commandment greater than these." (Mark 12:29-31)

LOVE

Greek: from *agape*—love, especially charity; the love of God for man and of man for God

Cambridge English: to have a strong affection for someone

Dictionary.com: a profoundly tender, passionate affection for another person

Merriam-Webster: strong affection or liking for someone or something; a passionate affection of one person for another

LOVING GOD

I'T'S TOUGH for us to admit that *we turn a blind eye* to God. In human terms, because of our sinful nature, it's impossible to achieve perfection in this area on this side of Heaven. That being said, we should never stop trying in all areas of our lives. Speaking for myself and being painstakingly honest, I have fallen short due to one word Jesus used three different times in this Scripture: *all*. When used as a noun, *all* means "the whole of one's energy or interest."[1] The Hebrew translation is the same, except it includes "the lot."

The best way for me to relate to the word is to use business as a comparison. When I am putting together a business deal, I am laser focused; I eat, drink and sleep that transaction. It has *all* my attention and dedication for weeks or even months until the deal is closed. I am a hundred percent confident that these ventures received my *all* or *the lot*.

When I compare my commitment to business to my commitment to loving God with *all* my heart, *all* my soul, *all* my mind, and *all* my strength as this Scripture commands, I personally fall short. Does this mean I love God any less than I did the day I got saved? Absolutely not. It simply means that I allowed something more important to me to take the place of God for a period of time instead of giving my all to God. My spiritual heart was damaged. I knew God was present and wanted to fellowship with me, but I chose to focus on other things.

How many men and women do the same thing in their careers? How many entrepreneurs are too busy building wealth instead of giving God their *all*? How many ministers are too busy taking the Kingdom by force and forget the greatest commandment? How about high school or college students who get caught up in campus life? I went through a "wilderness" experience in my own life when other "priorities" prevented me from obeying this Scripture.

It's not uncommon today to hear many folks profess to be Christians. In fact, according to Barna research, seventy-three percent of all Americans claim they are Christian;[2] yet if you let them talk for a while, you see that they produce very little fruit. When I have the opportunity, I ask about their spouse and kids; and they often confess their love for their spouse, brag on how wonderful she is, the precious time they spend together, the talks they have at night and how they would give up everything for their children, if required. These are all good feelings for sure—but such statements are also a perfect segue to this Scripture; I explain that we should have all those same feelings about God. I ask how much time they spend talking to God, bragging about how awesome He is, or reading His Word. I ask if they are willing to give up everything if needed for His purposes. At that point, many remind me of their church heritage and want to move on to another topic. I understand this because that was me at one time in my life. Thank God for His grace; regardless of my unwillingness to give Him *all* my love, He nevertheless loved me. The message people need to hear is that it is okay if we *turned a blind eye to God*. He still loves us. All we need to do is recognize it, then decide to give Him our *all*.

LOVING YOUR NEIGHBOR AS YOURSELF

In my mind, this concept is simple to understand but difficult to always follow. It boils down to what Jesus said in Matthew 7:12, *"So then, in everything treat others the same way you want them to treat you, for this is [the essence of] the Law and the [writings of the] Prophets."* If you love your fellow man as yourself, then you will always treat others the way you would treat yourself.

I have said and done things to people that I would never do to myself. It could be as trivial as when I take the garbage to the street every week and see my neighbor out of the corner of my eye doing the same, but choosing to look straight ahead, hoping that he or she does not acknowledge me because I'm busy. That neighbor may need to be encouraged due to life circumstances or simply recognized and shown that he or she matters. Perhaps that person is not saved, and God has appointed me to open the door through a conversation. Perhaps that person needs prayer. Every time I choose to ignore people and their potentials needs, I am *turning a blind eye.* I would never do that to myself much less would I want someone to do it to me.

I have also made remarks to people that I wish I could take back— words that were certainly not what I would have said to myself if I had been standing in front of a mirror. The moment those wrong words come out of my mouth, I am *turning a blind eye* to what I know is right to say. I have personally made a conscious effort to remember this before I act or speak to anyone. My eyes have been opened, and I am determined to treat others as I would treat myself.

REMOVING THE BLIND EYE

Loving God will all our heart, soul, mind and strength—the world bombards us with so many messages daily that it's easy for us to give God only a portion of ourselves instead of our all. For any of us to give God *all* (the whole of one's energy or interest) of our heart, soul, mind, and strength, we must come to the realization that this world is so temporal and fleeting, and that God our Father desires an affection for Him that is as profoundly tender and passionate as the one He has for us. If we strive to love God with every fiber of our being on earth with the anticipation of being with Him for eternity, much of what we consider important becomes trivial considering this revelation. Giving God our all requires an intentional decision to make it our life's mission during our short stay on earth to know Him and in turn feel His presence during every waking moment.

Psalm 42:1-2 says, "A*s the deer pants [longingly] for the water brooks, So my soul pants [longingly] for You, O God. My soul (my life, my inner self) thirsts for God, for the living God. When will I come and see the face of God?"* We must pant for God the moment we wake up and continue until we fall asleep. If you have ever been thirsty and panting for water, you know exactly what the Psalmist is saying. Does this imply that you go around talking to God out loud, praying nonstop or any other action that likely would cause people to think you're crazy? Of course not. It's more like seeing our daily lives from God's perspective instead of from a personal perspective. If we can do this, then every thought, word, action or reaction would be different; and our daily interactions would be viewed through God's lens instead of our own. That means God is on our hearts and minds all day, which would have a direct impact on our daily lives and those with whom we interact both personally and professionally.

So how do we take the necessary steps in working toward giving God our all? It starts with the one possession we all have, and that is *time*. First, we must purposely, diligently and daily fellowship with God in His Word. Secondly, we must purposely, diligently and daily fellowship with God through unbridled praise and worship. Thirdly, we must purposely, diligently and daily fellowship with God through prayer. This time in the Word followed by worshipping God through music and then ending in prayer will cause the love of God to pour out of our spiritual glands and mold us into being more Christ-like from the inside out. All three steps require effort followed by action, but they all manifest our love for God in a physical way. Let's discuss all three in a bit more detail.

Regarding the Word. Jesus said in John 1:1-2, *"In the beginning [before all-time] was the Word (Christ), and the Word was with God, and the Word was God Himself. He was [continually existing] in the beginning [co-eternally] with God."*

When I was in high school, we always had book assignments to complete. My problem at the time was that I did not like to read. So, I would go down to Interurban Pharmacy, which was the pharmacy of choice for our neighborhood, and purchase something called *Cliff Notes*. These were very short summaries of key points in the book, so by studying the notes, in theory, I could avoid reading the entire book and still submit a paper. Unfortunately for me, it rarely worked. A lot of people today would prefer the CliffsNotes on the Bible. Reading a chapter here and there would provide some benefits, but not the most benefit if your goal is to draw closer to God.

When referring to what Christians need to do with the Word, I use the term "study the Bible." Study includes reading one book at a time then breaking down the historical facts, the audience the writer was addressing, and then a deep dive into study helps like commentaries to gain further knowledge. Sad to say, many believers and most non-believers have no idea that there are 66 books in the Bible—39 in the Old Testament, and 27 in the New Testament. Many don't know that there were 40 authors or that chapters were introduced in AD 1238 and verses in AD 1551.

If our desire is to strive to love God with everything in us, all our heart, how do we do that without knowing every aspect of His written Word? The average American spent *only* 16.8 minutes a day reading for purposes other than work or school in 2017.[3] Even if that 16.8 minutes were used studying the Bible only, that's still not enough! Yet, even with that small amount of time spent reading, many people find time to read popular books recreationally. Let's compare the Bible to just a few of the best-selling books ever published.

Book	Word Count
Old Testament	622,700
New Testament	184,600[4]
The Gospels (Matthew, Mark, Luke and John)	83,680
The Gospels (merged without duplication)	65,493[5]
Jesus' Spoken Words (from all four gospels)*	31,426[6]
The Lord of the Rings series	698,045
Gone with the Wind	418,053
Harry Potter and the Order of the Phoenix	257,154
East of Eden	225,395
Moby Dick	206,052

Harry Potter and the Deathly Hallows.	.198,227
Lord of the Rings—The Fellowship of the Ring	.177,227
The Grapes of Wrath.	.169,481
A Tale of Two Cities	.135,420
The English Patient	. . 82,370
Old Yeller.	.35,968[7]

excluding duplicate words

So, for all of us who read *Old Yeller* when we were kids, that book contains more words than the recorded words of the Savior of the world in the gospels! On a more serious note, I believe this illustration puts into perspective the entire Bible, but certainly the New Testament and more importantly what Jesus himself said. At the end of the day, we all must purposely, diligently and daily fellowship with God in His Word even if it takes time from less important activities in our lives. The problem for most of us is not reading *per se* but rather what and how much time we spend reading other materials—whether the *Wall Street Journal*, a biography, a fiction novel, some best seller or any other written communication. All I know is when we make the Word of God the priority over any professional or recreational reading, something inside of us changes. Hebrews 4:12 says,

> *For the Word of God is living and active and sharper than any two-edged sword and piercing as far as the division of the soul and spirit, of joints and marrow, and able to judge the thoughts and intentions of the heart.*

Being exposed to and dwelling in the living and active Word of God causes DNA changes in the spiritual realm that impact the heart, soul and mind. The more of the Word we ingest, the more we pant for God. He begins to reveal His heart to us and ours to Him. That's what being in love is all about in the natural realm, and it's no different in the spiritual.

If you want to fall more deeply in love with God, camp out for starters on the 31,426 words that Jesus spoke, then sow the entire Word into your heart from all the Scriptures. In addition to the canonical Scriptures, I read other writings that are non-canonical such as the Apocrypha and what is known as *The Lost Books of the Bible*. Jesus was with God in the beginning and came down to earth in human form, and a significant portion of the first four gospels talks about our Heavenly Father. Remember, that's not the place to stop, but rather a place to start. Anyone, regardless of denomination, education, socio-economic status or country of origin, who commits purposely, diligently and daily to the entire Word of God will understand the love affair God wants with each of us on this side of Heaven as well as when our glorified bodies arrive in Heaven.

Secondly, we want to exercise unbridled praise and worship. To use an analogy, if the Word of God is the fuse, then worship is the match. Praise and worship are a vital part of expressing our love to God. Most believers associate praise and worship as part of a Saturday or Sunday church service and, like myself, really enjoy that part of the service. What has worked for me is to include praise and worship in conjunction with the time I spend in the Word. *Unbridled* simply means that I can worship God through music in the privacy of my own home without any reservation, fear or insecurity. In addition to listening to Blind Eye worship music, one of my favorites is Hillsong worship. I will use both as tools to seek God's presence with my heart full of the Word. I put on my headsets and sing some of the lyrics and other times just close my eyes and let the Holy Spirit do His work. The way I see it, since we're going to be praising God all the time in Heaven, we should practice here on earth and experience it now as an expression of love towards God. It's amazing that when we purposely, diligently and daily fellowship with God through praise and worship, our spiritual DNA changes much like it does when we take in the Word of God. I have also discovered that when you praise and worship God long enough when you're alone with Him, you can participate more freely when it comes time to worship with a congregation.

Another great opportunity to express our love of God through music is when we are driving around running errands, commuting to work or taking road trips. Depending on where you live, a commute to work can be ten minutes or two hours. How much music do we listen to? The average person listens to four and a half hours of music a day,[8] and my guess is that has something to do with long commutes. I turn on my favorite satellite worship station or take several CDs in my car and just worship God. Personally, I am not too concerned who sees me singing at the top of my lungs when I really get moved by a song. The practice of unbridled worship will cause you to focus on God so intently that you won't even notice if people are looking at you!

That third step is prayer. We will discuss prayer further in a subsequent chapter, but I believe that prayer is simply talking to God. It is unnecessary to make sure it's done "just right," or that the "correct" words are spoken because God already knows before you pray what you're going to say! Talking to God is not all about asking, although He wants us to do that; praising His goodness and reminding Him how much we love Him are equally important. We all should talk to God like we would our best friend, because He loves each of us as His children and longs for real conversation instead of pious formality.

Just to be clear, it's possible to express your love for God in other ways, including church attendance, fasting, fellowship, Bible studies, service work, evangelism and other forms not mentioned here. But in my experience and humble opinion, the three discussed here are foundational building blocks that enhance all the other forms. Rest assured, if these three are practiced daily, regardless of the amount of time spent, we will see a considerable difference in our heart, soul and mind as it relates to loving our God.

I think it should be no surprise why Jesus included loving your neighbor as yourself in the same text as loving God, nor should it surprise us that it is listed second. First, I believe He included it because loving others is the essence of God. 1 John 4:19 says, *We love, because He first loved us.* Secondly, if we strive to love God with all our heart, soul, mind, and strength then loving our neighbor should not be a problem. Let's consider what the word *neighbor* meant in Jesus' time. Our idea of neighbors is those who literally live next door to us, usually separated by a fence. When Jesus walked the earth, most people lived in villages where community was everything; and everyone was a neighbor. To gain a clearer understanding just how comprehensive the word neighbor is and how Jesus used it, let's look at Luke 10:25-37.

And a certain lawyer [an expert in Mosaic Law] stood up to test Him, saying, "Teacher, what must I do to inherit eternal life?" Jesus said to him, "What is written in the Law? How do you read it?" And he replied, "YOU SHALL LOVE THE LORD YOUR GOD WITH ALL YOUR HEART, AND WITH ALL YOUR SOUL, AND WITH ALL YOUR STRENGTH, AND WITH ALL YOUR MIND; AND YOUR NEIGHBOR AS YOURSELF." Jesus said to him, "You have answered correctly; DO THIS habitually AND YOU WILL LIVE." But he, wishing to justify and vindicate himself, asked Jesus, "And who is my neighbor?" Jesus replied, "A man was going down from Jerusalem to Jericho, and he encountered robbers, who stripped him of his clothes [and belongings], beat him, and went their way [unconcerned], leaving him half dead. Now by coincidence a priest was going down that road, and when he saw him, he passed by on the other side. Likewise a Levite also came down to the place and saw him and passed by on the other side [of the road]. But a Samaritan (foreigner), who was traveling, came upon him; and when he saw him, he was deeply moved with compassion [for him], and went to him and bandaged up his wounds, pouring oil and wine on them [to sooth and disinfect the injuries]; and he put him on his own pack-animal, and brought him to an inn

and took care of him. On the next day he took out two dena-
rii (two days' wages) and gave them to the innkeeper, and said,
'Take care of him; and whatever more you spend, I will repay
you when I return.' Which of these three do you think proved
himself a neighbor to the man who encountered the robbers?" **He**
answered, "The one who showed compassion and mercy to him."
Then Jesus said to him, *"Go and constantly do the same."*

Jesus asked the lawyer, "Which of these three do you think proved himself a neighbor?" (v. 36) He didn't say "*your* neighbor," but used the term to mean anyone; and in this case, the foreigner who helped the guy who was robbed and beaten proved to be his neighbor. Jesus was using *neighbor* interchangeably with fellow man. We're to love *everyone* with the same kind of love we have for God and with a love equal to the love we have for our own selves. Remember, these are the two greatest commandments according to Jesus.

So, how do we love our neighbor (fellow man) as ourselves and remove the *blind eye*? First, stop thinking only of ourselves; instead, think of others and their needs. Second, whatever love, respect, admiration, good will, generosity, courtesies, encouragement, hope, and help we like to receive, give the same to others. Again, if we love God like Jesus commands, then loving our fellow man should be a natural extension of God's love.

CHAPTER 4

MERCY

Blessed [content, sheltered by God's promises] are the merciful, for they will receive mercy. (Matthew 5:7)

MERCY

Greek: from *eleos*—mercy, pity, compassion

Cambridge English: kindness shown toward someone whom you have the right or power to punish

Dictionary.com: compassionate or kindly forbearance shown toward an offender, an enemy, or other person in one's power; compassion, pity, or benevolence

Merriam-Webster: compassion or forbearance shown especially to an offender or to one subject to one's power

MERCY CAN be a tricky concept. We can't fall into a trap that confuses it by associating it in the same context as judging, unforgiveness, retaliation or anger. You could be free of any of the latter and still not offer mercy. I believe the *Cambridge English Dictionary* describes mercy best as "kindness shown toward someone whom you have the right or power to punish."[1] Mercy is not getting something we deserve or unmerited favor. When we practice mercy, we recognize our right to punish or demand something owed to us but choose to reflect kindness and offer compassion instead. Thank goodness, I don't get most of what I really deserve. That's what God's mercy looks like in our own lives.

Mercy falls under one of the sowing versus reaping truths. If people do not show mercy to others, then it's guaranteed as a spiritual law that they will not receive the same mercy when they need it. That's how God determines when He shows mercy to us. Romans 9:16 says, *So then God's choice is not dependent on human will, nor on human effort [the totality of human striving], but on God who shows mercy [to whomever He chooses—it is His sovereign gift].* He shows mercy to whoever He chooses, and that is dependent on the mercy we show others.

Jesus said in Matthew 18:33, *"Should you not have had mercy on your fellow slave [who owed you little by comparison], as I had mercy on you?"* He says the same in Mark 5:19: *Jesus did not let him [come], but [instead] He said to him, "Go home to your family and tell them all the great things that the Lord has done for you, and how He has had mercy on you."*

When we don't give mercy to others, not only will we not receive mercy ourselves, but we could also receive judgment as well. Jesus' half-brother said in James 2:13, *"For judgment will be merciless to one who has shown no mercy; but [to the one who has shown mercy] mercy triumphs [victoriously] over judgment."* God's essence is many things, but mercy seems to stand out among all His awesome qualities. Psalm 100:5 says, *"For the LORD is good; His mercy and lovingkindness are everlasting, His faithfulness [endures] to all generations."* If God's mercies are everlasting, then shouldn't ours last while on this short journey through earth? I believe the answer to that question is a resounding yes.

REMOVING THE BLIND EYE

Since mercy can be extended by anyone, we have to be reminded of it every day. Proverbs 3:3 says, *"Do not let mercy and kindness and truth leave you [instead let these qualities define you]; Bind them [securely] around your neck, Write them on the tablet of your heart."* God told us to bind mercy around our neck so that we won't forget it! Some of us do this very same thing with a key we're prone to lose—we put it on a cord around our neck. We must not overlook this important takeaway. Mercy can be around your neck, but if it's not written in the tablet of your heart, it will never be used! We practice mercy every time we are given the opportunity to give it. Once you begin to exercise mercy on a daily basis, then it will become second nature and will be written on your heart.

CHAPTER 5

ANGER

You have heard that it was said to the men of old, "YOU SHALL NOT MURDER," and "Whoever murders shall be guilty before the court." But I say to you that everyone who continues to be angry with his brother or harbors malice against him shall be guilty before the court; and whoever speaks [contemptuously and insultingly] to his brother, "Raca (You empty-headed idiot)!" shall be guilty before the supreme court (Sanhedrin); and whoever says, "You fool!" shall be in danger of the fiery hell. (Matthew 5:21-22)

ANGER

Greek: from *orgízō*—Be angry, as expressing a fixed anger, enraged

Cambridge English: a strong feeling that makes you want to hurt someone or be unpleasant because of something unfair or unkind that has happened

Dictionary.com: a strong feeling of displeasure and belligerence aroused by a wrong; wrath; ire

Merriam-Webster: a strong feeling of displeasure and usually antagonism

Anger is one of the most common emotions exhibited by people throughout history. It's also one of the deadliest emotions in both the natural and spiritual world. We are all prone to become angry as humans, but the most important factor is what we do with that anger when it arises. Anger, similar to lust, must be stopped at the point of inception. We can't harbor anger and expect God to remain in our presence. Anger in the spiritual sense can be manifested in two ways. One sense is good, and the other is bad. Ephesians 4:26 says, *"Be angry [at sin—at immorality, at injustice, at ungodly behavior], yet do not sin; do not let your anger [cause you shame, nor allow it to] last until the sun goes down."*

Righteous anger is the good sense. It occurs when we are angry because we know people are going to Hell, injustice is taking place, immorality is rampant or ungodly behavior is present. Jesus expressed righteous anger Himself. This type of anger generates a positive effect by calling us to act in an attempt to make right the action that caused this emotion in the first place. This is why Paul said we could *"be"* angry, *"yet do not sin."*

Anger becomes sin when we manifest behavior that is consistent with strong feelings of anger that Jesus said is the same as murder. In other words, we're so angry that we have murdered the object of our anger in our heart. What follows are words that this Scripture points out that compound the issue even further. *Raca* is an Aramaic term that means "an empty-headed idiot and fool means a person lacking in judgment or prudence."[1]

Think of the last time you said or heard another believer call someone an idiot, fool or other ungodly words. It happens all too frequently. What this means to believers is that holding such a feeling in our hearts and expressing it with our words is just as sinful as the physical act of murdering someone. I believe Jesus was warning us to guard against any form of anger as a protection to ourselves. According to Scott A. Bonn,

EXTENSIVE research has shown that certain emotions are highly associated with crime, particularly acts of violence. Some of the primal and instinctual emotions associated with violence are pride, jealousy, lust and resentment. However, and consistent with the GST of crime, contemporary research reveals that the human emotion most likely to lead to violence is anger.[2]

In my opinion, this is why Jesus correlated murder to anger. If a person does not have self-control to prevent that anger, that's what leads to murdering another human being in many cases. Just read or watch the news on television or read it on the Internet, and you will see that truth played out.

It is no different in the spiritual sense. If a believer does not have the self-control to prevent anger, then it becomes sin that is manifested in the heart, then actions are taken through deeds or words, which negatively modifies our behavior. I have said many words in anger that I wish I could take back, but unfortunately that is not possible. The good news is that I never wanted to physically murder anyone when I did become angry in the flesh. The bad news is that I will have to answer to God for those times when I was angry enough in my heart, in the spiritual realm, to cause me to sin with my actions and words. This is why I strive to kill anger at the root, which is when I feel that emotion coming to the surface. Paul said that we should not let the sun go down on our anger, but I have to deal with it much sooner.

REMOVING THE BLIND EYE

Each one of us can relate to this issue of anger. It can be at work, in our homes or against total strangers. Road rage is a perfect example of anger gone wild. While we must recognize that we will feel the emotion of anger, many Christians downplay this display of anger as a natural reaction. However, it's not if it becomes sin. It helps to know where anger comes from and how to overcome it before we let it manifest itself in a sinful way.

It should not surprise anyone to learn that sinful anger comes from the same fallen angel from which all other destructive forces originate. God is the originator of righteous anger, but *Satan* is the originator of sinful anger. He uses it to incite both physical and spiritual violence. Paul warned us in Ephesians 4:27 when he wrote, "*And do not give the devil an opportunity [to lead you into sin by holding a grudge, or nurturing anger, or harboring resentment, or cultivating bitterness].*"

So, what is the first way we can prevent the devil from providing us the opportunity to sin with anger? What conquers all? The answer is one word: love. 1 Corinthians 13:4-7 gives us the answer:

Love endures with patience and serenity, love is kind and thoughtful, and is not jealous or envious; love does not brag and is not proud or arrogant. It is not rude; it is not self-seeking; it is not provoked [nor overly sensitive and easily angered]; it does not take into account a wrong endured. It does not rejoice at injustice but rejoices with the truth [when right and truth prevail]. Love bears all things [regardless of what comes], believes all things [looking for the best in each one], hopes all things [remaining steadfast during difficult times], endures all things [without weakening].

If love guides our heart every day, it's impossible to let the devil get a foothold when it comes to anger.

The second way to prevent giving Satan that opportunity is to get rid of fear. Generally, if we are angry with someone, it's likely due to a fear of something that affects us personally. 1 John 4:18-20 says,

There is no fear in love [dread does not exist]. But perfect (complete, full-grown) love drives out fear, because fear involves [the expectation of divine] punishment, so the one who is afraid [of God's judgment] is not perfected in love [has not grown into a sufficient understanding of God's love]. We love, because He first loved us. If anyone says, "I love God," and hates (works against) his [Christian] brother he is a liar; for the one who does not love his brother whom he has seen, cannot love God whom he has not seen.

Love drives out fear, disarming the devil and preventing us from hating the brother with whom we live so we can love the God with Whom we're going to dwell in eternity.

CHAPTER 6

LUST AND ADULTERY

You have heard that it was said, "YOU SHALL NOT COMMIT ADUL-TERY"; but I say to you that everyone who **[so much as]** *looks at a woman with lust for her has already committed adultery with her in her heart. If your right eye makes you stumble and leads you to sin, tear it out and throw it away* **[that is, remove yourself from the source of temptation];** *for it is better for you to lose one of the parts of your body, than for your whole body to be thrown into hell. If your right hand makes you stumble and leads you to sin, cut it off and throw it away* **[that is, remove yourself from the source of temptation];** *for it is better for you to lose one of the parts of your body than for your whole body to go into hell.* (Matthew 5:27-30)

LUST

Greek: from *porne*—to commit fornication, to act the harlot, (literally) indulge in unlawful lust (of either gender)

Cambridge English: a very strong sexual desire

Dictionary.com: intense sexual desire or appetite; uncontrolled sexual desire

Merriam-Webster: usually intense or unbridled sexual desire

I WILL NEVER forget a sermon I heard when the pastor stated that, "Lust has no face." I was immediately curious to know what he meant and fortunately didn't have to wait long to find out. He pointed out how our society puts so much of an emphasis on physical appearance, for both men and women. He went on to say that lust was an equal opportunity offender where "looks" don't always make a difference. He backed up his position by illustrating the men he personally knew who had beautiful wives in the world's eyes, yet they chose to put their marriage at risk by having sex outside their marriage with another woman. Why? Because lust is a spirit without a face, and we allow it in when we open up our hearts and minds to the very things we know can be fatal to our relationship. When we get too far down that rabbit hole, looks mean very little in most cases.

In this passage of Scripture, Jesus is talking about a man, but the same application can be made for women. Jesus said that if a man looks on a woman to lust for her, he has committed adultery. The key words here are *to lust for her*, which is not the same as *to look at her*. To *lust for* someone is "to have a very strong sexual thought or desire."[1] *To look at* someone is simply "to direct one's gaze toward a person."[2]

It's impossible in today's world not to notice the opposite gender—at work, on a business trip, on the sidewalks of New York City while on vacation or at the neighborhood park. The fact is that men and women are tightly interwoven in society today. The sin for a married person is when that gaze turns into staring then to thoughts of sexual desire or any other action that would violate the marriage relationship. **In other words, when we gratify ourselves mentally with thoughts of sexual pleasure or adoration for another person who is not our spouse is when we get into trouble.**

Sadly, the divorce rate among Christians is roughly the same rate as for the lost world.[3] Speaking from a male perspective, sexual activity or the lack thereof with our spouses does not cause divorce as is commonly believed. It may be a symptom of an unhealthy relationship, but it's not the cause. I recall several occasions when a friend has told me he didn't think his marriage was working and that he was considering a divorce. My next question, which usually shocked my friend, was simply, "What is her name?"

In most cases, a man doesn't leave his wife because his physical needs aren't being met. It's been my experience that such a man—long before he decides to end the marriage—has opened the door to his heart through his eyes by looking upon another woman with the same desire with which he once looked at his wife. Lust takes hold over time, then he gets drawn into the false illusion that "the grass is greener on the other side of the fence." Instead of recognizing the issues in his marriage that need to be addressed—which have very little, if anything, to do with his sex life—he first succumbs to the lust of the eyes, and then leads down a reckless path to the destruction of his marriage. Such a person falls short of Jesus' standard long before the physical act of lust. If you ask any man or woman who has been in such a predicament to pinpoint the precursor to their infidelity, they would likely tell you it all started with the eyes.

Keeping a marriage healthy takes a lot of work, and pornography has become a covenant cancer in this world. Pornography is so rampant, even among believers, that no defense is put up at the first thought. Then, thanks to the Internet, it's just a click away 24/7. Regardless of whether a person is married or single, once the door to pornography is opened up, it's difficult to close; that lustful spirit requires more and more to meet an insatiable appetite.

ACCORDING to *Covenant Eyes,* an Internet accountability software company, roughly 28,000 of their users are watching pornography every second. Their users are also spending around $3,000 on porn every second. For mobile Internet users, 1 out of every 5 mobile searches is for porn. Women aren't excluded from this heavy porn-watching either. Pornhub released information in 2017 that revealed women spend more time watching porn than men according to reports from the anti-porn advocacy group Fight the New Drug. Women were also more likely to search for harder versions of porn than men.[4]

Many people argue that these numbers suggest a natural need for humans to gratify themselves through porn. However, allowing porn as a social norm could have far-reaching consequences.

COVENANT *Eyes* states that 56 percent of divorce cases involved a partner's obsessive interest in porn sites. In addition, 64 percent of Christian men and 15 percent of Christian women report watching porn at least once a month. This is a departure from the teachings Christians adhere to in their worship.[5]

These statistics illustrate that pornography affects females as well as males. Many married couples watch pornography prior to being intimate. Think about it: these couples knowingly and deliberately choose to watch other men and women have sex (which is not making love), which allows fantasies to form that are counterproductive to a healthy marriage. Many a man will judge his wife's performance during intimacy by the woman's actions in the movie. I have heard men say to one another after watching porn either by themselves or with their spouses, "I wish my wife would do that" or "That woman was gorgeous."

And we wonder why marriages fail? If we can ignore the fact that watching porn causes a person to lust after someone other than a spouse, it's even more concerning that a relationship requires pornography to get a couple excited about being with one another sexually in the first place. Something is seriously wrong with such a scenario, but even more so when it involves Christians.

What married man or woman, whether or not a Christian, would ever step foot into a strip joint? Surprisingly, many people do—both Christian and non-Christian—and I was one of those men before I was saved. Believer or not, I can tell you that when I left that place, I had one thing and one thing only on my mind, and that was to satisfy the sexual desire caused by lust. Forget living up to the standard Jesus set, if I had known Him. That was gone the moment I walked from the entrance to the table by the stage.

At the end of the day, whether it's strip clubs, pornography, a lingerie store or even a sex scene in a movie, once you set your eyes on any of it, the spirit of lust will run rampant and the outcome is predictable. As a married man or woman, you have only three methods to satisfy that self-induced spirit of lust. You can have sex with your partner, have sex outside the marriage or satisfy the desire yourself. Only one of those answers is right, and that's to have sex with your partner; but your desire should never be due to any of the outside influences mentioned in this chapter or anything else that is contrary to Scripture. God sees lust and the acts we carry out due to it, even when we think they are done in "private."

Jesus raised the bar for those who are in a covenant relationship through marriage. As a man, if we lust after a woman with our eyes with the intent to commit a sexual act in our heart or inner-being, then it's no different than actually committing the physical act. That's a high bar to set, but the right one as well. If anyone has any doubt that lust is a spirit, ask a married man or woman why they went outside their marriage for a few minutes of physical pleasure that jeopardized not only their long-term relationship but also their entire family. The world labels such an act as a "one-night stand," but in reality, the person succumbed to lust in their heart long before the physical act occurred. Romans 6:12 says, *"Therefore, do not let sin reign in your mortal body so that you obey its lusts and passions."* Unfortunately, many people commit physical adultery then move on to other marriages; but in my experience, they regret that decision as they grow older, realize the effect on their children, and face their ultimate mortality.

Take idolatry as an example. The first manifestation is the spirit of greed, followed by covetousness. It's fair to say that a person doesn't just wake up one day and say, **"Today I will be an idolater."** That person opens the door to the spirit of greed through the eyes first, then idolatry becomes the end result.

Adultery based on Jesus' standard has a similar destructive path. What your eyes see (a woman or a man) goes directly into your mind. From the mind, thoughts (unhealthy desires that create lust) carry it directly into the spiritual heart (inner being) where the motive is formed (sexual desire), and corresponding actions are manifested (fantasies or act), and our behavior is determined (sin). The dots connect, and the outcome is always the same. What we tolerate, we accept. If we as the family of God *turn a blind eye* to this issue and fail to call it out for what it is, then we are destined to reap more broken marriages and families. In the end, we are no different than those in the world we're supposed to reach.

REMOVING THE BLIND EYE

It may be hard to believe, but we all can have victory over lust and avoid falling into adultery. The solution is right *above* our nose! It all starts with the eyes or what Jesus referred to as the "lamp of the body." Matthew 6:22 says, *"The eye is the lamp of the body; so if your eye is clear [spiritually perceptive], your whole body will be full of light [benefiting from God's precepts].* If we control what we choose to look at when we know it can be unhealthy to our spiritual heart, our sight becomes the first line of defense against it. In order to have a spiritual perspective, we must have the Word of God engrained deeply into our hearts so that when our eyes focus on something they shouldn't, our spirit is sensitive enough to adjust our line of sight.

As an example, if a man sees a pretty woman in revealing clothing walking down the street in his direction, he should immediately train his eyes on her face or simply look elsewhere. If he doesn't, his eyes will focus on her body in an inappropriate manner. When that happens, he has opened the door to lust in his heart. The same thing can happen to a woman who sees an attractive man on the beach. She admires his body and even takes a second look when he is not watching. This sounds like something teenagers do, but adults do it as well.

In reality, women are far less likely to engage in the physical side of attraction than men. In many cases, women first look to have their emotional needs met, and that is followed by their physical needs. They eventually get there, just as men do, but not quite as fast as men do. Job 31:1 says, *"I have made a covenant (agreement) with my eyes; How then could I gaze [lustfully] at a virgin?"* One of the most righteous men in history agreed that he must guard his eyes, otherwise he too could fall into this trap.

Jesus gave us a very gory metaphor in Matthew 5:29-30 as a solution to the problem in verses 27-28 concerning adultery. He said,

> *If your right eye makes you stumble and leads you to sin, tear it out and throw it away* **[that is, remove yourself from the source of temptation]**; *for it is better for you to lose one of the parts of your body, than for your whole body to be thrown into hell. If your right hand makes you stumble and leads you to sin, cut it off and throw it away* **[that is, remove yourself from the source of temptation]**; *for it is better for you to lose one of the parts of your body than for your whole body to go into hell.*

When most people read this, they tend to discount what Jesus meant to say because of the graphic detail of tearing out your eye and cutting off your arm—which He was not implying we should do in human terms. Keep in mind that Jesus was addressing men in Matthew 5:26-30, so he had to put this in terms that would grab their attention.

Men for the most part are stimulated sexually first by what they see through the eyes and then by what they feel through their hands. If you ever want to test the "eye" theory, just have a man's wife walk into the bedroom in a Victoria's Secret nightgown and, trust me, he will look no matter what NFL game he is watching at that moment. Once he sees with his eyes, then the "hand" theory kicks into high gear. The touch of the hand follows what he saw with the eyes, and when he makes physical contact with his wife and feels her flesh, the circuit is complete; and we all know what happens next. This process among married couples is natural and healthy; but when the same process is used on someone other than his spouse, the outcome can be devastating.

Jesus was saying, as the Amplified Version wonderfully illustrates, to remove yourself from the source of temptation by adjusting what you see—then the body will follow. If a married man or woman is full of the Word and has a spiritual perspective on what they see, they will benefit from God's precepts and not fall into the trap of lust and adultery. Paul said in Romans 13:14, "*But clothe yourselves with the Lord Jesus Christ, and make no provision for [nor even think about gratifying] the flesh in regard to its improper desires.*" You're covered with the strength of Jesus when you're covered in His Word. Jesus gave us a clear, cut-and-dried solution to avoid lust both in the heart and in the physical form; and it is centered on the eyes. Paul gave us one as well, but his solution deals with how we see someone relationally rather than in physical appearance. He offered a very practical solution in 1 Timothy 5:1-2 when he said,

> *D*o *not sharply reprimand an older man, but appeal to him as [you would to] a father, to younger men as brothers, to older women as mothers, to younger women as sisters, in all purity [being careful to maintain appropriate relationships].*

Once we have a "clear" eye, then what we do see in the opposite gender will be done in terms of a relationship rather than as an object.

Think about it this way. As a man, if you see a woman other than your spouse as a sister, then it's likely you will have an appropriate relationship. As a guy who has a sister, I can totally relate to what Paul was trying to say here. Married men should look at all women as sisters and married women should look at other men as brothers. This is possible if we have trained our eyes to see through a spiritual paradigm instead of a worldly one. Lust in any form is a battle. That's why Peter says in 1 Peter 2:11, "*Beloved, I urge you as aliens and strangers [in this world] to abstain from the sensual urges [those dishonorable desires] that wage war against the soul.*" Lust will wage war against your soul. This is a daily battle, but if fought with the power of the Holy Spirit by controlling what we allow to enter our minds through our eyes, it is a battle that can be won.

CHAPTER 7

DIVORCE

Now when Jesus had finished saying these things, He left Galilee and went into the part of Judea that is beyond the Jordan; and large crowds followed Him, and He healed them there. And Pharisees came to Jesus, testing Him and asking, "Is it lawful for a man to divorce his wife for just any reason?" He replied, *"Have you never read that He who created them from the beginning* MADE THEM MALE AND FEMALE, *and said, 'For this reason a man shall leave his father and mother and shall be joined inseparably to his wife, and the two shall become one flesh'? So they are no longer two, but one flesh. Therefore, what God has joined together, let no one separate." The Pharisees said to Him, "Why then did Moses command us to* GIVE HER A CERTIFICATE OF DIVORCE AND SEND HER AWAY?" *He said to them, "Because your hearts were hard and stubborn Moses permitted you to divorce your wives; but from the beginning it has not been this way. I say to you, whoever divorces his wife, except for sexual immorality, and marries another woman commits adultery." The disciples said to Jesus, "If the relationship of a man with his wife is like this, it is better not to marry." But He said to them, "Not all men can accept this statement, but only those to whom [the capacity to receive] it has been given."* (Matthew 19:1-11)

DIVORCE

Greek: from *aphistémi*—a forsaking, specifically (bill of) divorce

Cambridge English: to cause a marriage to a husband or wife to end by
an official or legal process

Dictionary.com: total separation; disunion

Merriam-Webster: the action or an instance of legally dissolving

I⸻T SEEMS silly to have to define divorce, because many of us know
what it means by the effect it has on our lives as children of divorced parents. Regardless of how silly it is and to stay true to the format
of this book, I did it anyway. It's estimated that thirty-eight percent of
Christian marriages who attend church regularly end in divorce. It goes
up to sixty percent for those who rarely attend church.[1] Any divorce in
the Christian or secular world has a negative impact on all parties involved to some extent. With that being said, it happens; and although
we have tools to assist married couples in getting through tough times
to honor their commitment before God, marriages don't always survive.

I have been married for over thirty-five years but if not for the
grace of God, my wife could have and likely should have divorced me
for a plethora of valid reasons. Unfortunately, in the church today,
those who have gone through divorce(s) are sometimes treated differently than those who have remained in their marriage. All of us know
that God hates divorce. It says so in Malachi 2:16,

> *"For I hate divorce," says the* LORD, *the God of Israel, "and him
> who covers his garment with wrong and violence," says the* LORD
> *of hosts. "Therefore keep watch on your spirit, so that you do not
> deal treacherously [with your wife]."*

You don't have to remind any divorced Christians of that because it's
been crammed down their throats.

Here is the deal: God does hate divorce, but He also hates lust, greed, the love of money, idolatry, lying and any other sin we are all capable of committing. Couples get divorced for many reasons, some being valid—like adultery—and others not specifically addressed in Scripture. Those include spousal abuse, domestic violence, violence against the children and even attempted murder. Why should grace and mercy be excluded from those who went through a divorce, for valid reasons or not?

Divorced people should not be excluded because God's grace, mercy and love is extended to all of us, even if we are wrong! Does that give any of us the right to pull the ripcord on our marriages because we found someone else who "understands" us? Absolutely not, but if that did happen, while there are consequences, God's forgiveness is still sufficient if there is true repentance.

REMOVING THE BLIND EYE

My parents divorced when I was a child. The negative impact it had on me was very evident in my behavior. Over the years and now that I have my own family, I still do not like to see my friends divorce; staying in a marriage should always be the priority. Yet, it happens and will likely continue in the years to come.

If I have the opportunity to counsel someone who is having a tough time in a marriage, I always advise them to look in the mirror and see what part they played in causing the discord. I try hard to convince them that their marriage before God is a solemn vow, but I don't beat them over the head with the Bible. They must make their own decision, then deal with the negative consequences of that decision.

We as Christians need to embrace those who have gone through divorce and give them hope that they can have a godly and fruitful marriage, despite their past. In the church community, though it might not be voiced, people quietly form judgments in their own minds about those who have been divorced. Often, those who have been married only once can feel superior in their spirit. Instead of focusing on the outcome of a person's previous marriage, we should focus on sharing God's solutions for the next one.

CHAPTER 8

VOWS

Again, you have heard that it was said to the men of old, "YOU SHALL NOT MAKE FALSE VOWS, BUT YOU SHALL FULFILL YOUR VOWS TO THE LORD [as a religious duty]." But I say to you, do not make an oath at all, either by heaven, for it is the throne of God; or by the earth, for it is the footstool of His feet; or by Jerusalem, for it is THE CITY OF THE GREAT KING. Nor shall you make an oath by your head, for you are not able to make a single hair white or black. But let your statement be, "Yes, yes" or "No, no" [a firm yes or no]; anything more than that comes from the evil one. (Matthew 5:33-37)

VOWS

Greek: from *horkos*—an oath

Cambridge English: to make a firm promise or decision to do something

Dictionary.com: a solemn promise, pledge, or personal commitment

Merriam-Webster: to promise solemnly

I BELIEVE WE all struggle in the area of keeping our word at one time or another. I have made promises that I haven't kept, even though I fully intended to do so when I made them. Although Jesus references the vows we make as being *"to the Lord"* in verse 33, I don't believe that's what Jesus was talking about in the ensuing verses. It's very common to hear both believers and unbelievers say, "I swear to God," "I swear on my mother's grave," or "I swear on my kids' lives." These are the types of vows Jesus was talking about in verses 34 through 37, and He pointedly tells us that we should refrain from making such vows.

Why someone would swear on their children's lives is beyond comprehension, but they do because they feel it validates their claim. Jesus made this command really simple—just say yes or no, and that's it. We have all seen a movie where some underling gets caught in a lie but declares he's telling the truth and adds, "I swear to God." But he suffers the consequences anyway, so his oath likely just reinforced the idea that he was lying in the first place. If he had uttered a simple "no" full of conviction, he probably would have stood a better chance of survival.

The same is true in the real world. We should never swear by anything, much less God or our families. The book of James always resonates with me, perhaps because he was Jesus' half-brother. He said in James 5:12:

> *B*ut above all, my fellow believers, do not swear, either by Heaven or by earth or with any other oath; but let your yes be [a truthful] yes, and your no be [a truthful] no, so that you may not fall under judgment.

If we hear a fellow brother or sister make such a vow—usually out of ignorance—we owe it to them to share what Jesus taught about this topic. It could change the trajectory of that person's life, as James stated, and keep them from judgment.

REMOVING THE BLIND EYE

While the habit of using foul language is usually a heart issue, I believe this to be a head issue that boils down to a simple lack of understanding. Who in their right mind would sacrifice any of their children based on a broken vow? Who would swear by an oath on the God that created them—a God who is in no way bound to back that pledge in the first place? Again, I don't believe anybody who is thinking straight would do either, so correcting this bad habit is simply a matter of stopping yourself before you make such a claim and instead responding with a simple yes or no. It's really not difficult to do if you think about it. Next time you feel the urge to swear an oath on your child's life, for example, picture the outcome if you broke the vow. That will change one's thinking very quickly.

CHAPTER 9

RETALIATION

You have heard that it was said, "AN EYE FOR AN EYE, AND A TOOTH FOR A TOOTH [punishment that fits the offense]." But I say to you, do not resist an evil person [who insults you or violates your rights]; but whoever slaps you on the right cheek, turn the other toward him also [simply ignore insignificant insults or trivial losses and do not bother to retaliate—maintain your dignity, your self-respect, your poise]. If anyone wants to sue you and take your shirt, let him have your coat also [for the Lord repays the offender]. And whoever forces you to go one mile, go with him two. Give to him who asks of you, and do not turn away from him who wants to borrow from you. (Matthew 5:38-42)

RETALIATION

Greek: from *antiloidoréō*—to *return* abusive insults; reproach, denigrate; detract from someone's honor (reputation)

Cambridge English: to hurt someone or do something harmful to someone because that person has done or said something harmful to you

Dictionary.com: to return like for like, especially evil for evil

Merriam-Webster: to repay in kind

THIS PASSAGE on retaliation has several different tracks to follow. Once again, Jesus began with Old Testament law—to which any Jewish person could relate—and raised that command to an even higher standard. If we as believers are even thinking about retaliation, we have not dealt with the core issue, which is anger in our hearts. If you love others, it's impossible to desire retribution. That being said, it's very important to understand the audience to whom Jesus was speaking regarding retaliation.

First, for the most part, these were Jewish peasants who were victims of humiliating acts. "Turn the other cheek" is from this era, but it is commonly misinterpreted by believers and unbelievers alike today who say that Jesus was advocating allowing yourself to be physically beaten up while offering no defense. But the meaning actually comes from first-century Judea, when one person would offer a backhanded slap on the right cheek to another who was deemed their inferior as a form of insult. A practicing Jew could not use his left hand because it was used only for unclean purposes. (They didn't have toilet paper back then!) If the slap was given with an open hand or fist, the implication was that the person was considered an equal and not inferior. So, to empower victims, the victim would "turn the other cheek" so the striker would be unable to use his right hand to backhand the left cheek. It took the power away from the striker and removed some of the humiliation from the victim.[1] Turning the other cheek in that culture does not in any way teach that we should turn ours today in a refusal to defend ourselves or our families from harm.

Secondly, the same was true when Jesus said to give your coat or outer garment also to someone who sued you for your shirt. Why? Anytime someone went into debt—which was common for the lower class in Jewish society in Bible times due to the oppression of the wealthy and the Romans—that person had nothing left to give but the shirt off his back. If he voluntarily gave the outer garments along with the inner garment, he was left standing naked in court. Jewish law placed more shame on the lender that forced a person to become naked than the debtor who was actually stripped of everything. This command was simply another way for the powerless to regain some measure of dignity from the oppressors. The lender would typically not allow that to happen, so he was left in a very difficult and embarrassing position.[2]

Third, the example of going two miles when asked to go one was related to the Roman soldiers requiring Jewish civilians to carry their heavy packs. The Roman government mandated that a civilian could be required to carry the pack for only one mile; when they reached that point, they could give the pack to the soldier and be free from their responsibility. Jesus said to tell the soldier you will carry the pack another mile because, if he accepted, the soldier who broke this law would be punished. Again, this put the soldier in a difficult position and restored some dignity back to the powerless.[3]

The fourth command about giving resources to those who ask and not turning away someone who wants to borrow was to ensure that the poor and powerless did not go hungry. Jewish law required those with means to take care of the poor and not to lend money expecting anything in return. Jesus was removing the burden from the oppressed in order to once again restore a level of dignity.[4]

All these examples involve not retaliating to gain advantage but countering retaliation by disarming the aggressor. We should have the same attitude today. We don't strike back like most people are prone to do, but rather respond in a way that exposes the true nature of the aggressor. Jesus did exactly that on the cross. 1 Peter 2:22-23 says,

> *H*E COMMITTED NO SIN, NOR WAS DECEIT EVER FOUND IN HIS MOUTH. *While being reviled and insulted, He did not revile or insult in return; while suffering, He made no threats [of vengeance], but kept entrusting Himself to Him who judges fairly.*

Peter made another reference to this in 1 Peter 3:8-9:

> *Finally, all of you be like-minded [united in spirit], sympathetic, brotherly, kindhearted [courteous and compassionate toward each other as members of one household], and humble in spirit; and never return evil for evil or insult for insult [avoid scolding, berating, and any kind of abuse], but on the contrary, give a blessing [pray for one another's well-being, contentment, and protection]; for you have been called for this very purpose, that you might inherit a blessing [from God that brings well-being, happiness, and protection].*

REMOVING THE BLIND EYE

Taking into account the context of this Scripture should allow us all to see the truth of how retaliation should be viewed in our world. Many believers have misinterpreted what Jesus was saying by believing they should be passive or non-responsive to aggression. Instead of accepting this misinformed view, the next time you are faced with a situation that could deserve a response, take heed to this Scripture and respond not in an evil retaliatory manner, but rather in love, which will cause the aggressor to have no other option but to walk away. The only weapon a powerful person has in this circumstance is the weapon we give them by our response.

CHAPTER 10

OUR ENEMIES

You have heard that it was said, "YOU SHALL LOVE YOUR NEIGH-BOR (fellow man) and hate your enemy." But I say to you, love **[that is, unselfishly seek the best or higher good for]** *your enemies and pray for those who persecute you, so that you may* **[show yourselves to]** *be the children of your Father who is in heaven; for He makes His sun rise on those who are evil and on those who are good, and makes the rain fall on the righteous [those who are morally upright] and the unrighteous* **[the unrepentant, those who oppose Him]**. *For if you love [only] those who love you, what reward do you have? Do not even the tax collectors do that? And if you greet only your brothers* **[wishing them God's blessing and peace]**, *what more* **[than others]** *are you doing? Do not even the Gentiles* **[who do not know the Lord]** *do that? You, therefore, will be perfect* **[growing into spiritual maturity both in mind and character, actively integrating godly values into your daily life]**, *as your heavenly Father is perfect.* (Matthew 5:43-48)

ENEMY

Greek: from *echthros*—hated, hostile

Cambridge English: a person who hates or opposes another person or tries to harm that person

---

Dictionary.com: a person who feels hatred for, fosters harmful designs against, or engages in antagonistic activities against another; an adversary or opponent

Merriam-Webster: one that is antagonistic to another

I FIND IT interesting that Jesus acknowledged that we are going to have enemies. He didn't say that we should avoid them at all costs, like He did when telling us not to become angry, make false vows or judge hypocritically. It's more along the lines of when He said, when you pray, or when you give alms, or when you fast. It's inevitable that we're going to have enemies (unless you are my wife!) just like Jesus did, so He gave us a solution in these verses for how we're supposed to deal with them from God's perspective, not man's.

Loving those who hate you or praying for those who persecute you—which can include personally, professionally, relationally or even spiritually—is very difficult. It goes against every fiber in our fleshly being to do either of these as Jesus commanded. I think it's the very reason why Jesus gave us a solution that was clear and to the point because He knows it is a challenge for us humans. When you love those who hate you or pray for those who persecute you, it certainly may provide a benefit to those individuals in this natural world; but what it does that's even more beneficial is help us in the spiritual realm. When we follow exactly what Jesus said by loving and praying, three things take place:

1) We are released from harboring negative emotions that could be detrimental to our walk with God,

2) It allows us more grace from God because, before we even pray, He knows what those individuals are doing to us,

3) It shows the world the character of God's people.

The saying, "Keep your friends close but your enemies closer" does not apply to us because we have already released them through love and prayer. They are no longer our enemies, but enemies only to themselves. If a person or a group of people hate you or persecute you, they are doing so as a result of bitterness, anger, spite, jealousy or some other ungodly motive. Galatians 6:7 says the following:

> *Do not be deceived, God is not mocked [He will not allow Himself to be ridiculed, nor treated with contempt nor allow His precepts to be scornfully set aside]; for whatever a man sows, this and this only is what he will reap.*

When you love and pray for your enemies, you have done your part by following what Jesus commanded. Once that happens, spiritual laws will take effect for the person who wronged you. Obviously, if we are wishing for judgment on that person, that's not true love. What I am saying is, eventually those who act this way will reap the same in their own lives. It's not *if,* but *when.* The world calls this "karma," but Christians know it as sowing and reaping.

Two concepts become evident when we break down this Scripture. Verse 44 tells us *what* we should do, and verses 45 through 48 tell us *why* we should do it. In verse 45, Jesus tells us that God causes the sun to rise and the rain to fall on both believer and unbeliever. So, when we love those who hate us or pray for those who persecute us, we are showing how God's children are supposed to act. In verse 46, God points out that we will have no reward from Him if we love only those who love us, since any human can do that. Verse 47 gives a similar illustration if we say hello to or offer well wishes only to those who think of us in the highest regard. But verse 48 is the sweet spot. If we do these things then, as the Amplified Bible says, we will be perfect *by growing into spiritual maturity both in mind and character, actively integrating godly values into our daily life.* **In other words, we would be imitating what God is doing and exactly what Jesus said He was doing when He**

walked the earth. That one benefit is worth it all, and we can reap that by loving and praying for our enemies.

REMOVING THE BLIND EYE

This command is one of the hardest to follow for many of us. I understand because, for the longest time, it was hard for me to accept. I heard it in my head, but I could not seem to get it into my heart. I can tell you that a peace came over me when I began to love those who didn't love me and pray for those who were persecuting me. It's hard to explain unless you just do it and experience this miracle for yourself. Your enemy might still be an enemy in *his own* eyes, but he is no longer the enemy in *your* eyes. This is literally removing the *blind eye* in real time.

Just take a moment on your knees to tell God that while you may not have the full understanding of the "what" of these verses, you believe that the "why" will make more sense as you choose to obey. Ask God for the strength to love your enemies, then pray for a blessing on those who may be persecuting you. Putting this command into practice will change you from the inside out.

CHAPTER 11

ALMS

Be [very] careful not to do your good deeds publicly, to be seen by men; otherwise you will have no reward [prepared and awaiting you] with your Father who is in heaven. So whenever you give to the poor and do acts of kindness, do not blow a trumpet before you [to advertise it], as the hypocrites do [like actors acting out a role] in the synagogues and in the streets, so that they may be honored and recognized and praised by men. I assure you and most solemnly say to you, they [already] have their reward in full. But when you give to the poor and do acts of kindness, do not let your left hand know what your right hand is doing [give in complete secrecy], so that your charitable acts will be done in secret; and your Father who sees [what is done] in secret will reward you. (Matthew 6:1-4)

ALMS

Greek: from *eleos*—mercy, pity, charity

Cambridge English: clothing, food, or money that is given to poor people

Dictionary.com: money, food or other donations given to the poor or needy; anything given as charity

Merriam-Webster: something (such as money or food) given freely to relieve the poor

To UNDERSTAND what role almsgiving plays in God's economic system, we must first understand the meaning and purpose for tithes and offerings. Legalism is a hot topic in the church regarding these two forms of giving financial resources, but I simply want to point out what Jesus said about it to allow people to make the decision for themselves.

Tithe means "one tenth of something." In today's terms, a tithe would equate to ten percent of one's gross income that is given to the local church or storehouse. Malachi 3:10 says,

> "*Bring all the tithes (the tenth) into the storehouse, so that there may be food in My house, and test Me now in this," says the LORD of hosts, "if I will not open for you the windows of heaven and pour out for you [so great] a blessing until there is no more room to receive it.*"

Jesus rebuked the Pharisees in Luke 11:42 for being legalistic about the tithe while neglecting justice and the love of God:

> *But woe (judgment is coming) to you Pharisees, because you [self-righteously] tithe mint and rue and every [little] garden herb [tending to all the minutiae], and yet disregard and neglect justice and the love of God; but these are the things you should have done, without neglecting the others.*

But He didn't say we shouldn't tithe and in fact confirmed we should when He stated, *"But these are the things you should have done, without neglecting the others."* I will say this about God's economic system: it is no different than the world's economic system in that it requires resources to make it work. This is the purpose of the tithe.

Offerings are financial gifts above and beyond the tithe. They can be given to a local church or any Christian organization. Jesus again acknowledges offerings in Matthew 5:23-24, which says the following:

So if you are presenting your offering at the altar, and while there you remember that your brother has something [such as a grievance or legitimate complaint] against you, leave your offering there at the altar and go. First make peace with your brother, and then come and present your offering.

Jesus wasn't confused; He didn't mistakenly call the tithe an offering. He was pointing out that an offering is independent of the tithe.

This leads us to God's third form of funding His kingdom, and that is almsgiving. Tithes *pay* for the kingdom of God, offerings *expand* the Kingdom of God, and alms *exemplify* the Kingdom of God. Personally, I believe all three should be practiced and that all should be done discreetly between you and God; but we are required to give alms in secret to receive the real reward from God. This form of giving is the purest practice of giving because it blesses someone in dire need while only God sees us do it. Pleasing Him is the only reward we should desire when giving alms.

REMOVING THE BLIND EYE

Any Christian can give alms and still not tithe or give offerings, though I don't recommend neglecting the tithe and offerings. With that said, almsgiving anytime is a wonderful thing to do for another human being. Even if you don't agree that we are commanded to pay tithes and give offerings in today's culture, you can certainly understand the need for and joy in helping others in their time of need. I am always looking for the opportunity to gives alms to someone—a homeless person or family, a single mother in need of food or a total stranger that God prompts me to bless. I always strive to figure out a way to give without the recipient knowing the gift came from me. I have left cash in envelopes on people's cars or given grocery cards anonymously; but when it's not possible to give anonymously, I specify that the gift be between the two of us and to please not tell anyone, including family members. I have often given alms without telling even my wife because I take to heart Jesus' command in Matthew 6:3-4:

> *But when you give to the poor and do acts of kindness, do not let your left hand know what your right hand is doing [give in complete secrecy], so that your charitable acts will be done in secret; and your Father who sees [what is done] in secret will reward you.*

You remove the *blind eye* in almsgiving by just doing it. Try it, and I promise your joy will abound, especially knowing it's between you and God only.

CHAPTER 12

PRAYER

Also, when you pray, do not be like the hypocrites; for they love to pray **[publicly]** *standing in the synagogues and on the corners of the streets so that they may be seen by men. I assure you and most solemnly say to you, they* **[already]** *have their reward in full. But when you pray, go into your most private room, close the door and pray to your Father who is in secret, and your Father who sees* **[what is done]** *in secret will reward you. And when you pray, do not use meaningless repetition as the Gentiles do, for they think they will be heard because of their many words. So do not be like them* **[praying as they do]***; for your Father knows what you need before you ask Him.* (Matthew 6:5-8)

PRAYER

Greek: from *proseúxomai*—towards, exchange, to *interact with* the Lord by switching *human wishes* (ideas) for *His wishes* as He imparts faith

Cambridge English: to speak to God or a god either privately or in a religious ceremony, especially to express thanks or to ask for help

Dictionary.com: to offer devout petition, praise, thanks, etc., to (God or an object of worship)

Merriam-Webster: to address God or a god with adoration, confession, supplication, or thanksgiving

PEOPLE SEEM to like a public demonstration of prayer. In many instances, such as a funeral, it's fitting and proper as long as the motives are pure. What Jesus was talking about in this Scripture as it relates to prayer is that if it's done publicly only to receive recognition or honor, then that person has received their only reward, and that is from man. I believe the most important part of this Scripture is centered on what we do privately as individuals. Jesus says that when (not if) we pray, go somewhere private where nobody can see us but God and reach out to our Father there. The reward for this kind of prayer activity is similar to the reward for giving alms or fasting in secret. If only God knows and sees, then our reward will be far greater than any human can give us.

Our private prayer time is not a ritual, but rather an opportunity to talk to God. Jesus pointed out in Matthew 6:7 that we need not use meaningless repetition because God already knows what we need before we ask. Prayer should never be viewed as a time to just ask God to give us things, but more importantly as a time to recognize and communicate to Him how awesome, wonderful, gracious, loving and real He is in our lives.

That's why Jesus told us to begin the Lord's Prayer with, *"Pray, then, in this way: 'Our Father, who is in heaven, Hallowed be Your name.'"* (Matthew 6:9) *Hallowed* means "set apart, devoted, consecrated, holy."[1] When you tell God how much you love Him and thank Him for who He is first instead of what He can provide, then you're praying in holiness and reverence. Prayer for me is talking to my Father in Heaven the same way I would talk to my father on earth. That's what Jesus did in the garden of Gethsemane when He cried out to God in Mark 14:36: He was saying, *"Abba, Father! All things are possible for You; take this cup [of judgment] away from Me; but not what I will, but what You will."* *Abba* is an Aramaic phrase from *Bar Abba*, which means "sons of the father."[2] Jesus was calling out to the Father He knew before the world was formed, assured He would hear him because of the personal relationship he had with God. We need to learn to have a conversation with God that is real—no formal, scripted words, but just a real conversation expressing the heart.

Can you imagine if one of your children approached you timidly, using long and formal words to address you? When a child and parent love each other, such formalities are not needed. You would be saddened and hurt that your child thought it was necessary to address you that way, and I believe God feels the same way when we approach Him that way. Yes, we are to have a reverence for God in our hearts that is shown by our actions; but when we go to God in prayer, we are going to Him as a child would go to his father on earth. Just as an earthly father does, our Heavenly Father gladly opens His heart, ears and arms and receives His child with eager expectation to meet his needs. When we see prayer through that lens, then we no longer need to wonder how much we should pray. The late Billy Graham said, "Every day has exactly 1,440 minutes; can't you find even 10 of them to be with your heavenly Father? Doesn't God deserve the best minutes of your day?"[3] Well said, Reverend Graham.

REMOVING THE BLIND EYE

We all need to place prayer back on the spiritual playing field. Talking then listening for God's voice through the Holy Spirit will build our faith, just as committing to reading the Word of God does. As 1 Thessalonians 5:17 says, *"Be unceasing and persistent in prayer."* If we're unceasing and persistent in talking and listening to God, then He will reveal Himself to us. I am not talking about a quick five-second prayer, although any prayer is better than no prayer at all, but rather a quiet time in a secluded place with just you and God. Another thing Billy Graham said that resonated with me is, "[Jesus] prayed briefly when He was in a crowd; He prayed a little longer when He was with His disciples; and He prayed all night when He was alone. Today, many in the ministry tend to reverse that process."[4] Our prayer time will enhance our intimacy with God. Carve out the time and grow closer to God by just talking to Him.

Also, if you commit to pray for someone, then do it. It's common to hear someone say, "Oh, that's terrible; I will pray for you, brother (or sister)." But you walk away knowing that it is unlikely that person will actually pray. People have good intentions perhaps but simply do not make the promise a priority. We are often guilty of giving an automatic promise to pray—similar to the response we give when somebody asks, "How are you doing?" We reply without thinking, "Just fine." In reality, our world may be falling apart, but we are conditioned to give that response. When it comes to something as holy and important as agreeing to pray for someone, such a promise should always be fulfilled with a sincere heart and never made without the serious intention to follow through.

CHAPTER 13

FORGIVENESS

For if you forgive others their trespasses [their reckless and willful sins], your heavenly Father will also forgive you. But if you do not forgive others [nurturing your hurt and anger with the result that it interferes with your relationship with God], then your Father will not forgive your trespasses. (Matthew 6: 14-15)

FORGIVE

Greek: from *charizomai*—to show favor, give freely

Cambridge English: to stop blaming or being angry with someone for something that person has done

Dictionary.com: to grant pardon for or remission of (an offense, debt, etc.); absolve

Merriam-Webster: to cease to feel resentment against (an offender)

THIS SCRIPTURE from Jesus' Sermon on the Mount is one of the most overlooked as far as practice is concerned, and I say this because most people forgive *from the head and not from the heart*. We say we forgive, but our actions say otherwise. When true forgiveness occurs—like the kind God gave us by faith in Jesus—our actions toward the other person show whether we offered real forgiveness, or only verbalized it. This is very similar to our salvation experience in that we confess Jesus as Lord with our mouths, yet at the same time we must believe in our hearts—otherwise, our confession is only fruitless words. Jesus makes this one proclamation very clear to us that if we don't forgive someone from the heart, then God will not forgive us of our own trespasses. That statement is worth noting. Matthew 18:35 says, *"My heavenly Father will also do the same to [every one of] you, if each of you does not forgive his brother from your heart."*

The word *trespass* comes from the Greek word *paraptóma*, which means "a falling away, lapse, slip, false step, trespass, or sin."[1] To put it bluntly, if we can't release someone from a wrong done against us, then God will not forgive the wrongs committed by us against Him. That should make all of us place forgiveness at the top of our list of principles to practice and follow in our daily lives. Paul echoes the same in Colossians 3:12-13, which says:

> *So, as God's own chosen people, who are holy [set apart, sanctified for His purpose] and well-beloved [by God Himself], put on a heart of compassion, kindness, humility, gentleness, and patience [which has the power to endure whatever injustice or unpleasantness comes, with good temper]; bearing graciously with one another, and willingly forgiving each other if one has a cause for complaint against another; just as the Lord has forgiven you, so should you forgive.*

We often hear the phrase, "I have forgiven that person, but I have not forgotten." That's not the forgiveness Jesus or Paul were talking about and should never be the attitude of a believer. If a person has not "forgotten," then their actions toward the offender will reflect such. What if God said to me, "Greg, I have forgiven you of that action, but I will never forget it"? I am one person who is grateful that God does not have a good memory when it comes to my own failings. Isaiah 43:25

says, "*I, only I, am He who wipes out your transgressions for My own sake, And I will not remember your sins.*"

REMOVING THE BLIND EYE

Just like love, forgiveness is a decision, not a feeling. If my wife loved me only when she felt like it, I would be in a world of hurt! My wife loves me in spite of myself and the stupid things I am capable of doing. Forgiveness works exactly the same way. We don't forgive because we "feel" like it; we forgive because God requires us to forgive, just as He forgave each of us. Take a moment to reflect on any person you have forgiven in the past or whom you need to forgive in the present. Ask yourself if you forgave from the heart instead of just in the head. You will know the difference by your actions, both in thought and in how you interact with them.

A good test is to ask yourself what emotion comes to the surface when you think about that person. If grace, mercy and goodwill come to mind, then you likely have forgiven them for your heart. If a slight bit of anger, resentment or ill-will comes to mind, then you should reconsider whether your forgiveness was truly the kind God asks of us.

Unforgiveness not only affects our relationship with God but also has negative consequences for our natural life. Unforgiveness in our hearts can cause physical illness as well as a root of bitterness, anger, hatred and other emotions we should never harbor in our hearts. If you think there is any chance that there is unforgiveness in your life, go to God in prayer and lift up that person(s) and ask God to give you the strength and ability to forgive just as God forgave you. The Holy Spirit can do for us what we cannot do for ourselves.

CHAPTER 14

FASTING

And whenever you are fasting, do not look gloomy like the hypocrites, for they put on a sad and dismal face [like actors, discoloring their faces with ashes or dirt] so that their fasting may be seen by men. I assure you and most solemnly say to you, they [already] have their reward in full. But when you fast, put oil on your head [as you normally would to groom your hair] and wash your face so that your fasting will not be noticed by people, but by your Father who is in secret; and your Father who sees [what is done] in secret will reward you. (Matthew 6:16-18)

FASTING

Greek: from *alpha* and *sitos*—without eating

Cambridge English: to have a period of time when you eat no food

Dictionary.com: to eat only sparingly or of certain kinds of food, especially as a religious observance

Merriam-Webster: to abstain from food

Fasting is a topic that we don't often hear addressed from the pulpit, usually because **nobody wants to do it**! Did you notice in the verse that Jesus said "when" you fast, not "if" you fast? We know that Jesus practiced fasting at the beginning of His ministry when He was in the desert for forty days and forty nights. What many miss is that it was no coincidence that it was right at the end of His fast that He was tempted by the devil. Fasting puts the devil on his heels. The reason Jesus taught and practiced fasting is because it's a critical task to complete in order to hear God and get the spiritual strength to fight our enemy on earth. When we fast even for a short period of time, our mind becomes clearer, our spirit more sensitive and we can more easily recognize the leading of the Holy Spirit.

> Acts 13:2-3 says, *While they were serving the Lord and fasting, the Holy Spirit said, "Set apart for Me Barnabas and Saul (Paul) for the work to which I have called them." Then after fasting and praying, they laid their hands on them [in approval and dedication] and sent them away [on their first journey].*

The disciples were able to clearly hear the Holy Spirit because they were fasting and in prayer.

Why did Jesus fast for forty days and forty nights? Forty is a very important number in the Bible. We all know the story of Noah, when it rained for forty days and forty nights. Moses spent forty days and forty nights fasting on top of Mt. Sinai when he received the Ten Commandments, and the Hebrew people spent forty years in the desert after they left Egypt. Jesus was with God when all these things occurred, so He was simply following in those footsteps. The nugget to understand here is that every time the number forty was used, a new beginning or a cleansing took place. Fasting is a cleansing of the mind, body and spirit and is always followed by a new birth.

Human beings can go sixty to seventy days without food before dying. Most people can survive one to three days without water if it's hot or six days at best under cooler conditions.[1] So when we fast, the idea is to abstain from anything that requires chewing and to drink plenty of water or other liquids that keep the body functioning. I have never completed a forty-day fast, but I have friends who have. When their fast is over, they truly seem impacted in a positive manner.

REMOVING THE BLIND EYE

We should all realize that fasting is as important to our spiritual life as prayer and faith. We usually avoid this practice because we don't want to be physically uncomfortable, so we pray, believe God and eat! You must start the practice of fasting in baby steps. I believe the best results are achieved by fasting for twenty-four hours. During that time, seek God in prayer as you go throughout your day and ask Him to reveal Himself to you and give you the knowledge of any weakness in your walk that would give the devil opportunity to come against you. After successfully completing twenty-four hours, then try forty-eight hours and build from there. God will honor your obedience and give you an entirely different perspective on spiritual warfare. Fasting is not a diet for overweight Christians but an act of obedience in seeking to hear the voice of God. Above all, don't tell anyone you're fasting, for then and only then can God reward you.

CHAPTER 15

IDOLATRY

Again, the devil took Him up on a very high mountain and showed Him all the kingdoms of the world and the glory [splendor, magnificence, and excellence] of them; and he said to Him, "All these things I will give You, if You fall down and worship me." Then Jesus said to him, "Go away, Satan! For it is written and forever remains written, 'You shall worship the Lord your God, and serve Him only.'" (Matthew 4:8-10)

IDOLATRY

Greek: from *eidololatria*—image worship

Cambridge English: very great admiration or respect for someone, often too great

Dictionary.com: excessive or blind adoration, reverence, devotion, etc.

Merriam-Webster: the worship of a physical object as a god

IN ORDER to understand the third temptation by the devil, we need to first understand what the word *worship* means. In today's English, *worship* is defined as "to regard with great or extravagant respect, honor or devotion."[1] The word *worship* in the Hebrew is the

verb *shachah*, which means "to prostrate in homage."[2] In the New Testament, the Greek word for *worship* that is used is *proskuneo,* which
means "to prostrate oneself."[3] So what the devil was saying to Jesus in
a translation is the following: I just showed You all the material kingdoms of the world (i.e. land, cities, treasuries, animals, gold, silver, precious metals, homes, finest jewelry, etc.) and their magnificent glory
(the satisfaction and praise You will receive when You have them), and
I will give it all to You if You bow down (put me ahead of all these
physical possessions and before God) and devote Yourself to me. Jesus
responded with the Word of God by saying, "No thanks, Satan, you are
a stinking liar; man will bow down only to the living God and devote
everything to Him. Now go back to Hades where you belong!"

I am amazed every time I read Matthew 4:1-11 and realize that
Satan showed his game plan by trying to get the Son of God to take
the bait. He tempted Jesus with satisfying His hunger, protecting His
health and well-being, and finally by thinking he could entice Him
to worship him in exchange for all the physical pleasures in life. Jesus, being divine and yet human, was easily able to combat the play
the devil tried to call on three different occasions and thank goodness for us that He did; otherwise, the outcome for our souls could
have been entirely different! If the devil is bold enough to try to
tempt the Son of God to worship him, how much more are we at risk
as mere humans?

Using a football analogy, when the devil called his three offensive
plays (satisfying three earthly cravings), Jesus countered with three
defensive plays (from the Word of God) that beat the devil at his own
game. He gave us the antidote to worshipping anything other than
God, thereby avoiding the creation of an idol in our lives; yet many
people today have been deceived by the devil and place other worldly
things above God.

In her book *Practicing Christian Doctrine*, Beth Felker Jones states
the following:

FOR sinful humans, idolatry is a basic feature of our situation. The human heart, according to John Calvin's diagnosis, is a factory of idols. The culprit in our lives that causes anyone to have an idol before God is self. It boils down to satisfying our carnal nature and an intense focus on gratifying ourselves.[4]

All forms of idol worship are summed up in 1 John 2:15-16:

Do not love the world [of sin that opposes God and His precepts], nor the things that are in the world. If anyone loves the world, the love of the Father is not in him. For all that is in the world—the lust and sensual craving of the flesh and the lust and longing of the eyes and the boastful pride of life [pretentious confidence in one's resources or in the stability of earthly things]—these do not come from the Father but are from the world.

In most cases that I have come across in my lifetime, and for me personally, that idol is materialism, which includes money, wealth, riches, status, possessions, praise from man and all the pleasures this temporal world has to offer. Materialism and the need for more and more stuff is an obvious idol that is fairly easy to point out. When God said in Exodus 20:4-5,

You shall not make for yourself an idol, or any likeness of what is in heaven above or the earth beneath or in the waters under the earth. You shall not worship them or serve them; for I, the Lord your God, am a jealous God, visiting the iniquity of the fathers on the children, on the third and fourth generations of those who hate me...

that is exactly what He meant. When Moses came down from the mountain, Aaron and the people had made a molten gold calf to be worshiped. We don't have golden calves today *per se*, but that doesn't mean we worship idols any less. God loves us so much that He gets jealous when we place anything above worshipping and serving Him. In addition to materialism, we can make an idol out of sex, ambition, work, ministry and even people.

I want to dig deep into materialism as an idol because I believe Christians and the world have blatantly *turned a blind eye* to this stronghold. The pattern I have discovered that causes people to develop materialism as an idol starts with *greed*, which is "an excessive or rapacious desire, especially for wealth or possessions."[5]

Once the spirit of greed takes hold, it is followed by *covetousness*, which means "to fix the desire upon, whether things good or bad; hence, to long for, lust after, covet evilly."[6] Materialism in all its forms becomes an obsession to covet because of greed; and in many cases it is masked by the delusion that the acquisition is for a better cause. Once covetousness takes hold, it becomes the idol so that nothing is more important—including God—than satisfying the need that was sparked by greed and sealed by covetousness. Once that happens, a material idol has been created. Colossians 3:5 tells us the following:

*So put to death and deprive of power the evil longings of your earthly body [with its sensual, self-centered instincts] immorality, impurity, sinful passion, evil desire, and **greed, which is [a kind of] idolatry [because it replaces your devotion to God]**.*

That is very clear, but Ephesians 5:5 also addresses this issue:

*For be sure of this: no immoral, impure, or greedy person—for that one is [in effect] an idolater—has any inheritance in the kingdom of Christ and God [**for such a person places a higher value on something other than God**].*

Then to put the nail in the idolatry coffin, Galatians 5:19-21 tells us,

Now the practices of the sinful nature are clearly evident: they are sexual immorality, impurity, sensuality (total irresponsibili-

ty, lack of self-control), **idolatry,** *sorcery, hostility, strife, jealousy, fits of anger, disputes, dissensions, factions [that promote heresies], envy, drunkenness, riotous behavior, and other things like these. I warn you beforehand, just as I did previously, that those who practice such things will not inherit the kingdom of God.*

An example in the New Testament that would resonate today is the story of the rich young ruler in Matthew 19:16-26. This man who was extremely rich and owned many properties thought he was doing all the rights things to gain eternal life. Jesus responded that to be "complete," he must go and sell all his possessions and give to the poor, then he could follow Jesus. Materialism was his identity and hence his idol, and he simply could not let it go in order to serve God. I believe the Bible says he went away grieved because he knew by his own actions and life choices that he had no desire to give up that idol. Many people who profess to know Jesus do the same thing 2,000 years later. They act the Christian part, attend church on Christmas and Easter, and might even throw a benevolent bone to the needy; but make no mistake—materialism is the idol in their life. Those are not my words, but straight out of Scriptures in both the Old and New Testaments. We must not *turn a blind eye* in our own lives or in the lives of others when the worship of materialism is clear and evident in the lives of fellow believers.

Some ask how to discern whether materialism is an idol in either their own life or someone else's. Beth Felker Jones gave insight to that when she wrote the following:

> REPEATEDLY, Scripture warns that we become like the gods we serve; in the assessment of G. K. Beale, worshippers reflect in their character the ungodly image of what they worship. Character is defined as one of the attributes or features that make up and distinguish an individual.[7]

Look at how a person reflects his or her character and determine whether money or material possessions distinguish them individually.

If so, perhaps it is an idol. As the saying goes, if something walks like a duck, quacks like a duck, and acts like a duck, it is likely a duck. Felker Jones goes on to say, "We are molded into the likeness of our false gods, people who make idols are like them; so are all who trust in them."[8] She points us to Psalm 115:8, *"Those who make them will become like them, everyone who trusts in them."*

I am a big fan of Billy Graham, and I love this quote: "I urge all of you to walk with the Lord in a life of separation from the world and to keep eternal values in view."[9] He also wrote regarding his and Ruth's financial commitment to God's kingdom: "From the beginning of our marriage, we determined that we would be tithers. We determined not to be preoccupied with material things, which leads to covetousness and which the Scriptures call idolatry."[10] This is a man who lived this out during the ninety-nine years he was on this earth. He knew what the Scriptures said and made a deliberate decision to avoid greed and covetousness, which lead to material idolatry.

I was recently touched when I read an article about Philip Ng of Singapore. He and his brother Robert are worth $12.1 billion dollars, yet he values his relationship with Jesus Christ more than anything else after years of searching. He said,

> WHAT I've discovered is that all of us are broken. We all have a missing piece, and for me, I discovered that the missing piece was God through Jesus Christ.... I was always in search for a better life, a better purpose, a better me, a better everything. I was just looking at all the wrong things, but I realized there is no better thing and no better me without Jesus. Then it all snapped into place. Maybe we have to look deeper. I treasure (my faith) more than anything, so I just wish for everyone to have that peace and joy. It sure beats a lot of money and material things that you may have.[11]

That is called keeping it in perspective.

REMOVING THE BLIND EYE

In order to deal with any form of idolatry and especially the monetary variety, you must address the two conditions that led to the false worship in the first place. If you don't "cure" the greed and covetousness problem, then idolatry will never be removed from the heart. It would be like treating symptoms of a bodily sickness instead of treating the actual disease. If someone believes they can just decide to no longer worship money or possessions without dealing with greed and covetousness, they will be sadly mistaken and will continue in a vicious cycle throughout their lives. It's very similar to addiction. If someone who struggles with alcohol or drugs takes one drink or that first pill after being sober for any length of time, then the craving kicks in and the vicious cycle returns. Drugs and alcohol are the symptom of the real problem, and until they discover what that is, they are destined to drink or use drugs again.

Idolatry is exactly the same. Once people realize that they are indeed greedy and covetous, and they understand how and why they became that way, then idolatry can be defeated. It's absolutely necessary to go back to the decisions that gave greed entrance into one's life. It generally starts with selfish ambition and self-gratification, often due to the messages communicated in the media, movies, radio or the news. Many children are taught at an early age that in order to be successful, they must strive to make as much money as possible, climb the corporate ladder—or, amazingly, that money itself can solve some or all of the life issues we encounter. We are told that if we don't achieve wealth ourselves, nobody will do it for us. That's a fertile ground in young people to nurture greed; then when they are thrown into the workplace, covetousness can take root and idolatry can grow unhindered.

When this all occurred or at what stage in life makes no difference, because we all have the opportunity to examine ourselves and determine if we fall into this category. If we do, after a deep dive into our decisions that reflect greed and covetousness, we have a way to tear down that idol in our lives by simply asking God for forgiveness and removing it from our lives. The same power of the Holy Spirit that will resurrect our earthly bodies can free us of any type of bondage, if we only ask. Then and only then can our future actions illustrate that God is first and everything else is secondary. This applies to any and all forms of greed that lead to covetousness then develop into idolatry.

CHAPTER 16

WEALTH

For what will it profit a man if he gains the whole world [wealth, fame, success], but forfeits his soul? Or what will a man give in exchange for his soul? (Matthew 16:26)

WEALTH

Greek: from *ploutos*—riches

Cambridge English: a large amount of money and other valuable possessions

Dictionary.com: a great quantity or store of money, valuable possessions, property or other riches; the state of being rich; prosperity; affluence

Merriam-Webster: much money or property, riches

A SURVEY WAS completed years ago that asked a sample population, "How much for a place in Heaven?" The survey claims that the wealthiest one percent of families in the U.S. (with a $250,000 annual income and/or a $2,500,000 net worth) were asked in a survey how much they would pay for various items. The most valuable item in the survey? **It was a place in Heaven**. The respondents said they would pay an average of $640,000 for that spot in Heaven. True

108 | *Turning a Blind Eye*

love came in a distant second at $487,000.[1] My guess is that now, many years later, the price of admission has surely gone up!

These one percenters, who certainly fit the definition of wealthy, thought they could put a price tag on eternal life. Forget the average "trip cost" of $640,000 and how they arrived at that figure, because that is not the point of the story. The point is that their financial status caused them to believe that money could get them into Heaven, *if given that option.* Most practicing Christians understand that all unbelievers, be they rich or poor, can never buy their way into the kingdom. Martin Luther's *95 Theses* that he nailed to the door of the All Saints church in 1517, which ushered in the Protestant Reformation, made this point clear. Only a saving relationship with Jesus Christ will get us to Heaven. This survey is symptomatic of how wealth is viewed in America. The good news from the survey is that they at least wanted to get there; but the bad news is that they had no idea how to do it. Bob Marley once said, "Money can't buy life."[2] There is no truer statement.

Wealth is neither good nor evil. What determines its true value is how it is used. Firearms are a good analogy. Guns don't murder people. It's the person in possession of the gun that carries out a murderous act. The gun is nothing more than a tool. It's the same with wealth; it has the power to do good—but if it's placed in the wrong hands, it has the power to destroy. Wealth, too, is only a tool.

A very good example of its power can be seen in lottery winners. Over the past couple of years, several news organizations have attributed a statistic to the National Endowment for Financial Education (NEFE), stating that seventy percent of lottery winners end up bankrupt within just a few years after receiving a large financial windfall.[3]

The story of Billy Bob Harrell, Jr., is so sad. He was a Pentecostal preacher working at a Home Depot. In June of 1997, he won the $31 million Texas Lottery jackpot. At first, all was great.

"HARRELL purchased a ranch. He bought a half dozen homes for himself and other family members. He, his wife and all the kids got new automobiles. He made large contributions to his church. If members of the congregation needed help, Billie Bob was there with cash," writes Steve McVicker in *The Houston Press*. "Then suddenly Harrell discovered that his life was unraveling almost as quickly as it had come together…everyone, it seemed—family, friends, fellow worshipers and strangers—put the touch on him. His spending and his lending spiraled out of control. In February those tensions splintered his already strained marriage." And tragically, twenty months after winning the lottery, Harrell committed suicide.[4]

Harrell said before his death that winning the lottery was "the worst thing that ever happened to him."[5] So, we have some who think they can use their wealth to get into Heaven and others who allow wealth to destroy them once they acquire it. Wealth can not only change people for good or for bad, but also be very deceiving.

People pursue wealth for three primary reasons. First, they pursue it out of pure greed and their personal desire to live the "good life." Second, they pursue it to fill a void in their heart that gives them a sense of self-worth. Third, they pursue it to make a difference in this world and use it for good. Understand that I did not say pursue earning an income, which is what we all should do to provide for our families. By pursuing wealth, I'm referring to the accumulation of earthly assets, none of which we can take with us. How we view wealth is how we view this temporal world. My favorite definition of *wealth* is found in the *Holman's Commentary*, which defines it "as physical resources God gives humans to control."[6] If that is our attitude and we walk it out, wealth has an entirely different purpose in our lives.

First, wealth for pure greed to live the good life seems to be the most common in our society. I love what Solomon said in Ecclesiastes 5:10,

"He who loves money will not be satisfied with money, nor he who loves abundance with its gain. This too is vanity (emptiness)." This is from a man who was one of the richest people of all time. We are all subconsciously taught at an early age the perceived importance of wealth. One of the most effective publications to validate this fantasy is the annual edition of the *Forbes 400*. This is by far the most popular edition the magazine produces. It highlights the net worth of the 400 richest people in the United States. This publication, as well as others that personify riches and possessions as the remedy to happiness, is what drives people to pursue wealth for pure greed and self-satisfaction. They have come to believe that wealth will give them the good life they deserve, and they will work all hours of the day and night to accomplish it, at any cost.

Proverbs 18:11 says, *"The rich man's wealth is his strong city, And like a high wall [of protection] in his own imagination and conceit."* The messages from the world tell people that it's okay to pursue wealth and is in fact even expected as part of the American Dream. The heart of the issue here is not the act of obtaining wealth itself, but at what cost and for what purpose. If a person is striving for wealth as a means to an end, then the cost will have many consequences. Those will include issues in their spirituality or lack thereof, relationships with their spouse and children, personal health, and social and professional relationships, just to name a few. Remember that Jesus said, *"For what will it profit a man if he gains the whole world* **[wealth, fame, success]***, but forfeits his soul? Or what will a man give in exchange for his soul?"*

I do not believe Jesus was asking that question because He didn't know the answer, but because His intention was for each of us to ask ourselves this question and then decide if this Scripture applies to our attitude toward wealth. You see, Jesus can't answer that question for us. We can answer it for ourselves only by digging deep into our spiritual hearts and determining what drives our desire to accumulate wealth.

Secondly, when someone pursues wealth to fill a hole in his or her heart and provide a false sense of self-worth, it can be just as devastating as pursuit for pure self-satisfaction. Don't get me wrong; this person enjoys the physical pleasures wealth can bring, but the driving force is what those possessions do for his or her self-image in their owns eyes and the eyes of others around them. Earthly wealth and the possessions it affords temporarily fill a void in the soul that only God can fill; people just don't know it.

Since wealth is subjective based on what part of the world you live in, it is not just those who are well-to-do who struggle with this issue. I have seen families with adequate but not substantial income by U.S. standards try to fill the same hole in their heart by borrowing the money to accomplish that goal. They have the same craving for self-worth, but since it's borrowed, the wealth is never really theirs in the first place.

Third, some pursue wealth to make a difference in this world and use their money for good. It's a fact that believers and unbelievers alike can use wealth to make the world a better place. I believe God uses men and women who may not yet know Jesus to bless His children. Proverbs 10:22 says, *"The blessing of the Lord brings [true] riches, And He adds no sorrow to it [for it comes as a blessing from God]."* The salient point in this verse is that the blessing of the Lord brings riches, not human effort or sheer will. God has a reason and purpose in mind to bless the righteous and unrighteous in this physical world that none of us will likely understand until we can ask God ourselves. I have a working theory that if believers cannot or will not make the financial effort to ease the world's pains, then God will use whoever He wishes to accomplish the task. God loves the entire human race as His children—and like parents in this natural world, He want His children taken care of and their needs met.

It's easy to say, "Well, if I were worth millions or billions, I would certainly use my wealth to do good." Nope, that's not the case. If we won't do it with what we have been given now, we will never do it if God decides to bless us beyond our wildest dreams. Did you know that many of the wealthiest people in the U.S. never set out to be wealthy or ultra-wealthy? Unless they inherited the money, they simply set out to make a difference in their respective fields and in many cases used their passion to change the world, thereby making it a better place for all. Wealth was a result of that desire, so when they did achieve it, they still had the same core principle in their hearts. Then they put their money where their heart was once they had the means to do it. This type of attitude toward wealth can be adapted by all of us even if we don't measure up to the world's standard of wealth.

REMOVING THE BLIND EYE

First, we must begin to look at wealth as a tool for God to use to advance His kingdom on earth. It's not a tool to use for self-gratification, to fill a hole in our hearts or give us a sense of self-worth; rather, it is a gift from God to use for His eternal purposes.

Secondly, everyone must take to heart what Jesus taught in the parable of the rich fool in Luke 12:15: *Then He said to them, "Watch out and guard yourselves against every form of greed; for not even when one has an overflowing abundance does his life consist of nor is it derived from his possessions."* Rest assured that if you ever have the opportunity to witness to someone who is about to die, that person typically doesn't talk about how wealth fulfilled his life. There are many believers today who chase the pursuit of wealth most their natural life instead of growing closer to their God; and when it comes time to die, they will likely experience fear instead of peace. If we can get that into our spirits and just begin to take baby steps toward this newfound attitude, our understanding of wealth will change. When it's our time to go, we will talk about the love for our families and friends and leave this world knowing that we used the resources God gave us to further His kingdom and make His world a better place during our journey.

PSALM 49:5-12, *Why should I fear in the days of evil, When the wickedness of those who would betray me surrounds me [on every side], Even those who trust in and rely on their wealth And boast of the abundance of their riches? None of them can by any means redeem [either himself or] his brother, Nor give to God a ransom for him—For the ransom of his soul is too costly, And he should cease trying forever— So that he should live on eternally, That he should never see the pit (grave) and undergo decay. For he sees that even wise men die; The fool and the stupid alike perish And leave their wealth to others. Their inward thought is that their houses will continue forever, And their dwelling places to all generations; They have named their lands after their own names [ignoring God]. But man, with all his [self] honor and pomp, will not endure; He is like the beasts that perish.*

This passage of Scripture alone will put wealth in its proper perspective if we will take it to heart.

CHAPTER 17

TRUE TREASURES

Do not store up for yourselves [material] treasures on earth, where moth and rust destroy, and where thieves break in and steal. But store up for yourselves treasures in heaven, where neither moth nor rust destroys, and where thieves do not break in and steal; for where your treasure is, there your heart [your wishes, your desires; that on which your life centers] will be also. (Matthew 6:19-21)

TREASURES

Greek: from *thesauros*—a storehouse for precious things; hence: a treasure, a store

Cambridge English: great wealth, especially in the form of a store of gold, silver, precious stones, or money; a treasure is also anything of great value

Dictionary.com: wealth or riches stored or accumulated, especially in the form of precious metals, money, jewels, or plates; wealth, rich materials, or valuable things; anything or person greatly valued or highly prized

Merriam-Webster: wealth (such as money, jewels or precious metals) stored up or hoarded; wealth of any kind or in any form; something of great worth or value

T HIS TOPIC—like those discussed in earlier chapters that deal with money, possessions, greed, covetousness, wealth and idolatry—likely hits a sensitive nerve for most readers because it concerns something dear to most people's hearts. A tragic misconception also exists—many miss that treasures in Heaven work much like treasures on earth, but for different purposes. Nearly everyone understands the basic economic principle of putting your money to work so that it will work for you and provide some form of temporal security for the future. Spiritual principles work exactly the same, but very few people see the similarities between the two.

What Jesus was saying in plain English is that if all our money, possessions and valuables are only accumulated on earth and used for earthly purposes, we're missing the boat. When a person transfers treasures from earthly accounts into heavenly accounts, those transfers are recorded by God Himself. If that were not the case, why would Jesus clearly demonstrate the difference between storing treasures on earth where they lose value and can be stolen versus in Heaven where they can't be devalued or stolen? The world is so focused on what a person's net worth is here on earth, especially in the United States. This focus on the measurement of worldly wealth is misguided because it measures wealth only from a natural perspective. The measurement should not change, but rather the place where it's stored and used. **Why don't we ever hear people inquire about our eternal net worth?**

Paul said in Philippians 4:17, "*Not that I seek the gift itself, but I do seek the profit which increases to your [heavenly] account [the blessing which is accumulating for you].*" He was specifically speaking of a heavenly account, but even more exciting is that our treasure there accumulates over time! I have no doubt in my mind that, just as we will be accountable to God for every word, deed and action, He will also reward us for all the material transfers we make into our accounts in Heaven.

Jesus said it again in Matthew 19:21:

Jesus answered him, "If you wish to be perfect [that is, have the spiritual maturity that accompanies godly character with no moral or ethical deficiencies], go and sell what you have and give [the money] to the poor, and you will have treasure in heaven; and come, follow Me [becoming My disciple, believing and trusting in Me and walking the same path of life that I walk]."

We all have issues with what our finite minds can understand, and storing treasures in Heaven is no exception. It's fairly easy to tell where a person's heart is based on how much treasure is stored on earth instead of where it belongs, which is in Heaven managed by God for His purposes.

REMOVING THE BLIND EYE

Every person should take an inventory of all their assets on earth and compare them to their assets in Heaven. We transfer our financial treasures from earthly accounts into heavenly ones in three ways—through tithes, offerings and alms. When we pay our tithe to our local church, give offerings to worldwide ministries and provide alms to those in need in secret, we are indeed building our heavenly portfolio.

Scripture confirms this awesome fact in Acts 10:1-4,

*Now at Caesarea [Maritima] there was a man named Cornelius, a centurion of what was known as the Italian Regiment, a devout man and one who, along with all his household feared God. He made many charitable donations to the Jewish people and prayed to God always. About the ninth hour (3:00 p.m.) of the day he clearly saw in a vision an angel of God who had come to him and said, "Cornelius!" Cornelius was frightened and stared intently at him and said, "What is it, lord (sir)?" And the angel said to him, "Your prayers **and gifts of charity have as-***

cended as a memorial offering before God [an offering made in remembrance of His past blessings]."

It doesn't matter if you're the average Joe, wealthy or ultra-wealthy, how much you give should be proportionate to how much you have been given. **Stated another way, it's not just the amount you give but the amount you keep**. It is really that simple. So, take an inventory of how much of your income has been transferred to God or how many possessions you have on earth that could be monetized and used for eternal purposes instead of your own satisfaction. Like the old saying goes, "You will never see a hearse pulling a U-Haul," and 1 Timothy 6:7 is even more clear: "*For we have brought nothing into the world, so [it is clear that] we cannot take anything out of it, either.*"

Most of what has been covered thus far in this chapter specifically relates to money, but let me clarify that there are other ways to lay up treasures in Heaven that have nothing to do with financial resources. For instance, you can invest your time here on earth for the Lord's work. You could also use your talents for God to build your heavenly account. Regardless of which method someone uses to transfer earthly assets into their heavenly account, what's most important is to just do it!

CHAPTER 18

SERVING GOD OR MAMMON

*Do not store up for yourselves [**material**] treasures on earth, where moth and rust destroy, and where thieves break in and steal. But store up for yourselves treasures in heaven, where neither moth nor rust destroys, and where thieves do not break in and steal; for where your treasure is, there your heart [**your wishes, your desires; that on which your life centers**] will be also. The eye is the lamp of the body; so if your eye is clear [**spiritually perceptive**], your whole body will be full of light [**benefiting from God's precepts**]. But if your eye is bad [**spiritually blind**], your whole body will be full of darkness [**devoid of God's precepts**]. So if the [**very**] light inside you [**your inner self, your heart, your conscience**] is darkness, how great and terrible is that darkness! No one can serve two masters; for either he will hate the one and love the other, or he will be devoted to the one and despise the other. You cannot serve God and mammon [**money, possessions, fame, status, or whatever is valued more than the Lord**]."* (Matthew 6:19-24)

MAMMON

Greek: from *mamonas*—money, treasure, or personified riches, which are opposed to God

Cambridge English: the force that makes people try to become as rich as possible, and the belief that this is the most important thing in life

Dictionary.com: riches or material wealth; a personification of riches as an evil spirit or deity

Merriam-Webster: riches regarded as an object of worship and greedy pursuit

LET ME make something clear from the very start, and please pay attention! Money itself is not evil, nor is it the enemy unless it becomes *the* focus in your life; then it becomes both evil and your enemy.

> *For the love of money [that is, the greedy desire for it and the willingness to gain it unethically] is a root of all sorts of evil, and some by longing for it have wandered away from the faith and pierced themselves [through and through] with many sorrows.* (1 Timothy 6:10)

Money is like a knife. It can be used for good, like to prepare food, or it can be used for evil to take a life. Just as using a knife for an evil purpose has natural consequences involving the earthly legal system, loving money as a god on this earth has spiritual consequences in the next life when we are judged by the Creator of the universe. *Money is neither good nor bad; its true value is determined by how you use it.* I have often said, to the consternation of many, that if you want to know whether you love God or your money the most, you only need to look in your checkbook. Rich or poor, our bank account tells us a lot about our priorities.

The best example of this is found in Mark 12:41-44 when Jesus and His disciples were sitting down by the treasury:

And He sat down opposite the [temple] treasury and began watching how the people were putting money into the treasury. And many rich people were putting in large sums. A poor widow came and put in two small copper coins, which amount to a mite. Calling His disciples to Him, He said to them, "I assure you and most solemnly say to you, this poor widow put in *[proportionally]* more than all the contributors to the treasury. For they all contributed from their surplus, but she, from her poverty, put in all she had, all she had to live on."

The rich gave out of their surplus, but the widow emptied her bank account.

If you got to know me, you would discover that I love expresso. In fact, I usually go to Starbucks or another local coffee shop every day to get my five espresso shots over ice with a splash of milk. If you looked at my bank statement, you would see all the charges throughout the month. Based on this alone, you would then realize—whether you knew me or not—that I love expresso. How would you know? Because I spend the time as well as the money to go get it every day.

You can tell the same about our love for money by examining where our resources are invested. If all you see when you look at your bank statement is resources spent on yourself, your family, your vacations, your primary home, your second home, multiple cars(s) and other earthly possessions and nothing sown into God's Kingdom on earth, you might be serving mammon—or at the very least making earthly possessions a priority over loving God. I understand that loving God is not based only on how you spend money, *but* for those critics who will scoff at this, it's a really good barometer. I see way too many business folks who quickly claim they are Christians, but their conversation is dominated by a discussion of current and future possessions, the need for their bank accounts to remain at a certain level to sleep well at night, and their desire to make even more money. Someone like this might even throw God a bone and speak of feeling so blessed; but if you investigate that person's bank account, you would likely conclude that God is nowhere in the picture.

If people profess to be Christians but it is not reflected in how they use God's resources, then they have a love of money and are serving the god of mammon. Does that mean such people will not have eternal life? Matthew 19:23 says, *Jesus said to His disciples,* "I assure you and most solemnly say to you, it is difficult for a rich man [who clings to possessions and status as security] to enter the kingdom of heaven." He said it was difficult, but that is for God to judge; He is the only one who knows everyone's heart and motive. God loves everyone equally, but with that being said, you still have to ponder His statement that you cannot serve two masters. Every person must make a choice between serving God or serving mammon. One sure test is how a person's resources are used and whether their security comes from money or from God.

Exodus 20:3 says, "You shall have no other gods before me." If money is the priority in your life or provides a security blanket to cover up with at night, it has become your idol. Saying that money is your idol certainly won't help anyone be voted most popular, but it's just that plain and simple. Jesus made this one point very clear. Money makes a terrible master.

Money and thorns seem to go together, and we see that expressed in Mark 4:18-19:

And others are the ones on whom seed was sown among the thorns; these are the ones who have heard the word, but the worries and cares of the world [the distractions of this age with its worldly pleasures], and the deceitfulness [and the false security or glamour] of wealth [or fame], and the passionate desires for all the other things creep in and choke out the word, and it becomes unfruitful.

In my experience, many with good intentions fall prey to the thorns Jesus mentioned, which causes them to serve the world's values versus God's values. Let's dig deeper into all four pathways with the primary focus being on the thorns.

The first path is described in Mark 4:14-15:

The sower sows the word [of God, the good news regarding the way of salvation]. These [in the first group] are the ones along the road where the word is sown; but when they hear, Satan immediately comes and takes away the word which has been sown in them.

From this passage, we know for certain that this group of people heard the Word, but as Jesus pointed out, Satan *immediately* comes and takes away the Word, thus preventing salvation for the hearer. I have shared the gospel with businessmen at their desks, in conference rooms and even in an escalator when it's evident from their reaction to me that Satan is present! The Word went into their spirit, but Satan came immediately to take it away; so the conversation is short, and I am asked to move along. Most of these men were focused on **religion versus a relationship** but were diligent to attend church on Christmas and Easter like I did. It's as though they felt they had a free pass because of this religious affiliation and had a salvation insurance card next to their health insurance card in their wallet.

The second group is described in Mark 4:16-17:

*In a similar way these [in the second group] are the ones on whom seed was sown on **rocky** ground, who, when they hear the word, immediately receive it with joy [but accept it only superficially]; and they have no real root in themselves, so they endure only for a little while; then, when trouble or persecution comes because of the word, immediately they [are offended and displeased at being associated with Me and] stumble and fall away.*

Satan is not specifically mentioned in the rocky places, but Jesus did say *"in a similar way,"* which implies that Satan did the same thing, but it was not immediate. Once again, we are certain that these people heard the Word. Satan waited until affliction or persecution arose due to the Word, then dispatched a demon to steal that Word, causing these to *"fall away."*

Those who received the seed sown in rocky places fell away because of affliction and persecution, which is clearly why they fell away. I have preached the Word to this group of people and, in my experience, most fell away due to persecution from work peers or current friends because of the Word of God. When they brought up the Word, they were shamed or laughed at or perhaps even demoted or denied promotions.

The third group described in Mark 4:18-19 speaks of the seeds sown among the thorns:

> *And others are the ones on whom seed was sown among the* *thorns; these are the ones who have heard the word, but the wor-* *ries and cares of the world* [the distractions of this age with its worldly pleasures]*, and the deceitfulness* [and the false security or glamour] *of wealth* [or fame]*, and the passionate desires for* *all the other things creep in and choke out the word, and it be-* *comes unfruitful.*

In this short passage, Jesus revealed three tactics the devil uses to deceive human beings. For a third time, Scripture is clear that these people heard the Word—but three barriers come into play.

First, *the worries of the world* choke the Word. The word *worry* as a verb means "give way to anxiety or unease; allow one's mind to dwell on difficulty or troubles." As a noun it means "a state of anxiety and uncertainty over actual or potential problems."[1]

These are the same worries Jesus mentioned in Matthew 6:25-34, which is as follows:

*Therefore I tell you, stop being worried or anxious (**perpetually uneasy, distracted**) about your life, as to what you will eat or what you will drink; nor about your body, as to what you will wear. Is life not more than food, and the body more than clothing? Look at the birds of the air; they neither sow [seed] nor reap [the harvest] nor gather [the crops] into barns, and yet your heavenly Father keeps feeding them. Are you not worth much more than they? And who of you by worrying can add one hour to [the length of] his life? And why are you worried about clothes? See how the lilies and wildflowers of the field grow; they do not labor nor do they spin [**wool to make clothing**], yet I say to you that not even Solomon in all his glory and splendor dressed himself like one of these. But if God so clothes the grass of the field, which is alive and green today and tomorrow is [**cut and**] thrown [**as fuel**] into the furnace, will He not much more clothe you? You of little faith! Therefore do not worry or be anxious (**perpetually uneasy, distracted**), saying, "What are we going to eat?" or "What are we going to drink?" or "What are we going to wear?" For the [**pagan**] Gentiles eagerly seek all these things; [**but do not worry,**] for your heavenly Father knows that you need them. But first and most importantly seek (aim at, strive after) His kingdom and His righteousness [**His way of doing and being right—the attitude and character of God**], and all these things will be given to you also. So do not worry about tomorrow; for tomorrow will worry about itself. Each day has enough trouble of its own.*

My guess is that when Jesus mentioned the worries of the world in Mark 4:19, He was speaking of those concerns centered on the previous Scripture. The remaining two points in verse 19 deal with the deceitfulness of riches and the desire for other things, which certainly imply money; so it makes sense that the worries of the world deal with the same. This can include food, clothing, drinks, bank accounts, credit card bills, mortgage payments, car payments, kids' college tuition, etc. We as believers should be concerned about the resources God gives us so we can be good stewards, but we should not worry. Peter says in 1 Peter 5:7, *Casting the whole of your care (all your anxieties, all your worries, all your concerns, once and for all) on Him, for He cares for you affectionately and cares about you watchfully.*

I believe Jesus is talking here not about those who do believe and walk in His ways, but rather those who choose not to believe because of these obstacles. In other words, the message was sown, but due to the seed being thrown into the thorns where worry, deceitfulness of riches and desire for worldly things are present, the Word is unfruitful.

Secondly, *the deceitfulness of riches* chokes the Word. In my opinion, no other Scripture gives a better description of the person who is blinded by the deceitfulness of riches than Matthew 19:16-26.

And someone came to Him and said, "Teacher, what [essentially] good thing shall I do to obtain eternal life [that is, eternal salvation in the Messiah's kingdom]?" Jesus answered, "Why are you asking Me about what is [essentially] good? There is only One who is [essentially] good; but if you wish to enter into eternal life, keep the commandments." He said to Jesus, "Which commandments?" And Jesus answered, "YOU SHALL NOT COMMIT MURDER; YOU SHALL NOT COMMIT ADULTERY; YOU SHALL NOT STEAL; YOU SHALL NOT GIVE FALSE TESTIMONY; HONOR YOUR FATHER AND MOTHER; AND LOVE YOUR NEIGHBOR AS YOURSELF" [that is, unselfishly seek the best or higher good for others].The young man said to Him, "I have kept all these things [from my youth]; what do I still lack?" Jesus answered him, "If you wish to be perfect [that is, have the spiritual maturity that accompanies godly character with no moral or ethical deficiencies], go and sell what you have and give [the money] to the poor, and you will have treasure in heaven; and come, follow Me [becoming My disciple, believing and trusting in Me and walking the same path of life that I walk]." But when the young man heard this, he left grieving and distressed, for he owned much property and had many possessions [which he treasured more than his relationship with God]. Jesus said to His disciples, "I assure you and most solemnly say to you, it is difficult for a rich man [who clings to possessions and status as security] to enter the kingdom of heaven. Again I tell you, it is easier for a camel to go through the eye of a needle, than for a rich man [who places his faith in wealth and status] to enter the kingdom of God." When the disciples heard this, they were completely astonished and bewildered, saying, "Then who can be saved [from the wrath of God]?" But Jesus looked at them and said, "With people [as far as it depends on them] it is impossible, but with God all things are possible."

Oh, my! This rich young ruler had God in the flesh standing there—yet he still refused the answer he received about how to obtain eternal life. If he could be so foolish, how much more easily are we to be deceived by riches in this present world? Mark's account of this same story relates that, *"A man ran up to him and knelt before him"* (10:17). This verse tells me the rich man knew Jesus was a king, otherwise he never would have knelt down! Did Jesus literally mean his young ruler must go and sell all his real estate holdings right then when he said go? I have no idea but, in my mind, Jesus was making it clear that he had to make a decision. What I do know, though, is that this young man should have been willing to do so; his refusal revealed he was plagued by the deceitfulness of riches, which simply means he chose to serve mammon over God.

If I had been in the rich young ruler's shoes, I believe I would have responded, "I will do that, Jesus, if that's what it takes to spend eternity with You." As I walked away to go hire my real estate broker,

I believe Jesus would have said, "Greg, stop. I just wanted to see if you would lay down everything to follow Me." Then I like to think I would have come up with a plan on how to sell some of the property immediately to fund Jesus' ministry as well as help the poor, followed by a long-term plan for the balance while I preached the gospel to other business leaders.

You must ask yourself, like I did, what would your own personal response have been in that same situation? Remember, Jesus was in the flesh and likely less than two feet away from you. If your answer is the same as mine, then it should be the same in this present time. I find it so very troubling that Scripture said this man went away grieving. *Grieving* in this passage is used as a verb and means "implying deep mental suffering often endured alone and in silence but revealed by one's aspect."[2] Synonyms include h*urt, wound, pain, sting, gall, sadden, upset, distressed* and *devastated.* This man was absolutely devastated and likely walked away with his head hung low, realizing he had just walked away from eternal life. He *turned a blind eye* to salvation because of the *love* of money.

Jesus gave us the roadmap to become complete when it comes to money.

1) Go. This implies action and requires a decision.

2) Sell. Be willing to give it all for the kingdom.

3) Give. Once you gain that liquidity, give to the poor or into His kingdom.

4) Lay up treasure. You just opened your heavenly bank account.

5) Follow. Live for Him and not yourself.

The problem that I have seen countless times is that most business professionals are simply unwilling to follow this roadmap because they are attempting to accumulate wealth in their own strength.

Jesus talked about how *"difficult"* it is for a person to get saved if he or she is deceived by riches using the comparison of a camel and a sewing needle. Some say that the "eye of the needle" was a small gate in one of the twelve gates that surrounded Jerusalem. Those entering the city would use this gate at night to prevent being conquered by their enemies when they opened the main gate. The camel would have to literally bend down to get through the small opening after the rider removed his entire load. This analogy implies that you must remove the bond of money and possessions before you can go through the eye of the needle and have eternal life. The analogy goes back as far as the fifteenth century, but some historians claim that such a gate never existed. Frankly, I could care less. I get the point whether the gate existed or not. The camel was one of the largest animals in that time, and a sewing needle was one of the smallest openings you can imagine. The fact is that a camel could never fit through a sewing needle.

Jesus first said it was *"difficult."* The Bible says the disciples were *"astonished"* and asked Him, *"Then who can be saved?"* His answer was short but to the point when **He replied that with people, it's impossible, but with God all things are possible.**

The bottom line here according to Jesus is that unless a person gains an eternal perspective to money and possessions by a revelation from God Himself, it will never happen. Any man would exchange his life for the life of his wife or children. He would lay it down for their benefit because of his love for them. Yet, when it comes to money, which is temporal, men simply can't give it all on their own unless the Holy Spirit moves on their heart.

Many businessmen and even a few friends remind me of this rich young ruler. This guy thought he was doing everything he needed to do to gain eternal life by following the commandments. He likely was a respected pillar of society in the Jewish community, had many "friends," several houses, a stable of camels and knew all the right people. Yet, when faced with the ultimate test, he failed because he loved money and was deceived by those riches.

I think Hades (intermediate state after death) and ultimately Hell (permanent place after the final judgment) might be full of people who were well intentioned and thought they did all the right things to have eternal life, but at the end of the day failed to recognize that when Jesus said, *"You cannot serve both God and Mammon,"* He really meant it in a literal sense; we are saved by grace and not by works because of God's love and mercy for us. With that being said, this Scripture and the many others in this book on this topic should compel us to look deep into our hearts to see if we or others we know are *turning a blind eye* to being deceived by riches by not completely giving ourselves to God.

Thirdly, *a desire for other things* chokes the Word. I have pondered this statement many times and often wondered what these other things could be. After all, the worries of the world and the deceitfulness of riches covered a lot of ground! When He is saying "other things," it is my belief that he is talking about the stuff people desire to accumulate and the pleasures in life.

Many people are kept out of the kingdom because of their desire for the pleasures of the world. These are the folks who desire everything the world has to offer which gives them temporary pleasure. These things become their primary focus in life and cause the Word to be unfruitful.

Beginning at a very young age, the world bombards us with the false narrative that more is better—that if you have this item or that item, you will be elevated in status and your needs will be fulfilled. This is counterintuitive to our Christian walk. God does want to bless in all areas of our life, including meeting our material needs, but when we place these desires above God, believers will choke the Word and hinder the growing seed and become unfruitful in their walk.

When Christians do this, the seed that was planted has a hard time growing at all and they have no chance for the Word to have any impact on their lives. Is there anything wrong with having nice things during our journey through earth? No, unless these riches and a desire for these things control your life.

Jesus summed up this entire chapter about serving mammon versus serving God in Matthew 16:24-26:

> *Then Jesus said to His disciples,* "If anyone wishes to follow Me [as My disciple], *he must deny himself* [set aside selfish interests], *and take up his cross* [expressing a willingness to endure whatever may come] *and follow Me* [believing in Me, conforming to My example in living and, if need be, suffering or perhaps dying because of faith in Me]. *For whoever wishes to save his life* [in this world] *will* [eventually] *lose it* [through death], *but whoever loses his life* [in this world] *for My sake will find it* [that is, life with Me for all eternity]. *For what will it profit a man if he gains the whole world* [wealth, fame, success], *but forfeits his soul? Or what will a man give in exchange for his soul?*"

I always try to remember that Jesus was faced with the same temptation in the wilderness that the devil tries to use on the unbeliever and believer alike here on this earth. Matthew 4:8-11 says,

> *Again, the devil took Him up on a very high mountain and showed Him all the kingdoms of the world and the glory* [splendor, magnificence, and excellence] *of them; and he said to Him,* "All these things I will give You, if You fall down and worship me." *Then Jesus said to him,* "Go away, Satan! For it is written *and forever remains written,* 'YOU SHALL WORSHIP THE LORD YOUR GOD, AND SERVE HIM ONLY.'" *Then the devil left Him; and angels came and ministered to Him* [bringing Him food and serving Him].

You see, the devil tried to deceive Jesus. He wanted Jesus to believe he could give Him the entire world if He just bowed down and worshipped him. But Jesus knew the truth and rebuked Satan. Then, to add insult to injury, He reminded Satan on His way out that, *"You shall worship the Lord your God, and serve Him only."* Jesus countered Satan's punch with the Word of God, and then His angels came to minister to the Lord. Jesus knew what He came to earth to do and bowing down to Satan to gain the world was not one of them.

Make no mistake, Satan and his demons are doing the same thing today. In most cases, a person doesn't audibly hear what Satan is saying like Jesus did. Nevertheless, the devil entices people by promising he will give them the world if they just fall down and worship riches. If he can successfully get someone to do that, he has enabled that person to build the idol of money or mammon and worship it instead of God.

When someone is worshipping mammon instead of God, mammon controls that's persons financial behavior much like lust controls someone's physical behavior. Mammon manifests itself in someone's life through one or more of these characteristics: anxiety about ones possessions and/or the fear of losing them, finding security in wealth instead of God, spending more than necessary on the world's goods, forgetting that God is the source of all wealth, loving money as if it's a person, greed in all its forms and boasting about wealth in a prideful way, just to name a few.

REMOVING THE BLIND EYE

Where do we start? This explanation could be an entirely separate book! How do we determine if we are serving God or serving mammon? Just ask yourself three questions. First, do you have the same worries of the world? Secondly, are you deceived by riches to the point that most of your treasures are here on earth? Thirdly, do you desire other things above God? These three very straightforward questions are the hardest for most of us to answer.

Many assume this is a "gray area" open for interpretation. In reality, the opposite is true. As much as I would like to say otherwise, it's really black or white—an absolute truth versus a relative truth, if we are very honest as we evaluate this area of our lives. If we worry about anything financially instead of having a healthy concern, then we have *turned a blind eye*. If we have little to show in our heavenly bank accounts and all our treasures are on this earth, then we have *turned a blind eye*. If we desire to accumulate things that are wants versus needs, then we have *turned a blind eye*. We could be serving mammon and not even realize it.

We're talking about living in such a way that money has become a deity in our lives, and we worship it in a greedy pursuit to have more than is needed. The *Cambridge English Dictionary* defines greed in simple terms that I can understand: "the force that makes people try to become as rich as possible and the belief that this is the most important thing in life."[3]

King David said in Psalm 62:10, "*If your riches increase, do not set your heart upon them.*" It's an issue of the heart, and all the evidence we need is to listen to what we talk or think about, look at where we spend our money, and determine whether our goals are centered on the world. As pointed out in the chapter on idolatry, if we walk like a duck, quack like a duck and act like a duck, then we're probably a **mammon-loving duck**! Is this harsh? Yes. It was meant to be when Jesus drew the line in the sand and clearly stated that a man cannot serve God and mammon. That's why He spent more time talking about money and possessions than any other topic during His ministry.

Did you know that nineteen of the thirty-nine parables are about money and possessions? Jesus knew money would be a stronghold for us all. Does this mean we're to be poor Christians who are broke all the time? I don't believe so, but in many cases, this happens because of poor stewardship of the resources God gives us. Many Christian business leaders who run large corporations choose to use their resources to first advance God's kingdom then modestly bless themselves and their families. They dedicate all money generated first and foremost to transferring their treasures from earth into Heaven by using God's resources to further His kingdom. They "wire" money into their heavenly accounts on a regular basis not to earn any sort of favor from God but because of their desire to impact the world for Jesus. I can promise you these men and their companies are clearly serving God and not mammon because they have plenty of money to use in whatever way they wish.

We must push the spiritual reset button on our understanding of what it means to serve God or mammon. Answering the three questions mentioned above is a good start. Ask for the thoughts of someone you are close to and walk together with the Lord. If you're convicted that you have this money thing all wrong, go to God and receive forgiveness. Then, take action that will reflect that God is first and money is somewhere down the line. We can no longer *turn a blind eye* to this epic issue in believers' lives. The evidence is there—one way or the other—if we will only look.

CHAPTER 19

WORRY

Therefore I tell you, stop being worried or anxious (perpetually uneasy, distracted) about your life, as to what you will eat or what you will drink; nor about your body, as to what you will wear. Is life not more than food, and the body more than clothing? Look at the birds of the air; they neither sow [seed] nor reap [the harvest] nor gather [the crops] into barns, and yet your heavenly Father keeps feeding them. Are you not worth much more than they? And who of you by worrying can add one hour to [the length of] his life? And why are you worried about clothes? See how the lilies and wildflowers of the field grow; they do not labor nor do they spin [wool to make clothing], yet I say to you that not even Solomon in all his glory and splendor dressed himself like one of these. But if God so clothes the grass of the field, which is alive and green today and tomorrow is [cut and] thrown [as fuel] into the furnace, will He not much more clothe you? You of little faith! Therefore do not worry or be anxious (perpetually uneasy, distracted), saying, "What are we going to eat?" or "What are we going to drink?" or "What are we going to wear?" For the [pagan] Gentiles eagerly seek all these things; [but do not worry,] for your heavenly Father knows that you need them. But first and most importantly seek (aim at, strive after) His kingdom and His righteousness [His way of doing and being right—the attitude and character of God], and all these things will be given to you also. "So do not worry about tomorrow; for tomorrow will worry about itself. Each day has enough trouble of its own." (Matthew 6:25-34)

WORRY

Greek: from *merimna*—care, anxiety

Cambridge English: to think about problems or unpleasant things that make you anxious, or to make someone feel anxious

Dictionary.com: to torment oneself with or suffer from disturbing thoughts; to fret; a cause of uneasiness or anxiety; trouble

Merriam-Webster: troubled state of mind, anxiety

WHEN WE worry or are anxious about anything in the natural world, the primary cause of this emotion boils down to a lack of trust in God and His purposes for our lives. We all do it, though some more than others. Because most Christians are embarrassed to recognize it, they suppress it and *turn a blind eye* to this in their lives. In many people's minds, sharing their anxiety with a fellow believer is a sign of weakness. That belief only hurts that individual who is struggling and is the work of the enemy.

On the flip side of that coin is a believer who worries about everything and is more than happy to share those worries with anyone who will listen, including those outside of the faith. That hurts our witness and affects anyone who is curious about the gospel because, as Jesus stated above, that's what the pagan world seeks—**so the believer who is a worrier is no different than the unbeliever who is anxious**.

Refusing to share with fellow believers and sharing with the unbelieving world are both harmful to the Christian walk. In addition, many Christians even medicate themselves to control the symptoms of their worry. While medicine can be beneficial temporarily, if anxiety is a permanent situation, a deeper spiritual cause might be at the root of the problem.

Some believe that because we are commanded not to worry or be anxious, worry and anxiety evidence a lack of trust in God that is sinful. I have no idea whether God considers worry a sin; frankly, that should not be the focal point. If someone is really struggling with worry, the last thing they want to hear is that it's sin. If someone commits adultery, call it sin. If someone is worrying, help them build their faith to overcome this devil-induced emotion. I think the best Scripture in the New Testament, besides what Jesus said Himself, is found in Philippians 4:6-7, which says,

> Do not be anxious or worried about anything, but in everything [every circumstance and situation] by prayer and petition with thanksgiving, continue to make your [specific] requests known to God. And the peace of God [that peace which reassures the heart, that peace] which transcends all understanding, [that peace which] stands guard over your hearts and your minds in Christ Jesus [is yours].

Obviously, God does not want us to worry. When my children were younger, they would sometimes come into the bedroom and say, "Daddy, I'm scared and worried the monster will get me." My kids knew they could come to their father, and I would make everything okay. It's the same with God. The reason why Paul knew this is because he had many opportunities to tell God about his worries when he was imprisoned, beaten and uncertain of his future. He knew he could ask God to give him the peace in any circumstance and that the peace he felt surpassed all natural understanding. Paul said in Philippians 4:11, *"Not that I speak from [any personal] need, for I have learned to be content [and self-sufficient through Christ, satisfied to the point where I am not disturbed or uneasy] regardless of my circumstances.*" I don't believe that verse describes someone who is worried or anxious.

Jesus conveys the same message throughout Scripture. He said if we abide in Him (His Word), we can ask for anything and it will be granted. Why? So, His Father can be glorified. Does worry and anxiety glorify God? It does not, and Jesus reminds us that worry can't add a single hour to our lives anyway!

Some dismiss this Scripture by saying, "Well, that was Jesus saying that. He was the Son of God, but I am all human and can't help it." That's exactly why I point out the apostle Paul. He was just like all of us, yet he found the remedy for worry and anxiety. The apostle Peter who worried about everything before he was filled with the Holy Spirit says in 1 Peter 5:6-7:

> *Therefore humble yourselves under the mighty hand of God [set aside self-righteous pride], so that He may exalt you [to a place of honor in His service] at the appropriate time, casting all your cares [all your anxieties, all your worries, and all your concerns, once and for all] on Him, for He cares about you [with deepest affection, and watches over you very carefully].*

Worry is not from God but from our earthly enemy, the devil. If your mind is full of worry and anxiety, then that is what will rule your life. If it's full of faith and what the Word says about your circumstances, then peace, joy, certainty, hope, contentment, sureness and calm will rule your life. **The battle is in our minds.**

Let me be clear that worry is different than fear, which we will discuss in more detail in a later chapter. Fear precedes worry and anxiety. **In other words, worry and anxiety are by-products of fear.** That fear is typically what causes the root problem of not trusting God and His plans for our lives. A healthy concern is a good thing. To fret or have a troubled state of mind is a bad thing. Let me illustrate. An aviation company has designed a light airplane with a parachute just in case of

138 | *Turning a Blind Eye*

catastrophic failure. If the pilot cannot remedy the problem, he can pull the chute and the plane will slowly descend to the ground and hopefully land safely. I have seen a video of this invention in action, and it's both cool and comforting at the same time!

In such an aircraft, while a passenger might have a healthy concern that the pilot is qualified and the plane is in good working condition, that backup chute would eliminate the fear of crashing—in turn eliminating worry and anxiety throughout the flight. The flip side of that coin is boarding a commercial flight with no parachute after reading in the news that another plane crashed with no survivors. When that plane gets into the air and then hits major turbulence soon after takeoff, a passenger might become fearful the plane will crash because there is no parachute and the plane appears to be outdated. That fear causes immediate worry and anxiety, which likely would continue throughout the flight even after reaching the cruising altitude. The passenger who was not worried or anxious in the plane with the parachute feels differently now.

That's exactly what we do in our minds with everyday life issues such as our finances, jobs, children, illness and a host of other examples. When we're worried or anxious due to fear, we believe there is no parachute to help us land safely when, in fact, there is—God Himself. The devil will try to tell us otherwise, and fear will dominate our minds if we allow it and will have a negative impact on our lives. **Just as anxiety and worry are a by-product of fear, peace and contentment are a by-product of trust in God or faith.** As surely as you trust that when you flip that light switch electricity will flow and light up the room, you can be sure that God will remove worry and anxiety if you ask and trust in Him.

When I was diagnosed with a rare form of leukemia in 2007, I really was not anxious or worried. Why? Because I had no fear of death. I believed God would heal me either supernaturally or through the medication that the medical professionals developed through the mind

God gave them. I have always said, "If physical death is my worst-case scenario, that's fine with me." I didn't fear death, so the enemy could not penetrate my mind and cause worry and anxiety. Now, I struggle in other areas of my life and have to fight the good fight of faith to overcome those emotions; but with my health at that time, I had perfect peace.

REMOVING THE BLIND EYE

It's imperative that we determine what the spiritual root cause is for any circumstance that causes worry and anxiety. If we don't get to the root cause of the fear we're experiencing that is causing worry and anxiety, then we will never know what we need to ask God to remove. The first step is not to *turn a blind eye* to that issue for any reason at all. Search your heart and write down the fears you have and why you are concerned. I think it is very helpful to make your list then sit down with a "faithful friend" and spill the beans! That person can help unwind the tangled web the devil has created in your mind. Once you have done that and discovered the root cause, you can then come into agreement with your friend and ask God to remove it. Once the root cause is gone, then the by-products of worry and anxiety will be gone as well.

Secondly, a person needs to stop verbalizing what he or she is worried about and thus giving the enemy a foothold. He cannot read your mind. He can only activate his schemes based on the words you speak. Stop saying things like, "I'm worried sick" or "That worries me to death" or any other form of a confession contrary to God's Word. Instead, *"Do not be anxious or worried about anything, but in everything [every circumstance and situation] by prayer and petition with thanksgiving, continue to make your [specific] requests known to God."* (Philippians 4:6) Instead of verbalizing your worries to someone else, take them to God in prayer because only He can do something about your situation. The trust we exhibit in God and the confession of our faith in God's Word instead of worrying is setting a good example to others that our trust is in the Lord and not the world, so anyone sitting on the fence will be inspired to ask how we live so peacefully in light of worrisome circumstances. That's a great segue into the Gospel and might perhaps give you the opportunity to preach the good news.

Finally, be sensitive to others who maybe struggling with worry and anxiety. If you sense someone is worried or anxious based on their countenance or words, ask directly. Don't *turn a blind eye* and not inquire about the fears that might be causing the worry and anxiety. Trust me, people will thank you. Proverbs 12:25 (NASB) says, *Anxiety in the heart of a man weighs it down, but a good word makes it glad.*

CHAPTER 20

JUDGING

Do not judge and criticize and condemn [others unfairly with an attitude of self-righteous superiority as though assuming the office of a judge], so that you will not be judged [unfairly]. For just as you [hypocritically] judge others [when you are sinful and unrepentant], so will you be judged; and in accordance with your standard of measure [used to pass out judgment], judgment will be measured to you. Why do you look at the [insignificant] speck that is in your brother's eye, but do not notice and acknowledge the [egregious] log that is in your own eye? Or how can you say to your brother, "Let me get the speck out of your eye," when there is a log in your own eye? You hypocrite (play-actor, pretender), first get the log out of your own eye, and then you will see clearly to take the speck out of your brother's eye. (Matthew 7:1-5)

JUDGE

Greek: from *anakrinó*—to examine, investigate

Cambridge English: to form, give, or have as an opinion, or to decide about something or someone, especially after thinking carefully

Dictionary.com: to form an opinion or estimate

Merriam-Webster: to form an estimate or evaluation of

A MAJOR MISCONCEPTION exists regarding the subject of judging others in the church and the world in general. I hear people say, "Stop judging me" or "We accept people and don't judge them." Most of the time, these statements come from people who either don't want to stop what they are doing or are open to compromise regarding sin. Jesus never said we could *not* judge, but He clearly stated that before we do, we are to make sure we have judged ourselves on the issue we bring to light to another person. He is talking about hypocrites who judge others for exactly what they are doing themselves. If that is the case, then the measure we give out will come back on our heads in like measure.

Over the past forty years, "not judging" has allowed so many compromises in the body of Christ and society as it relates to the indisputable Word of God. Additionally, so many church leaders have had very public moral failings that we have lost the right to genuinely try to help someone who can't see that "speck" in their eye. Some use John 3:17 to justify their position on not judging when Jesus said, *"For God did not send the Son into the world to judge and condemn the world [that is, to initiate the final judgment of the world], but that the world might be saved through Him."* **In this verse, Jesus is talking about salvation, not lifestyle choices.** He goes on to say in John 5:30, *"I can do nothing on my own initiative or authority. Just as I hear, I judge; and My judgment is just (fair, righteous, unbiased), because I do not seek My own will, but only the will of Him who sent Me."* Paul expanded on the subject further in Romans 2:1 when he wrote,

> *Therefore you have no excuse or justification, every one of you who [hypocritically] judges and condemns others; for in passing judgment on another person, you condemn yourself, because you who judge [from a position of arrogance or self-righteousness] are habitually practicing the very same things [which you denounce].*

Most people ignore verse five when they discuss this topic, which says, *"You hypocrite (play-actor, pretender), first get the log out of your own eye, and then you will see clearly to take the speck out of your brother's eye."* (Matthew 7:5) I can tell you that I wish someone had judged me and helped me to see the error of my ways before it was too late. Jesus said in paraphrase, "Hey, if you see a brother or sister stumbling, then make sure you have dealt with that issue in your own life (the log) before you confront the person about the issue (the speck) in their life."

A good example in my life centers on my driving habits. I have a heavy foot, and I sometimes exceed the speed limit. My wife will say, "Greg, the speed limit is such and such. Do you want to get a ticket?" Well, the instant she says that, my temperature rises; I want to tell her not to judge me, but my wife literally never speeds. She has never received a speeding ticket in her life, so she has no log in her eye. I am powerless to refuse her advice because I know I am guilty of having a speck in my own eye. I also know she is trying to help me not break the law.

My analogy may seem silly, but it's no different with any other shortcoming, fault or sin that we realize a fellow believer needs to correct. If we're walking it out ourselves, then we owe it to others to help them see what they could change.

REMOVING THE BLIND EYE

We need to stop being fearful of pointing out issues in other believer's lives that need to be addressed. Most folks are simply too uncomfortable to face a person and humbly address the issue. As a practical example, let's say I see one of my brothers in Christ not treating his wife with honor and respect. What I would do first is ask my wife if I treat her with honor and respect. She would say that I do, so I have met one condition. Then I am likely to ask a close friend who has seen me interact with my wife and get his opinion. If he agrees that I treat my wife appropriately, then I am free, and frankly obligated, to go to that brother and bring up the issue. **I can't control how someone else receives it, but I can control how I deliver it.** I can then with a pure heart know before God that I didn't *turn a blind eye* to it and sincerely tried to help a fellow brother in the Lord. James 5:19-20 says,

> *My brothers and sisters, if anyone among you strays from the truth and falls into error and [another] one turns him back [to God], let the [latter] one know that the one who has turned a sinner from the error of his way will save that one's soul from death and cover a multitude of sins [that is, obtain the pardon of the many sins committed by the one who has been restored].*

James was addressing Hebrew Christians who lived outside of Palestine. These believers had fallen into some sort of sin. James said if we *"judge"* in similar situations and enable others to see the folly of their ways and turn back, we will cover a multitude of sins. We owe it to our brothers and sisters to point out character defects in their lives so they can grow in their faith. We just need to make sure we are not being hypocritical and practicing the same deed.

CHAPTER 21

THE SPIRIT OF GREED

Then He said to them, "*Watch out and guard yourselves against every form of greed; for not even when one has an overflowing abundance does his life consist of nor is it derived from his possessions.*" (Luke 12:15)

GREED

Greek: from *pleonexia*—Greedy desire to have more, covetousness, avarice

Cambridge English: a strong desire to continually get more of something, especially money

Dictionary.com: excessive or rapacious desire, especially for wealth or possessions

Merriam-Webster: desiring more than one needs or deserves

CONTRARY TO what Gordon Gekko said in the movie *Wall Street*, greed is not good. His exact quote was, "*Greed*, for lack of a better word, is *good*." A follower of Christ should never hold that worldview. Another word for *greed* is *covetousness*, which *Merriam-Webster* defines as "marked by inordinate desire for wealth or possessions or for another's possessions, having a craving for possessions."[1] So many of us *turn a blind eye* when it comes to greed; in fact, most the time, we try to justify our accumulation of possessions, our work to gain status or our maneuvering to get power. While nothing is wrong with these things if we're trying to achieve them for God's purposes with a right heart, Matthew 23:12 says, *"Whoever exalts himself shall be humbled; and whoever humbles himself shall be raised to honor."* We all have been humbled in some form or fashion and learned this lesson the hard way.

It's interesting that in Luke 12:15, Jesus said, *"all forms of greed."* This implies that there are ways to be a greedy person other than just being stingy with money like Scrooge in Dickens' *Christmas Carol*. So, what forms of greed should we open our eyes to and what are some of the consequences of greed? First, we must understand that greed begins at a very early stage of life.

As early as the age of two, my children began to demand that everything they touched was theirs by saying, "Mine!" They were usually after a toy or snack that belonged to another child. They were convinced it was theirs and would throw a fit to get their way.

Just as a firecracker must have a lit fuse before exploding, greed must desire something before rearing its ugly head. 2 Peter 2:14 mentions having a heart trained in greed: *"They have eyes full of adultery, constantly looking for sin, enticing and luring away unstable souls. Having hearts trained in greed, [they are] children of a curse."* This implies that just as a dog can be trained to obey, our hearts can be trained to obey greed and all its forms. I break down greed into four forms that meet the definition of more of something:

1) Material

2) Power

3) Prestige

4) Influence

MATERIAL GREED

At its core, this is simply desiring materialistic gains that a) are not yours, or (b) you don't need, or (c) you took from others to enrich yourself at the expense of somebody else. How many stories have we all read or heard on the news about someone stealing another's possessions or, in other words, taking what is not theirs? It's so common that shows like "American Greed" have enough content available to air to last until Jesus returns! Although there are many ways to steal, one driving force usually causes it to happen—greed. The spark that ignites greed is usually the desire for money or possessions. Some will even kill in order to get what they want, despite the potential consequences and the effect on other people's lives.

How much is enough? This question is valid when considering whether we want more than we really need. I witness this form of greed most often in my business life. I see people who have enough resources to last several lifetimes, yet they continue to accumulate material possessions for their own pleasures. The parable of the rich fool in Luke 12:13-21 should cause every believer to rethink his strategy if this is an issue in life. This passage gives us a clear look at what greed and covetousness look like in our world and church today.

> *Someone from the crowd said to Him, "Teacher, tell my brother to divide the family inheritance with me." But He said to him, "Man, who appointed Me a judge or an arbitrator over [the two of] you?" Then He said to them, "Watch out and guard yourselves against every form of greed; for not even when one has an overflowing abundance does his life consist of nor is it derived from his possessions. Then He told them a parable, saying, "There was a rich man whose land was very fertile and productive. And he began thinking to himself, 'What shall I do, since I have no place [large enough in which] to store my crops?' Then he said, 'This is what I will do: I will tear down my storehouses and build larger*

ones, and I will store all my grain and my goods there. And I will say to my soul, "Soul, you have many good things stored up, [enough] for many years; rest and relax, eat, drink and be merry (celebrate continually)." But God said to him, 'You fool! This very night your soul is required of you; and now who will own all the things you have prepared?' **So it is for the one who continues to store up and hoard possessions for himself and is not rich [in his relationship] toward God."**

The weight the bolded verse (21) carries is because Jesus said it Himself and that is what brought me to my knees. When we decide to store up treasure for ourselves on this earth without thought of what those resources can do for others while we dwell in our earthly tents, it is simply greed. Those who live like this have no understanding of the eternal treasures they will receive by transferring their wealth from earth into Heaven. It's all about satisfying a craving for more when they already have enough. I know this to be true because it happened to me. Does this imply that wealth or personal possessions are wrong? Of course not, but it does reflect what is important to us and certainly causes most believers to be shortsighted.

You see, *love* of money is the spark that causes this form of greed.

For the love of money [that is, the greedy desire for it and the willingness to gain it unethically] is a root of all sorts of evil, and some by longing for it have wandered away from the faith and pierced themselves [through and through] with many sorrows. (1 Timothy 6:10)

A great analogy I like to use to help folks see that they are *turning a blind eye* to this issue involves my wife. I love my wife, and if you spend any time around me you will hear me talk about her and what a wonderful wife and mother she is to my family. If you are around us, you likely will witness my getting a bit "frisky" with her, which drives my five children crazy. I think about her, pray for her and do my best to provide for her. Bottom line is, I love her, and you can see that she is a priority in my life.

The same holds true about physical possessions and money. All some people talk about is money—how much they have in one account or another, deals that will increase those balances many times over, new cars, new houses and new toys they purchased. You clearly know they *love* those possessions because they talk about them all the time and describe the joy they get from them. They take care of these possessions, think about them regularly and make sure that they get paid for if they took out a loan. The bottom line is that they *love* their money and possessions. This is greed—and this type of greed is idolatry.

> Colossians 3:5 says, *So put to death and deprive of power the evil longings of your earthly body [with its sensual, self-centered instincts] immorality, impurity, sinful passion, evil desire, and greed, which is [a kind of] idolatry [because it replaces your devotion to God].*

How can you love the Lord your God with all your heart, all your soul, all your mind, and all your strength if there is an idol before Him? The answer is that it's impossible. God said in the first two commandments in Exodus 20:3-4,

> *You shall have no other gods before Me. You shall not make for yourself any idol, or any likeness (form, manifestation) of what is in heaven above or on the earth beneath or in the water under the earth [as an object to worship].*

When we "worship" money and possessions, we have idols in our lives.

We need to look no further than Solomon when we struggle with financial greed. In Ecclesiastes 5:10-11 he says,

> *He who loves money will not be satisfied with money, nor he who loves abundance with its gain. This too is vanity (emptiness).*

When good things increase, those who consume them increase. So what advantage is there to their owners except to see them with their eyes?

Keep in mind Solomon was the richest king ever and likely one of the wealthiest people in the history of the world. If he wasn't satisfied with money, then none of us will be either.

POWER GREED

This greed can be just as destructive as material greed, but it is tolerated by more people. *Power* is defined as "possession of control, authority, or influence over others."[2] When used in the right way, power can be a good force; but when used for the wrong motive, power can cause destruction not only in that person's life but also in the lives over which that person has authority. We often hear someone say, "He is on a power trip." In layman's terms, it simply means the person is relishing that authority, which amounts to greed. In most cases, people who act in such a way crave even more power than they are currently given. Jesus said in Mark 10:42-45,

> *Calling them to Himself, Jesus said to them, "You know that those who are recognized as rulers of the Gentiles lord it over them; and their powerful men exercise authority over them [tyrannizing them]. But this is not how it is among you; instead, whoever wishes to become great among you must be your servant, and whoever wishes to be first and most important among you must be slave of all. For even the Son of Man did not come to be served, but to serve, and to give His life as a ransom for many."*

A desire for power does not apply only to the high-powered CEO, the successful entrepreneur or the ultra-rich, which make up the top one percent of our society. According to CNBC, the average income of the top one percent nationwide is $1.32 million. The other ninety-nine percent, on the other hand, earn an average of $50,107 a year.[3] Can people earning $50,107 a year, which by the world's standards makes them rich in most other countries, have greed for power? Absolutely! Greed for power is not biased towards an individual's socioeconomic status. You can be relatively free from material greed yet have an insatiable appetite for power. Regardless of class, Jesus made it clear we are not to "lord" over anyone under our authority. When power is used as a good force, those with authority will take on an attitude of servant-hood and earn the respect due the position of authority given to them. Conversely, if the motive is to exercise power to satisfy a greed for respect/power, they will eventually become a slave to themselves, which turns into a destructive force. Proverbs 16:18 says, "*Pride goes before destruction, and a haughty spirit before a fall.*"

Merriam-Webster defines *haughty* as "blatantly and disdainfully proud: having or showing an attitude of superiority and contempt for people or things perceived to be inferior."[4] If you ever run across a person who has greed for power, this definition will fit them to a tee. A haughty spirit is the left jab that causes a boxer to stumble, but pride is the uppercut that knocks him to the mat and destroys him. Simon, a former practicing magician, was saved through a message from Philip and then baptized in water. Peter and John came down from Jerusalem to lay hands on the new converts to receive the Holy Spirit. Acts 8:16 says, *For He had not yet fallen on any of them; they had simply been baptized in the name of the Lord Jesus [as His possession].* So, Simon, a new believer who formerly seemed to take great joy in astonishing the crowds through his magic, is a good example of believers "letting down their guard" to greed. This is what happened.

ACTS 8:17-24, *Then Peter and John laid their hands on them [one by one], and they received the Holy Spirit. Now when Simon saw that the Spirit was given through the laying on of the apostles' hands, he offered them money, saying, "Give me this authority and power too, so that anyone on whom I lay my hands may*

> *receive the Holy Spirit." But Peter said to him, "May your money*
> *be destroyed along with you, because you thought you could buy*
> *the [free] gift of God with money! You have no part or share in*
> *this matter, because your heart (motive, purpose) is not right be-*
> *fore God. So repent of this wickedness of yours, and pray to the*
> *Lord that, if possible, this thought of your heart may be forgiven*
> *you. For I see that you are provoked by bitterness and bound by*
> *sin." But Simon answered, "Pray to the Lord for me both of you,*
> *so that nothing of what you have said will come upon me."*

So, Simon watched the apostles lay hands on folks who then received the power of the Holy Spirit, and he wanted that **power.** He was even deceived into thinking he could pay money for it.

PRESTIGE GREED

Prestige greed is the cousin to power greed. *Merriam-Webster* defines *prestige* as "standing or estimation in the eyes of people; weight or credit in general opinion; a commanding position in people's mind."[5] Jesus made it a point to show us what this looked like when He rebuked the Pharisees and Scribes. He said the following in Matthew 23:5-8:

> *They do all their deeds to be seen by men; for they make their*
> *phylacteries (tefillin) wide [to make them more conspicuous] and*
> *make their tassels long. They love the place of distinction and honor*
> *at feasts and the best seats in the synagogues [those on the plat-*
> *form near the scrolls of the Law, facing the congregation], and to be*
> *greeted [with respect] in the market places and public forums, and*
> *to have people call them Rabbi. But do not be called Rabbi (Teach-*
> *er); for One is your Teacher, and you are all [equally] brothers.*

Those who crave a commanding or favorable position in people's minds may not have greed for material possessions or greed for power. They seem to want to portray themselves as having everything together through the way they look and sound. They are very concerned about how people view them and strive daily to make sure they portray the right image. They surround themselves with material possessions not because they necessarily lust for them, but rather because of what those possessions silently communicate to other people. The house they occupy doesn't necessarily need to be the most expensive, but it must be in the "right" neighborhood. The car they drive, the watch they wear, and even the type of credit card they display must match their image. Even the title on their business card is important to them.

Obviously, nothing is wrong with Christians driving a nice car or wearing a nice watch, but God wants us to prosper for His purposes. Simply put, Christians can own material wealth as long as those possessions don't own us. Sadly, many Christians seem to have a misplaced motive for desiring prestige and all the bling required to present such an image. In fact, many believers go into deep debt just to maintain a lifestyle that is a manifestation of this form of greed. It's likely that such a person who lost his possessions would not be nearly so devastated by the material losses as by what such loss would do to his image or even his self-worth. This person uses material possessions as a means to an end—just to fill a void in their lives.

Even seemingly generous people might donate money for construction projects, for example, but require the building to have their name on it. Perhaps they want to have the right picture with an important figure or someone famous or the name of their company plastered all over the place. To some, having a seat in the front row at church or at a conference creates the right optics.

I know this happens because this was me. The idea of prestige and what people thought about me from the outside looking in was very important to me. I was more concerned about the image that others saw instead of what God was seeing in me. It became all-consuming and took my eyes off Jesus; this type of greed caused me to look instead to others for my affirmation or approval.

We can expect this type of validation to be important to those who don't know Christ, but as believers, we must evaluate whether this is true of us—and change if needed. It's just as destructive, although more insidious, than any other form of greed. It affects family, business, relationships and other areas of life. In my humble opinion, it is the form of greed that often results in suicide. The ultimate betrayal by the devil is the loss of a carefully crafted image—so when that happens, people decide to take their life because all is lost in their own mind. That's a lie straight from the pit of hell. Many spouses, children, parents, grandparents, friends and church leaders have faced this reality when it was too late to help. I know that from personal experience. We owe it to this type of person not to *turn a blind eye* when we see them steering off course.

INFLUENCE GREED

We all have seen these individuals who "know all the right people." They believe they are the gatekeepers to decision makers and hold the only key to making something happen. They have an address book the size of the Book of Life that they are constantly refining and are more than happy to tell you about it. It might be an executive, a co-worker, church member, committee member, neighbor or even your spouse. They have an insatiable desire to have influence in their sphere of life. *Merriam-Webster* defines *influence* as "the capacity to have an effect on the character, development, or behavior of someone or something, or the effect itself."[6] The three greatest examples of influence greed can be found in business, politics and the church.

Take for example business, which is much like the Italian mob. All mobsters say they "know a guy who knows a guy" who can get something you need—and there is always the guy in business who knows a guy or knows a guy who knows a guy to get a deal accomplished. This person claims to have all the connections to influence any part of the transaction. In fact, in many encounters in my professional life, this person didn't need to "know the guy who knows the guy" because he already had direct access—whether to company owners, investors, bankers, decision makers, etc. This person has spent his or her professional life building "influence" for the exact right opportunity.

In some cases, such an individual is truly connected and produces results. At other times, the person is exaggerating and only thinks he has influence. In either case, such a focus is detrimental to a person's well-being if used for personal motives. You find the person with influence greed in all forms of organized business. He or she spends an enormous amount of time wining and dining folks at the best restaurants, taking lavish vacations with the influencer, donating to all the political parties to gain access to events and meet even more well-placed people. This person is always very close to his targets to remind them of their importance, and he bends over backwards to do whatever these people require in an attempt to gain influence. The need to gain influence overrides anything else in his professional or personal life. Politics has the same framework but is much less forgiving. Influence jockeying in this arena resembles a blood sport in terms of its aggression, tactics and lack of boundaries.

It's so easy for many of us to *turn a blind eye* to the real solution, which is to understand that we earn influence by our walk, and that allows us to gain the capacity to influence other people's lives. The Reverend Billy Graham was a perfect example of being influential in ordinary people's lives as well as to many world leaders. He didn't seek the influence or jockey, posture or manipulate to gain it. He earned his influence by his own good character, which allowed him to have a positive impact on millions of lives.

Greed in any form should have no place in any person's life, regardless of their faith. Greed is harmful, in spite of what the world believes about it. In fact, the Bible describes *greed* as *idolatry* (Colossians 3:5), *sinful* (Isaiah 57:17), *trained* (2 Peter 2:14), *improper*

(Ephesians 5:3), *a mask* (1 Thessalonians 2:5), *a trap* (Proverbs 11:6), and *deadly* (Acts 5:1-10).

The most important consequence of greed is that it can keep a person from having eternal life.

> *Do you not know that the unrighteous will not inherit or have any share in the kingdom of God? Do not be deceived; neither the sexually immoral, nor idolaters, nor adulterers, nor effeminate [by perversion], nor those who participate in homosexuality, nor thieves,* **nor the greedy,** *nor drunkards, nor revilers [whose words are used as weapons to abuse, insult, humiliate, intimidate, or slander], nor swindlers will inherit or have any share in the kingdom of God.* (1 Corinthians 6:9-10)

Luke 12:15 relates this warning from Jesus: *Then He said to them, "Watch out and guard yourselves against every form of greed; for not even when one has an overflowing abundance does his life consist of nor is it derived from his possessions."* He said to guard ourselves, which would imply that we can be tempted to fall into one of the four categories of greed—otherwise why guard against it? How do we stand guard against greed?

1) Recognize before you take any action the real motive and purpose behind that action.

2) Ask your heavenly Father to protect you from greed.

3) Just stand and wait for the Holy Spirit to guide like He promised.

If, like many people, you find yourself already walking in some form of greed, recognize it, talk to your heavenly Father, repent and change.

REMOVING THE BLIND EYE

For all four forms of greed, the first step to removal is recognizing it as a stronghold in your life. If you feel the need to have to ask yourself if you're greedy, that may be a telling sign. Be honest with yourself or, better yet, have someone close to you be honest with you. The solution for removing the *blind eye* is different for each of the four types of greed, but none will be effective until we first realize the problem exists.

Removing the Blind Eye to Material Greed

Material greed is the most prevalent form of greed in the church and world today. It's intertwined throughout our lives, and the devil has been able to put a spin on it that the means justifies the end. When someone asks how much stuff is enough, it is typically meant to be subjective in nature; but from a biblical point of view, it's the right question to ask, and the answer we give determines the condition of our heart. If anyone wants to determine if they have any degree of material greed in their heart, there is an easy way to find out. Just take a look at your tax return to see how much you're giving and your bank statement to see where you're spending. If you're one of the one, five or ten percenters, then look at your balance sheet as well and see what you're accumulating. The fact of the matter is, regardless how you measure it, if you are doing so through the lens of "how much stuff is enough," you will get a totally different perspective and possibly the answer to that question.

The antidote for material greed is generosity. Even if you're rich, generosity and material greed cannot co-exist. **I believe that a materially greedy person lives for this world, but a generous person is living for the next one**. A generous person can let go of the false illusion that more is better while on this earth. Generous people do estate planning both for earthly and eternal reasons. A generous person understands that every deed done on this side of Heaven will have a reward when they reach the other side. Jesus said in Matthew 6:21, *"For where your treasure is, there your heart [your wishes, your desires; that on which* *your life centers] will be also."* The person whose treasure is stored on earth in the form of multiple houses, cars, jewelry, etc. without having the ledger balanced with treasures in Heaven is greedy. The person with a generous heart is always considering how every possession on earth, regardless of its value, can be used to bless others besides himself and his immediate family.

Freedom from material greed requires action and a paradigm change in how you view money. It's literally renewing your mind in this area of your life, then determining to be steadfast in seeing all your income and current or future possessions in light of eternal benefits instead of earthly, temporal benefits. If someone's attitude is, "You can't take any of it with you, so get as much as you can now and enjoy it," that wrong perspective misses the entire point. We all know you will take absolutely nothing physical into the afterlife. But if someone has determined to use what God has given in all material things to bless others because "you can't take it with you," God will bless that perspective. Believers who embrace a life filled with material greed will die a sad death because the joy they received from living for themselves will all be left behind; there will be very little to celebrate when they see Jesus. For unbelievers, it really doesn't matter because the rich and poor die alike, without any hope of an eternal home in Heaven. Proverbs 22:2 says, *"The rich and poor have a common bond; The LORD is the Maker of them all."*

Removing the Blind Eye to Power Greed

The unquenchable thirst for power is the undoing of many people. The quest is like a "silent-killer" disease—the disease can be killing you, but you just don't know it yet. The lust for power does the same thing.

It's common to hear someone who is materially greedy brag about their possessions or openly speak of their lust for more to anyone who will listen. Just as material greed is an internal drive that manifests externally in possessions and lack of generosity, the greed for power is an internal drive that manifests externally through actions that are the polar opposite of servitude. **The antidote for power greed is servanthood.** In the world's system, people can obtain brute power by self-determination and a disregard for all the body bags left in their wake. In the spiritual world, power is earned and comes in the form of a servant instead of a master.

We can find power greed in ourselves or in others within the Christian community. Do we *turn a blind eye* to that in ourselves to obtain power at the expense of others including our families and co-workers? Perhaps you know someone who is greedy for power whose motives you have never had the nerve to question? As a believer, thirst for power is ultimately a two-edged sword that will come back to bite at some point. It's not **if** but **when.** Paul tells us what Jesus said in 2 Corinthians 12:9,

> *But He has said to me, "My grace is sufficient for you [My lovingkindness and My mercy are more than enough—always available—regardless of the situation]; for [My] power is being perfected [and is completed and shows itself most effectively] in [your] weakness." Therefore, I will all the more gladly boast in my weaknesses, so that the power of Christ [may completely enfold me and] may dwell in me.*

Power given to advance the Kingdom of God in our earthly functions should be earned and not demanded, because that's the only kind of power that will last.

Removing the Blind Eye to Prestige Greed

Prestige greed is the one form of greed that everyone slides under the mat and more often than not *turns a blind eye* to it. Many Christians (including yours truly years ago) strive to build a certain image in other people's minds that usually centers around their perceived status. The Scripture that comes to mind as it relates to possessions is in Proverbs 13:7, *There is one who pretends to be rich, yet has nothing at all; Another pretends to be poor yet has great wealth.* The body of Christ is no different than the world when it comes to this. In fact, we have the same propensity to borrow money in order to acquire material possessions to present the false illusion of status.

In other ways, prestige greed has nothing to do with material possessions. Status in not limited only to monetary gain—it could manifest as sitting on the front row in church, who someone is seen with in church and in the community, or deeply caring what other people think of you. Most folks who have prestige greed are people pleasers who find it critical to keep all the puzzle pieces in the right place to maintain the illusion. **The antidote for prestige greed is to die to self and look up to God and not man.** Striving for prestige is pointless when you have God on your side. Proverbs 18:16 says, *A man's gift [given in love or courtesy] makes room for him, and brings him before great men,* so it's the gift that God gives each of us that earns us prestige—not something created by our own minds.

Jesus gave us the answer to this issue in John 12:24-25:

> *I assure you and most solemnly say to you, unless a grain of wheat falls into the earth and dies, it remains alone [just one grain, never more]. But if it dies, it produces much grain and yields a harvest. The one who loves his life [eventually] loses it [through death], but the one who hates his life in this world [and is concerned with pleasing God] will keep it for life eternal.*

If we die to striving to gain prestige in this world by our own will, we will not care how the world perceives us—which in turn will cause us to look up at Jesus instead of looking into the mirror. The reflection from looking at Jesus is totally different than the one the mirror gives.

We should not care what others think about the car we drive, the house we live in, the company we work for, or anything else for that matter. These all are symbols of status in this world that mean nothing for the next world. We must ask ourselves if trying to keep a certain status or image is affecting our walk with God. Such greed could manifest as burdensome consumer debt, having to own a certain piece of jewelry or clothing, or something as simple as having to constantly spin stories to validate your worth in your own eyes as well as in the eyes of those around you. Such actions are totally unnecessary because God loves us in whatever station of life we find ourselves today.

Removing the Blind Eye to Influence Greed

Influence greed is personified by the "movers and shakers" in both the church and the world at large through business, politics, or some other avenue. You know these folks because they are always angling for the right position. They attempt to connect the dots of life to ensure they are in the center of the sphere of influence. These are good people whose priorities are out of whack. They believe they are necessary in order to make the world go around—both theirs and everyone else's. **The antidote for influence greed is humility.**

When you see yourself as a conduit for God, who is more than capable of making the right connections, you are immediately humbled and realize you have no more influence than what God gives you. 1 Peter 5:6 says, *Therefore humble yourselves under the mighty hand of God [set aside self-righteous pride], so that He may exalt you [to a place of honor in His service] at the appropriate time.* God also said He is opposed to the proud but gives grace to the humble (James 4:6). If you feel like you have to work to gain influence, that idea is not from God. Humility allows us to see just how small we are in this world and realize that apart from Jesus we can do nothing of ourselves. This realization will result in more influence than we ever imagined—influence that will advance God's agenda instead of our own.

CHAPTER 22

COVETOUSNESS

*For from within, [**that is**] out the heart of men, come base and malevolent thoughts and schemes, acts of sexual immorality, thefts, murders, adulteries, acts of greed and covetousness, wickedness, deceit, unrestrained conduct, envy and jealousy, slander and profanity, arrogance and self-righteousness and foolishness (poor judgment).* (Mark 7:21-22)

COVETOUSNESS

Greek: (noun) from *pleonexia*—greedy desire to have more, covetousness, avarice; (verb) from *epithumeo*—to desire, lust after[1]

Cambridge English: wanting to have something too much, especially something that belongs to someone else

Dictionary.com: inordinately or wrongly desirous of wealth or possessions; greedy, eagerly desirous

Merriam-Webster: greedy, acquisitive, grasping, avaricious; having or showing a strong desire for especially material possessions; *covetous* implies inordinate desire, often for another's possessions

GREEDINESS AND covetousness are often mentioned in the same sentence. In the Greek, the noun derivative is the same for both words. That being said, when *covet* is used as a verb, it adds an additional meaning that I believe is important today. Someone controlled by the spirit of greed has an excessive or rapacious desire, especially for wealth or possessions. That definition can apply to covetousness as well, but my focus here is on the word when used as a verb. To covet is not always about only money or possessions. While it can refer to money and possessions, it can also be for another person's spouse, a co-worker's job and even someone's position in the ministry. When Jesus said, *"deeds of coveting"* in Mark 7:22, He said it in the plural, which in my mind covers more than just money and possessions. I am convinced that anyone can covet, even if they are not greedy or do not have a love for money.

The fact that Jesus included covetousness as one of the thirteen sins that defile a person warrants attention.

> MARK 7:20-23 says, *And He was saying, "That which proceeds out of the man, that is what defiles the man. For from within, out of the heart of men, proceed the evil thoughts, fornications, thefts, murders, adulteries, **deeds of coveting** and wickedness, as well as deceit, sensuality, envy, slander, pride and foolishness. All these evil things proceed from within and defile the man."*

Listed among the other commandments relating to man, Exodus 20:17 says the following:

> *You shall not covet [that is, selfishly desire and attempt to acquire] your neighbor's house; you shall not covet your neighbor's wife, or his male servant, or his female servant, or his ox, or his donkey, or anything that belongs to your neighbor.*

Keep in mind that *neighbor* doesn't mean only the person that lives next to you, but rather the community in general.

Just as the spirit of greed can lead to covetousness, the spirit of covetousness can lead to adultery, murder, theft, lying and a host of other sins we are commanded not to practice. The most common example today that illustrates the path of destruction taken by coveting something we should not is coveting another person's spouse. Think about it. Any man or woman, before committing adultery, must first desire another person's spouse. It's coveting something that doesn't belong to us that leads to the act of adultery. Adultery occurs in two ways that is the same sin in God's eye. It can occur in the heart or be a physical act, but either way, we have committed sin. As common as adultery is in our churches today, it really makes me grateful for the blood of Jesus and the opportunity He gives to turn from that—or any sin, for that matter—and be forgiven. Coveting sexually is just one of the many "deeds" to which we can fall prey, but because it can lead to adultery—which shatters families, reputations and a person's very soul—it seems to be one of the most destructive. Coveting someone's house or cars, position in a company or ministry, power or status are all equal opportunity offenders; but these sins usually come with far fewer earthly consequences. That is not to say the spiritual repercussions are any less costly, but those are often faced when we face judgment before God.

REMOVING THE BLIND EYE

I view defeating covetousness before an earthly or spiritual consequence occurs is a lot like defeating cancer. You *must* catch this sin in its early stages; otherwise, it could be too late. Regarding coveting a person sexually, we must deal with that thought in our mind first before it turns into an openly committed sin. The battle is in the mind, and it requires discipline and the Word of God to renew our minds. We know such thoughts *are not* from God and, without a doubt, are from the enemy.

As a man, sexual desire is stimulated by sight and touch. Since the eyes are the gateway to the heart, man must guard what he sees at all times. Usually a man sees, then fantasizes, and that is followed by some action as the next step. Once touching occurs, the situation is typically way past the point of return. The key is to stop a lustful thought before it becomes a fantasy. When such a thought comes to mind, a man must immediately rebuke it in Jesus' name and refuse to go there. The thought might have originated because of watching a movie or television show that glorified such behavior, or perhaps because of staring too long while hanging out at the pool when another man's wife was swimming with her kids. It doesn't matter what *precipitated* the covetous thought; we must kill it at its root, which is when it enters the mind.

The same is true of all the other forms of covetousness as well. We must stop the first thought in its tracks before it takes root. If a person continues to struggle with any type of covetousness, he or she needs to share that struggle with a trusted Christian brother or sister. This is one *blind-eye* issue that could cause life-changing consequences if ignored.

CHAPTER 23

LOVING THE WORLD

If you belonged to the world, the world would love [you as] its own and would treat you with affection. But you are not of the world [you no longer belong to it], but I have chosen you out of the world. And because of this the world hates you. (John 15:19)

WORLD

Greek: from *kosmos*—pertaining to this world

Cambridge English: the planet on which human life has developed

Dictionary.com: the class of persons devoted to the affairs, interests or pursuits of this life

Merriam-Webster: the concerns of the earth and its affairs as distinguished from Heaven and the life to come

F AR TOO many Christians are in love with this world without any regard for the next one to come. These are some of the same folks who do not and will not risk offending anyone in this world. If you are speaking about God and certainly Jesus, it is virtually impossible for you to be loved by those in the secular world. I John 3:13 says, *"Do not be surprised, believers, if the world hates you."* This is exactly what Jesus was saying to His disciples in the Scripture at the beginning of this chapter. During the time Jesus walked the earth, He was the target of most people's anger, but His disciples were equally hated for following Him. Jesus told us why in John 17:16, *"They are not of the world, just as I am not of the world."*

Believers as well as unbelievers who love this world have allowed God and Jesus to be slowly removed from our social, educational and government functions—despite the fact that this country was founded on biblical principles. Any believer who exercises his or her faith today is ridiculed and, in many instances, even hated for their stance. Believers who love this world will never mention Jesus or God, so they conform to the world's standards and rarely take a stance for righteousness. This allows them to have many "friends" and be loved and accepted by those of the world.

Loving the world involves more than simply loving the material things of the world. It's a deeper issue of the heart where apathy becomes the standard. James 4:4 says,

You adulteresses [disloyal sinners—flirting with the world and breaking your vow to God]! Do you not know that being the world's friend [that is, loving the things of the world] is being God's enemy? So whoever chooses to be a friend of the world makes himself an enemy of God.

Christians are not supposed to hate the people of the world. Instead, we are to loathe the "things" of this world and the effect the lost worldview can have on our hearts and minds. James 1:27 says the following:

Pure and unblemished religion [as it is expressed in outward acts] in the sight of our God and Father is this: to visit and look after the fatherless and the widows in their distress, and to keep oneself uncontaminated by the [secular] world.

This may sound a little morbid, but my position is that I am so excited to one day get to the eternal world that this physical world gives me little pleasure anymore. That's not to say I don't enjoy being with my family, spending time with my grandchildren, doing business and fellowshipping with my close friends. I do all these things and enjoy them immensely; but I understand that if I allow myself to love this world and everything in it and what it stands for, then the benefits of the next world are minimized.

Many successful people in business delight in the fact that they are living "the good life." In this world the term "good life" usually means they have lived well materially due to their success. Being financially successful can be a good thing if used for the right purposes. Unfortunately, when a person has this "good life" mindset, it usually means they are living for this world and not the next one. All too often, that bubble is burst when they face challenges in life—especially related to their health—which puts it all in perspective.

John 12:25-26 tells us what it looks like from Jesus' perspective not to love the world and what it has to offer:

> *The one who loves his life [eventually] loses it [through death], but the one who hates his life in this world [and is concerned with pleasing God] will keep it for life eternal. If anyone serves Me, he must [continue to faithfully] follow Me [without hesitation, holding steadfastly to Me, conforming to My example in living and, if need be, suffering or perhaps dying because of faith in Me]; and wherever I am [in heaven's glory], there will My servant be also. If anyone serves Me, the Father will honor him.*

Now, that is living for the next world in a practical way. If we focus on pleasing God by becoming Christ-like, we're called to "hate" this life. I love what Paul said in Galatians 6:14, *But far be it from me to boast [in anything or anyone], except in the cross of our Lord Jesus Christ, through whom the world has been crucified to me, and I to the world.* Dying to our flesh and this world and focusing on Jesus is what gives us all true purpose of life.

REMOVING THE BLIND EYE

The best way not to love this world is to understand how temporary it is so you can have a better appreciation for the next one to come. As believers, we are assured that our ultimate destiny is to live with God in the new heaven. Physical life is short, but spiritual eternity lasts forever. King David understood this when he said in Psalm 39:5, "*Behold, You have made my days as [short as] hand widths, And my lifetime is as nothing in Your sight. Surely every man at his best is a mere breath [a wisp of smoke, a vapor that vanishes]!*" When we really get this revelation that David spoke of, we begin to look at the world as we know it now as a stumbling block to living for the next one.

Equally important is to make a decision to stop wanting to please man. Once we start living to get recognition or accolades from anyone or anything but God himself, then we're destined to mold ourselves to this world to feed our fragile egos. Jesus said in Luke 16:15,

> *So He said to them, "You are the ones who declare yourselves just and upright in the sight of men, but God knows your hearts [your thoughts, your desires, your secrets]; for that which is highly esteemed among men is detestable in the sight of God."*

If we realize how short life is and that pleasing man in this world is futile, we will not be afraid to proclaim the gospel, influence the nations or take necessary stances for our faith because we care less about this existence and all its temporal pleasures and focus on loving the world to come. As John said in 1 John 2:16,

> *For all that is in the world—the lust and sensual craving of the flesh and the lust and longing of the eyes and the boastful pride of life [pretentious confidence in one's resources or in the stability of earthly things]—these do not come from the Father but are from the world."*

Let's start focusing on what comes from the Father; then it becomes easier to fall out of love with this world.

CHAPTER 24

BLASPHEMY

Therefore I say to you, every sin and blasphemy [every evil, abusive, injurious speaking, or indignity against sacred things] will be forgiven people, but blasphemy against the [Holy] Spirit will not be forgiven. Whoever speaks a word against the Son of Man will be forgiven; but whoever speaks against the Holy Spirit [by attributing the miracles done by Me to Satan] will not be forgiven, either in this age or in the age to come. (Matthew 12:31-32)

BLASPHEMY

Greek: from *blasphemia*—defamation or evil speaking in general

Cambridge English: something you say or do that shows you do not respect God or a religion

Dictionary.com: impious utterance or action concerning God or sacred things; irreverent behavior toward anything held sacred, priceless, etc.; an act of cursing or reviling God

Merriam-Webster: profane speech, writing or action concerning God or sacred things

UNDERSTANDING THE horrific sacrifice Jesus made on the cross on our behalf makes it personal to me when believers and unbelievers blaspheme our Lord. We hear people say *Jesus Christ* in conjunction with some vulgar word prior to or after making a point, or they even add an expletive after God's name. We also hear vulgar or crass words added to the word *holy*. The third commandment in Exodus 20:7 says,

> **Y**ou shall not take the name of the LORD your God in vain *[that is, irreverently, in false affirmations or in ways that impugn the character of God]; for the* LORD *will not hold guiltless nor leave unpunished the one who takes His name in vain [disregarding its reverence and its power].*

Isaiah 52:5 says,

> *"***B**ut now, what do I have here," declares the LORD, "seeing that My people have been taken away without reason? Those who rule over them howl [with taunting and mockery of salvation]," declares the* LORD, *"****and My name is continually blasphemed all day long.***"*

Romans 2:24 says, *For, "***T**HE NAME OF GOD IS BLASPHEMED AMONG THE GENTILES BECAUSE OF YOU*," just as it is written [in Scripture].* Astoundingly Paul turned over two followers to Satan to teach them not to blaspheme as recorded in 1 Timothy 1:20: *"Among these are Hymenaeus and Alexander, **whom I have handed over to Satan, so that they will be disciplined and taught not to blaspheme.***"* I love what Jesus' half-brother James said in James 2:6-7,

> **B**ut you [in contrast] have dishonored the poor man. Is it not the rich who oppress and exploit you, and personally drag you into the courts of law? Do they not blaspheme the precious name [of Christ] by which you are called?

When you hear someone blaspheming, and you can count on it that you will, don't *turn a blind eye* and simply say nothing. In love, remind the speaker that he or she is talking about your (and perhaps his or her) Lord, Savior, Holy Spirit or Heavenly Father—and you would appreciate them showing respect to you and reverence to God. I clearly understand that God can defend Himself, but our love for Jesus and God should be so great that hearing his name cursed is no different than if someone chose to curse someone else that we dearly love—like husband, wife, parent or child. If that happened, it would generate an entirely different response with most people. I am not suggesting that someone throw a punch, but if it were me, I would tell the speaker he had crossed a line and needed to move on.

Why don't we react similarly when someone blasphemes our Lord and Savior or uses God's name in vain? This should not happen, and it's up to us to point out such error. Jesus forgives people when they use His name like this, but it still does not make it right—especially among believers. Unfortunately for some, and according to Matthew 12:31, there is no forgiveness for those who blaspheme the Holy Spirit. The Pharisees had blasphemed against the Holy Spirit by attributing to Satan the power by which Jesus did miracles instead of crediting the Holy Spirit. This is a serious *blind-eye* issue that is rarely addressed. We should do so in love but also in truth.

REMOVING THE BLIND EYE

During the time of Jesus, people who blasphemed God could be put to death. Today in some parts of the world, blasphemy in the Muslim faith carries the same death penalty. Thank God for Jesus and our Christian faith, which does not require any earthly consequence like death, but leaves judgment in the hands of God.

If a person confesses to be a believer then blasphemes, we owe it to that person to say something. Proverbs 27:5 says, *"Better is an open reprimand [of loving correction] Than love that is hidden."* **How can we as believers use God's or His Son's name during the week to punctuate a sentence—likely due to anger, disbelief or some other negative emotion—then use the same name in church on Sunday**

to praise Him? A gentle discussion to explain this to believers could have a big impact in their lives, but most people don't like confrontation, so they fail to do anything.

Whenever I realize someone is about to finish the name of Jesus with a curse word, before they can finish, I say, "my Lord and Savior." I receive a lot of funny looks, but that's one way to open the door with someone who doesn't know the Lord. Other times, especially with believers, I confront them head on and just let them know why such speech likely grieves God and what the Word specifically says about it. In many cases the Holy Spirit and the Word convict them, and they stop and only use His name in reverence.

CHAPTER 25

CONFESSING JESUS

Therefore, the one who confesses and acknowledges Me before men [as Lord and Savior, affirming a state of oneness with Me], that one I will also confess and acknowledge before My Father who is in heaven. But the one who denies and rejects Me before men, that one I will also deny and reject before My Father who is in heaven. (Matthew 10:32-33)

CONFESS

Greek: from *homologeo*—to speak the same, to agree

Cambridge English: to acknowledge

Dictionary.com: to acknowledge or avow

Merriam-Webster: to tell or make known

IT OFTEN amazes me how seldom we hear the name of our Lord used in church. The word *deny* means that one "refuses to admit the truth or existence of."[1] These two verses are part of the forty-two verses in Matthew 10 when Jesus was instructing His disciples. Before this, He said in verses 28-31,

Do not be afraid of those who kill the body but cannot kill the soul; but rather be afraid of Him who can destroy both soul and

body in hell. Are not two little sparrows sold for a copper coin? And yet not one of them falls to the ground apart from your Father's will. But even the very hairs of your head are all numbered [for the Father is sovereign and has complete knowledge]. So do not fear; you are more valuable than many sparrows.

Jesus was basically warning the disciples of the persecutions coming their way and reminding them to remain faithful to Him and His name. Many believers around the world, especially in Middle Eastern countries, face the reality of persecution every day. They are tortured and beaten in an attempt to get them to deny their faith and accept a twisted ideology. Many die and others are scarred for life after this experience.

For those of us fortunate enough to be believers in the United States, it's unlikely that we will face this type of persecution and be forced to deny our faith or face death. With that being said, we can deny Jesus in a more insidious manner. It's very common to see believers who are timid or even scared to use the name of Jesus when the greatest consequence is that they might make someone uncomfortable or, horror or horrors, angry. **I believe that we all can be guilty of denying Jesus by simply not acknowledging Him in our everyday lives.**

The definition of *deny* doesn't imply that one must be asked in order to deny the truth or existence of something. If you are refusing to admit something—which is defined as "confess to be true or to be the case, typically with reluctance,"[2] then our failure to confess the name of Jesus means we are in one way denying Him by saying nothing at all. Should we not all be so full of Jesus that we can't keep ourselves from admitting or confessing Him in some form or fashion?

Before I was saved, I ran with a crowd of guys who didn't have a high degree of moral character, and that included me. I was married then, and most of my friends were married as well. Some of them would take off their wedding ring and put it in a pocket as we entered bars or clubs just in case they met a pretty woman. These friends want-ed to leave the option open of being able to deny they were married. In all likelihood, women wouldn't inquire about a spouse if they didn't see a ring. My friends who took off their rings were not acknowledging their wives, so by default they were denying them—at least until the bars closed.

In the same way, we all *turn a blind eye* to the name of Jesus by simply *not* recognizing Him in our daily lives. I remember when we had each one of our five children; immediately after each birth, I was telling anybody who would listen about my new child and what we named him or her. Should I not be that excited everyday about Je-sus and look for opportunities to mention His name and how much I love Him and how much joy He has brought into my life? Of course, I should, but I don't do it nearly enough.

Does that mean when I enter a Starbucks to get my daily five shots of espresso over ice that I should be yelling the name of Jesus as I walk in, then do the same when I am leaving? No, that's not what I am say-ing. People would think I was crazy, and any opportunity to minister to someone while getting my espresso would fly out the window. Co-lossians 4:5 says, "*Conduct yourself with wisdom in your interactions with outsiders (non-believers), make the most of each opportunity [treat-ing it as something precious]*." What the Lord wants from us is not to deny Him by failing to mention Him and use His name as we go about each day. Philippians 2:9-11 says,

For this reason also [because He obeyed and so completely hum-bled Himself], God has highly exalted Him and bestowed on Him the name which is above every name, so that at the name of Jesus EVERY KNEE SHALL BOW [in submission], of those who are in heaven and on earth and under the earth, and that every tongue will confess and openly acknowledge that Jesus Christ is Lord (sovereign God), to the glory of God the Father.

Again, we see in Acts 4:12, "*And there is salvation in no one else; for there is no other name under heaven that has been given among people by which we must be saved [for God has provided the world no alternative for salvation].*" So we all should wake up each morning and decide that we are not going to *turn a blind eye* to the name of Jesus and ask God to give us opportunities through conversation, meetings or any other way to mention His Son.

Paul said to Timothy in 2 Timothy 1:8,

> *So do not be ashamed to testify about our Lord or about me His prisoner, but with me take your share of suffering for the gospel [continue to preach regardless of the circumstances], in accordance with the power of God [for His power is invincible],*

and Paul added the following in 2 Timothy 1:12,

> *This is why I suffer as I do. Still, I am not ashamed; for I know Him [and I am personally acquainted with Him] whom I have believed [with absolute trust and confidence in Him and in the truth of His deity], and I am persuaded [beyond any doubt] that He is able to guard that which I have entrusted to Him until that day [when I stand before Him].*

Can we boldly say the same?

REMOVING THE BLIND EYE

You can go to any major sporting event in this country and hear people yelling at the top of their lungs for one team or the other. They are fanatics about their team, and they are not afraid to let you know. Yet, if we hear someone shouting the name of Jesus in a church service, I find it very sad that we feel that is totally inappropriate. We can talk about our favorite team or player and how they won or lost a game, but we are too scared to mention the name of our Lord. People are dying for their faith for simply mentioning the name of Jesus in other countries, but we are more concerned about being politically correct or "sensitive" to others. Do you know what is wrong with the name of Jesus? Nothing! If all of us looked at Jesus like many look at a rock star, we would hear His name spoken *everywhere*.

I am convinced that if more believers recognized our failure to mention His name as *turning a blind eye* that many people's lives could be changed. The church seems to be playing spiritual charades by giving every hint in the book and hoping someone picks up on it versus just saying His name! Remember Matthew 10:33 when Jesus said, *"But the one who denies and rejects Me before men, that one I will also deny and reject before My Father who is in heaven."*

Personally, I will never be ashamed or in fear of using the name that is not only the name above all names but also the reason why I will be able to live with God in eternity. Proudly and confidently share the name of Jesus, and don't worry about how the world perceives you.

CHAPTER 26

THE ULTIMATE SACRIFICE

And Jesus answered them, "The hour has come for the Son of Man to be glorified and exalted. I assure you and most solemnly say to you, unless a grain of wheat falls into the earth and dies, it remains alone **[just one grain, never more]**. *But if it dies, it produces much grain and yields a harvest. The one who loves his life* **[eventually]** *loses it* **[through death]**, *but the one who hates his life in this world* **[and is concerned with pleasing God]** *will keep it for life eternal. If anyone serves Me, he must* **[continue to faithfully]** *follow Me* **[without hesitation, holding steadfastly to Me, conforming to My example in living and, if need be, suffering or perhaps dying because of faith in Me]***; and wherever I am* **[in heaven's glory]**, *there will My servant be also. If anyone serves Me, the Father will honor him. Now My soul is troubled and deeply distressed; what shall I say? 'Father, save Me from this hour* **[of trial and agony]**'? *But it is for this* **[very]** *purpose that I have come to this hour* **[this time and place]**." (John 12:23-27)

SACRIFICE

Greek: from *thysía*—properly, an offering (sacrifice); an official sacrifice prescribed by God; hence an offering *the Lord accepts* because it is *offered on His terms*

Cambridge English: to give up something for something else considered more important

Dictionary.com: to surrender or give up, or permit injury or disadvantage to, for the sake of something else

Merriam-Webster: a giving up of one thing for the sake of another

J ESUS SIMPLY gave up His life so we could have eternal life. Saying it and doing it are two different things. Jesus did it, and what He had to endure should be seared into the hearts and minds of all believers. It's my opinion that most Christians want to *turn a blind eye* to the real suffering Jesus endured while being tried in court then ultimately led to the cross. It's like turning our eyes away from a bad accident on the highway. If I don't see it, then I won't think about it. How many sermons do you hear that describe in detail the time between Jesus' arrest and crucifixion?

Here is a recap: After His arrest, He was beaten beyond recognition, scourged, and spat upon. His beard was plucked out, and a crown of one- to three-inch thorns was placed on his head. He received repeated blows to His face and was slapped. He was beaten on the head with a reed, given sour wine, mocked, blindfolded, stripped naked, and forced to walk to His own execution carrying a hundred-pound crossbeam at least a portion of the way to the site of His own crucifixion. Once there, the horrific crucifixion preparation began prior to Him being hung naked on the cross in the heat of the day for six hours. The following information describes the process and effects of crucifying a human being. Take a moment to read and reflect what happened physically to our Lord and Savior for our benefit. The barbaric torture that Jesus had to endure for me causes a welling up of emotion from deep within my soul, and, yet at the same time, a heartfelt gratitude for the salvation I inherited from His selfless act.

CRUCIFIXION sometimes began with a scourging or flogging of the victim's back. The Romans used a whip called a flagrum, which consisted of small pieces of bone and metal attached to a number of leather strands. The number of blows given to Jesus is not recorded; however, the number of blows in Jewish law was 39 (one less than the 40 called for in the Torah, to prevent a counting error). During the scourging, the skin was ripped from the back, exposing a bloody mass of tissue and bone. Extreme blood loss occurred, often causing death, or at least unconsciousness. In addition to the flogging, Jesus faced severe beating and torment by the Roman soldiers, including the plucking of His beard and the piercing of His scalp with a crown of thorns. After the flogging, the victim was often forced to carry his own crossbar, or patibulum, to the execution site. The patibulum could easily weigh 100 pounds. In the case of Jesus, the record shows that He may have carried His patibulum a distance of more than two football fields. In a weak and tormented state, it's no wonder the record establishes that Jesus needed a great deal of assistance. At the execution site, the patibulum was put on the ground and the victim was forced to lie upon it. Spikes about seven inches long and three eighths of an inch in diameter were driven into the wrists. The spikes would hit the area of the median nerve, causing shocks of pain up the arms to the shoulders and neck. Already standing at the crucifixion site would be the seven-foot-tall post, called a stipes. In the center of the stipes was a crude seat to "support" the victim. The patibulum was then lifted on to the stipes, and the victim's body was awkwardly turned on the seat so that the feet could be nailed to the stipes. At this point, there was tremendous strain put on the wrists, arms and shoulders, resulting in a dislocation of the shoulder and elbow joints. The position of the nailed body held the victim's rib cage in a fixed position, which made it extremely difficult to exhale, and impossible to take a full breath. Having suffered from the scourging, the beatings and the walk with the patibulum, Jesus was described as extremely weak and dehydrated. He was probably losing significant amounts of blood. As time passed, the loss of blood and lack of oxygen would cause severe cramps, spasmodic contractions and probably unconsciousness.

Ultimately, the mechanism of death in crucifixion was suffocation. To breathe, the victim was forced to push up on his feet to allow for inflation of the lungs. As the body weakened and pain in the feet and legs became unbearable, the victim was forced to trade breathing for pain and exhaustion. Eventually, the victim would succumb in this way, becoming utterly exhausted or lapsing into unconsciousness so that he could no longer lift his body off the stipes and inflate his lungs. Due to the shallow breathing, the victim's lungs would begin to collapse in areas, probably causing hypoxia. Due to the loss of blood from the scourging, the victim probably formed a respiratory acidosis, resulting in an increased strain on the heart, which beats faster to compensate. Fluid would also build up in the lungs. Under the stress of hypoxia and acidosis, the heart would eventually fail. There are several different theories on the actual cause of death for Jesus. One theory is that the pericardium filled with fluid, which put a fatal strain on the ability of His heart to pump blood. Another theory states that Jesus died of cardiac rupture. Still others theorize that Jesus' death was "multifactorial and related primarily to hypovolemic shock, exhaustion, asphyxia and perhaps acute heart failure." Regardless of the actual medical cause of final death, the historical record is very clear that Jesus suffered numerous hours of horrible and sustained torture on the cross of Calvary.[1]

I can't imagine any other way to die that would be worse than a human crucifixion. There were no drug cocktails like we have today that just made a person go to sleep then die shortly thereafter. No propofol to knock Him out to avoid the pain. What if we had been there to witness it firsthand? Would it be like what we do today when coming upon a car accident and seeing mangled bodies on the road? Would we just turn our heads, so we wouldn't have to deal with the pain and suffering? I am certain that I would have had great difficulty enduring or even watching what happened to Jesus. I believe many Christians feel the same today regarding the brutality of Christ's death. We know He died; we just don't want all the details. When you read the Crucifixion account, something inside you must rise and recognize the cost He paid that day for our sins. Just because the crucifixion happened over 2,000 years ago does not make it any less real or relevant today.

REMOVING THE BLIND EYE

The movie *The Passion of Christ* was released in 2004 and became a box office hit, grossing over $611,899,420 million worldwide.[2] Mel Gibson was the director, and, against all studio wisdom, the movie was produced for only $30 million. It has ministered to both saved and unsaved from all walks of life. The reason why has very little to do with the common methods others use when they produce a blockbuster or even receive an Academy award. In fact, the movie had very few words spoken during the entire 127-minute run time. The reason why it touched so many people is because it humanized and portrayed the gruesome price Jesus paid when He was crucified on our behalf. The movie focused on the last twelve hours of Jesus' life, followed by the resurrection. Viewers would stand and begin preaching during the credits, people were saved, and the world was able to see the closest depiction of what really happened to our Lord ever produced.

We have heard the slogan "Never forget 9-11," in reference to the day when terrorists attacked our homeland. During the first five to ten years after that tragic day, the memory was at the forefront of people's minds. After a decade passed, that battle cry diminished, and now we have to be purposely reminded to keep 9-11 in the forefront of our minds.

When it comes to what Jesus suffered at the time of His crucifixion on the cross, we seem to be in the same dilemma as we are in regarding 9-11. We have forgotten the horrific pain and suffering Jesus endured as a human being. We *turn a blind eye* and rarely reflect or share the historical facts of his suffering. Here in Texas we say, "Remember the Alamo" and, as a native Texan, that event is seared into my mind. Christians should have those last twelve hours of Jesus's earthly life seared into our minds so that we can be grateful during every waking moment for the sacrifice He made on our behalf.

CHAPTER 27

THE SPIRIT OF FEAR

"Peace I leave with you; My [perfect] peace I give to you; not as the world gives do I give to you. Do not let your heart be troubled, nor let it be afraid." [Let My perfect peace calm you in every circumstance and give you courage and strength for every challenge.] (John 14:27)

FEAR

Greek: from *phebomai* (to be put to flight)—panic, flight, fear, terror

Cambridge English: a strong emotion caused by great worry about something dangerous, painful, or unknown that is happening or might happen

Dictionary.com: a distressing emotion aroused by impending danger, evil, pain, etc., whether the threat is real or imagined; the feeling or condition of being afraid

Merriam-Webster: anxiety caused by real or possible danger, pain, fright

As addressed in the chapter on worry, fear is the root source that causes worry and anxiety. Without the fear of something, how can you be worried or anxious? According to the Billy

Graham Evangelistic Association, "An estimated forty million people in the United States feel trapped or crippled by fear. They live as prisoners to their own anxiety."[1] This is just in the United States, so the numbers worldwide would be staggering. I have come to expect that those who do not know the Lord Jesus Christ will struggle with fear in their lives because they have not yet received the revelation of who God is and what He is capable of doing in their lives. What surprises me is how many true believers suffer from the same fear in their own lives even when they know how mighty God is and that He is active in their daily affairs.

I too have suffered from fear in certain areas of my life, so I can understand; but more importantly, God understands as well. Even though Jesus said in John 14:1, *"Do not let your heart be troubled; believe in God, believe also in Me,"* we still let fear creep into our lives. When we live in fear, which causes worry and anxiety, we are not only forgetting what Jesus said but also forgetting all the promises of God. **As a believer, fear is faith in the enemy's ability because all forms of fear come from our enemy, the devil.**

We should all have a healthy fear of God. Paul said in 2 Corinthians 7:1, *"Therefore, since we have these [great and wonderful] promises, beloved, let us cleanse ourselves from everything that contaminates body and spirit, completing holiness [living a consecrated life—a life set apart for God's purpose] in the fear of God."* When we fear God, we do so not with the expectation of punishment, but rather with reverence for Him and who He is in our lives. Psalm 33:8 spells it out so clearly: *"Let all the earth fear the LORD; Let all the inhabitants of the world stand in awe of Him."* If we have a healthy fear of God, we can't help but be in awe of Him. Many fear God for the wrong reasons, and others have no concept of awe because they do not allow Him to dominate their lives. In our society, it's more common to be in awe of a successful man or woman than of the one who created those individuals as well as the universe.

Personal fear, as opposed to the fear of God, is not a feeling but a powerful spirit that wreaks havoc on a believer's life. Scripture tell us that is a fact in 2 Timothy 1:7, which says,

> *For God did not give us a spirit of timidity or cowardice or fear, but [He has given us a spirit] of power and of love and of sound judgment and personal discipline [abilities that result in a calm, well-balanced mind and self-control].*

Just like the spirit of faith produces positive results, the spirit of fear produces negative results. You don't have to look any further than Job during the time he was going through the worst adversity a human could endure. He said in Job 3:25-26,

> *For the thing which I greatly fear comes upon me, And that of which I am afraid has come upon me. I am not at ease, nor am I quiet, And I am not at rest, and yet trouble still comes [upon me].*

Job said the very things he allowed himself to fear had come to pass in his life. This was said by a person who was righteous in God's eyes. How often do we verbalize our fears and give the devil a foothold into our minds?

What we should all do when fear comes upon us is to immediately get into the Word and confess what God says about the situation, not what the devil says. Jesus said to the Pharisees in John 8:44,

> *You are of your father the devil, and it is your will to practice the desires [which are characteristic] of your father. He was a murderer from the beginning and does not stand in the truth because there is no truth in him. When he lies, he speaks what is natural to him, for he is a liar and the father of lies and half-truths.*

Since we know God would never put a spirit of fear on our lives, by the process of elimination, that fear must come from the father of lies, the devil. When he peddles the spirit of fear and you buy it, then he will come back and do it again and again.

Whenever we realize this spirit is trying to come on us, we should counter it with our faith and the promises of God. Hebrews 11:1 (NASB) says, "*Faith is the assurance of things hoped for, the conviction of things not seen.*" Faith will dig out the root of fear so that its ugly cousins, worry and anxiety, will not befall us in spite of our circumstances. Fear will tell you that you're going to die unexpectedly, lose your job, get a serious disease, die of cancer, have an unfaithful spouse, and on and on until you stand firm against the schemes of the devil. He will always try to pedal doubt and unbelief so your focus will turn inward based on circumstances that have not even occurred, which in turn causes worry and anxiety. If life throws you a curve ball, as they say, and your heart is full of faith and the promises of God instead of fear, you will be able to have peace even during adversity and trust God for the outcome. The question is not whether we're going to have physical, emotional, and spiritual trials on earth, because we will. The question is when they do come, how will we handle them. James 1:2-4 says,

> *Consider it nothing but joy, my brothers and sisters, whenever you fall into various trials. Be assured that the testing of your faith [through experience] produces endurance [leading to spiritual maturity, and inner peace]. And let endurance have its perfect result and do a thorough work, so that you may be perfect and completely developed [in your faith], lacking in nothing.*

Therein lies the answer!

That's what I did when I was diagnosed with leukemia. If you don't believe me, then believe what Jesus said Himself in Mark 11:20-24:

> *In the morning, as they were passing by, the disciples saw that the fig tree had withered away from the roots up. And remembering, Peter said to Him, "Rabbi (Master), look! The fig tree which You cursed has withered!" Jesus replied, "Have faith in God [con-*

*stantly]. I assure you and most solemnly say to you, whoever says
to this mountain, 'Be lifted up and thrown into the sea!' and does
not doubt in his heart [in God's unlimited power], but believes
that what he says is going to take place, it will be done for him
[in accordance with God's will]. For this reason I am telling you,
whatever things you ask for in prayer [in accordance with God's
will], believe [with confident trust] that you have received them,
and they will be given to you."*

Jesus was saying that faith moves mountains—not fear, doubt or
unbelief. Realize that God is for you and not against you. Isaiah 41:10
says the following:

*Do not fear [anything], for I am with you; Do not be afraid, for
I am your God. I will strengthen you, be assured I will help you;
I will certainly take hold of you with My righteous right hand [a
hand of justice, of power, of victory, of salvation].*

If we accept this Scripture as fact, which it is, fear has no place as we
walk with the Lord.

REMOVING THE BLIND EYE

It's important to recognize that you are afraid in some area of your
life and refuse to *turn a blind eye* to it any longer. Go to your secret
place and tell God what fear(s) you are struggling with, then thank
Him for your deliverance.

Secondly, ask yourself who is the author of the spirit of fear you
are struggling to overcome. That's somewhat of a rhetorical question
because we know who it is, and we can use God's own words to defeat
that fear. Jesus gave us the solution when He was tempted by the devil
for forty days and forty nights in the desert prior to the beginning
of His ministry. The event is covered in Matthew 4:3, and here is the
bottom line. The Bible states, *"And the tempter came and said to Him.*
Satan will always show his hand by *saying* it first." If you hear that voice

in your head, you know who it is and that it's a total lie because God would never say that to any true believer. Then in Jesus' response, He says, *"It is written,"* then *speaks* the Word of God to the devil. That was the end of the ball game, the devil left, and angels came to minister to Jesus. We have that exact same power today to get the devil and his spirit of fear to flee if we use it. Tell Satan what the Scriptures say instead of what the world says. Then you will see results.

The final step is to accept deep in your inner being (your spiritual heart) that God loves you and wants you to fear nothing except to have a healthy fear of Him while you live in this world. When you accept that love from God, then show that same love to others, fear cannot coexist. 1 John 4:18 says,

> *There is no fear in love [dread does not exist]. But perfect (complete, full-grown) love drives out fear, because fear involves [the expectation of divine] punishment, so the one who is afraid [of God's judgment] is not perfected in love [has not grown into a sufficient understanding of God's love].*

When we're perfected in love, it casts out any fear because not only are we receiving God's love, but we are also loving others. These three steps can usher us into freedom!

CHAPTER 28

MORTALITY

But God said to him, "You fool! This very night your soul is required of you; and now who will own all the things you have prepared?" (Luke 12:20)

MORTALITY

Greek: from *thnetos*—subject to death

Cambridge English: the way that people do not live forever

Dictionary.com: the state or condition of being subject to death

Merriam-Webster: the quality or state of being mortal

FATIMA ALI, the fan favorite of a previous season of Bravo's *Top Chef*, died recently after a nearly year-long battle with cancer, according to the network. She was 29. She said prior to her death, "It's funny, isn't it? When we think we have all the time in the world to live, we forget to indulge in the experiences of living." Ali wrote the following on the website *Healthyish*:

> WHEN that choice is yanked away from us, that's when we scramble to feel. I am desperate to overload my senses in the coming months, making reservations at the world's best restaurants, reaching out to past lovers and friends, and

smothering my family, giving them the time that I so selfishly guarded before.[1]

It's so easy for any human being to take life for granted, especially those who are young. The thought that any day could be our last really never enters our subconscious minds, so we live accordingly which usually results in regrets. What if we all lived like King David who said the following in Psalm 39:4 (NASB):

> LORD, *make me to know my end and what is the extent of my days; Let me know how transient I am. Behold, You have made my days as handbreadths, And my lifetime as nothing in Your sight; Surely every man at his best is a mere breath. Selah. Surely every man walks about as a phantom; Surely they make an uproar for nothing. He amasses riches and does not know who will gather them."*

I am certain that anyone who knew it was their last day on earth would likely wish they had lived differently. That is *turning a blind eye* to our own mortality.

If you're one of the minority who would not change anything if you knew you were about to die, then praise God! As believers, we should all understand that God has an appointed time for each of us to enter eternal life. We need to be encouraged by the fact that Jesus said in Luke 12:7, *"Indeed the very hairs of your head are all numbered. Do not be afraid; you are far more valuable than many sparrows."* Psalm 139:13 says, *"For You formed my innermost parts; You knit me [together] in my mother's womb."* God knew us while we were in our mother's womb, and He knows every hair on our heads. He also knows the exact moment we will take our last breath. If God revealed when our death would occur, then we would be inclined to live less by faith and more for the time we had left on earth.

Psalm 91:16 says, *"With a long life I will satisfy him and I will let him see my salvation."* This Scripture tells us that God will give some people a long life; however, for reasons unknown, some will have shorter lives. We must recognize and accept the sovereignty of God over life and death. I often think about the eleven disciples and other followers of Jesus who were martyred in what many would consider to be the prime of their life. I am highly confident that after accepting Christ prior to His crucifixion and after being filled with the Holy Spirit after His ascension hardly any of His followers realized that they would someday suffer brutal deaths. Perhaps they all thought they would be preaching into their later years despite what Jesus told them. Why was John spared execution and died of natural causes versus the other eleven? What about Stephen? How about the apostle Paul? It's really simple. God had a plan for each of their lives that served a purpose for Him. It didn't matter what each of them thought about how or when their lives would end. It only mattered when the time came that what happened to them was for the glory of God.

I find it interesting that only God knows when Heaven and earth as we know it today will be destroyed and our new eternal world will be ushered into existence. Even Jesus or the angels don't know! He said in Matthew 24:36, *"But of that [exact] day and hour no one knows, not even the angels of heaven, nor the Son [in His humanity], but the Father alone."* The fact is that if we knew when Jesus was coming back, our entire outlook on life would change—but we should always live as though it were our last day on earth and do so with a gusto for the kingdom of God. Then whether we go home to be with the Lord or Jesus comes back, we will have *no regrets.* We can say we lived life well versus saying we lived a good life.

My first brush with my mortality came on December 20, 2007, when I developed hairy cell leukemia. Though I was forty-seven years old, I had never really contemplated the fragility of life. Although I knew God would heal me, I was fortunate that a treatment had been developed that can put this rare form of leukemia into remission.

When this disease was first discovered, it was potentially fatal. When I was diagnosed, I had to stop and reflect about the fragility of life. I had been saved for seventeen years, married for twenty-four years, and had fathered five awesome children; but there is no doubt I would have done many things differently if I'd had the opportunity. I am still a work in progress, but I can say that my outlook on this life and my eternal purpose changed significantly at that point in time. The question I had to ask myself was why did it take a disease to make that happen? That's where I missed the mortality boat, if you will, by taking so many things for granted, including life itself. I now understand that I want to have a life well lived for my family and friends, the needy, the lost, and most importantly for God. I still can make people mad and do stupid things that I regret, but the difference is that I am aware of it now and can make it right, so I am less likely to do it again.

When my wife was diagnosed with breast cancer in May 2018, thoughts of mortality reared its head again. I can attest, though, that she would have few regrets because she has always had a life well lived ever since I met her and is loved by everybody. What her diagnosis did for me was to make me even more grateful than I already am to have her in my life, which enriched our earthly journey more than I thought possible. If we can learn to live without regrets before we encounter a possibly life-changing event, we will have a richer and more fulfilling life on this earth.

REMOVING THE BLIND EYE

My mother always used to say to me, "Stop and smell the roses, Greg." That means don't be too busy to enjoy life—slow down and appreciate the beauty around you. Stop and smell the roses or life will pass you by. When I was young, I viewed this saying more as an admonition not to miss opportunities to take in the pleasures of life, which, as an adolescent, was important to me. Now that I am much older, I interpret the saying to mean that we should stop and reflect on life and the brevity of it before others are smelling the roses on our coffin!

Removing the *blind eye* to mortality is nothing more than acknowledging the fact that life is a gift and the time we have on earth is predestined by God, so we need to appreciate every breath we take while living on this earth. If you really believe that with *all* your heart, then your actions will follow to reflect that reality. This is how you have a life well lived.

Although my regrets would have been different, I believe I understand what Fatima Ali was trying to say to all of us. Live like you're dying (because you are), then you will know how to live in a way that makes a difference both in this present world and in the next. 1 Peter 1:17 says, *"If you address as Father, the One who impartially judges according to each one's work, conduct yourselves in [reverent] fear [of Him] and with profound respect for Him throughout the time of your stay on earth."*

CHAPTER 29

THE FEAR OF DEATH

Jesus said to her, "*I am the Resurrection and the Life. Whoever believes in (adheres to, trusts in, relies on) Me [as Savior] will live even if he dies; and everyone who lives and believes in Me [as Savior] will never die. Do you believe this?*" (John 11:25-26)

DEATH

Greek: from *thanato*s—death, physical or spiritual

Cambridge English: the end of life

Dictionary.com: the act of dying; the end of life; the total and permanent cessation of all the vital functions of an organism

Merriam-Webster: a permanent cessation of all vital functions; the end of life

WHAT A great question Jesus asked this woman. Do we believe this? If we do, then the fear of *physical* death should not be present in our lives. Yet, death is a subject to which most people—including believers—prefer to *turn a blind eye*. It's sad to think that some people suffer from a medical condition called *necrophobia*, which *Merriam-Webster Dictionary* defines as "an exaggerated fear of death or horror of dead bodies."[1] Many Spirit-filled believers have a fear of death but likely will not admit it or want to talk about it. Everyone wants to talk about living, but few want to discuss the inevitable truth that we will die. Hebrews 2:14-15 says,

> *Therefore, since [these His] children share in flesh and blood [the physical nature of mankind], He Himself in a similar manner also shared in the same [physical nature, but without sin], so that through [experiencing] death He might make powerless (ineffective, impotent) him who had the power of death—that is, the devil—and [that He] might free all those who through [the haunting] fear of death were held in slavery throughout their lives.*

Paul said in Philippians 1:21-24,

> *For to me, to live is Christ [He is my source of joy, my reason to live] and to die is gain [for I will be with Him in eternity]. If, however, it is to be life here and I am to go on living, this will mean useful and productive service for me; so I do not know which to choose [if I am given that choice]. But I am hard-pressed between the two. I have the desire to leave [this world] and be with Christ, for that is far, far better; yet to remain in my body is more necessary and essential for your sake.*

Paul clearly had an eternal perspective and never doubted his outcome even as he was beheaded.

Jesus said we will *not* die, but we *will* live forever. If we believe that to be true, then why would any of us fear dying? I believe fear of death can be divided into two camps. In the first camp is the fearful believer who struggles with the idea of a spiritual existence after natural death. In the other camp are those who accept the afterlife but fear the process of dying rather than death itself.

The core issue with the first camp is that they have yet to grasp the truth and promises in Scripture about our immediate destiny at the time of our natural death. They read what is clearly laid out in the New

Testament about where the soul goes and comprehend in the mind, but that understanding doesn't seem to penetrate the heart. If it were in the heart in the same way as their confession of faith that resulted in salvation, any doubt or fear would be removed. Perhaps they believe that Christ came to earth through the virgin birth and was crucified for our sins, but have trouble accepting with the finite mind (as opposed to believing in the heart) the reality of the resurrection.

I believe Jesus understood that some believers would struggle with doubt, so He made sure there were many confirmations by others of His presence before He ascended to Heaven following the resurrection. He appeared to Mary Magdalene at the tomb (John 20:11-18), He appeared to the "other Mary" and to Mary Magdalene again as they left the empty tomb (Matthew 28:1, 8-10), He revealed Himself and broke bread with two people on the way to Emmaus (Luke 24:13-32), and He appeared to several of His disciples while they were fishing on the sea of Galilee (John 21:1-14).

The apostle Paul stated the truth of the resurrection so clearly in 1 Corinthians 15:3-9, which says:

> *For I passed on to you as of first importance what I also received, that Christ died for our sins according to [that which] the Scriptures [foretold], and that He was buried, and that He was [bodily] raised on the third day according to [that which] the Scriptures [foretold], and that He appeared to Cephas (Peter), then to the Twelve. **After that He appeared to more than five hundred brothers and sisters at one time**, the majority of whom are still alive, but some have fallen asleep [in death]. Then He was seen by James, then by all the apostles, and last of all, as to one untimely (prematurely, traumatically) born, He appeared to me also. For I am the least [worthy] of the apostles, and not fit to be called an apostle, because I [at one time] fiercely oppressed and violently persecuted the church of God.*

It's not sin to doubt, but it is a critical part of our theology that we accept the resurrection as fact. Keep in mind that the eleven disciples themselves had a hard time believing Jesus was raised from the dead, so Jesus had to appear to them to set them straight. He said in Mark 16:14,

> *Later, Jesus appeared to the eleven [disciples] themselves as they were reclining at the table; and He called them to account for their unbelief and hardness of heart, because they had not believed those who had seen Him after He had risen [from death].*

We overcome any reservation in our hearts by first accepting and admitting the doubt. That's exactly what Thomas did when he said the following to his fellow disciples in John 20:25,

> *So the other disciples kept telling him, "We have seen the Lord!" But he said to them, "Unless I see in His hands the marks of the nails, and put my finger into the nail prints, and put my hand into His side, I will never believe."*

When Jesus appeared to the disciples again and Thomas was present, we learn that Jesus lovingly erased any of Thomas's doubts. John 20:26-28 says,

> *Eight days later His disciples were again inside the house, and Thomas was with them. Jesus came, though the doors had been barred, and stood among them and said, "Peace to you." Then He said to Thomas, "Reach here with your finger, and see My hands; and put out your hand and place it in My side. Do not be unbelieving, but [stop doubting and] believe." Thomas answered Him, "My Lord and my God!"*

The good news for all of us is that we don't have to see as the disciples did in order to believe: Jesus said to him, *"Because you have seen Me, do you now believe? Blessed [happy, spiritually secure, and favored by God] are they who did not see [Me] and yet believed [in Me]."* (John 20:29) This statement recorded by the apostle John was meant for you and for me.

One might still argue that it's easier for the disciples to believe because Jesus walked with the disciples for three years of His earthly ministry then appeared to them after His death in a bodily form. Additionally, they were all able to see Him ascend into the clouds and back to Heaven, so of course they would have believed! We all have heard the expression "Seeing is believing," and in this technological world we live in today, it's become the standard for evidence. Yet, for followers of Christ, it should have nothing to do with the use of our eyes or any of the other four senses God gave us. The foundation of our evidence comes from the historical facts as presented in Scripture. The fact that these accounts of the life of Jesus and specifically his resurrection were written between AD 50-100 should have no impact on their validity.

The New Testament is humanity's most reliable ancient document.[2] All ancient manuscripts were written on papyrus, which didn't have much of a shelf life. So people hand copied originals to retain the message and circulate it to others. Few people doubt that Plato wrote *The Republic*, a classic written around 380 BC. The earliest copies we have of it are dated AD 900, which is 1,300 years after it was written. Only seven copies exist today. Caesar's *Gallic Wars* was written around 100-44 BC. The ten copies in existence today are dated 1,000 years after he wrote it. When it comes to the New Testament, which was written between AD 50-100, more than 5,000 copies exist today. All are dated within 50 to 225 years of the original writing. Furthermore, when it came to Scripture, scribes (monks) were meticulous in their copying of original manuscripts. They checked and rechecked their work, to make sure it perfectly matched. What the New Testament writers originally penned is better preserved than any other ancient manuscript. We can be more certain of what we read about Jesus' life and words than we are of the writings of Caesar, Plato, Aristotle and Homer.[1] Based on these facts, every believer should be convinced that because of the resurrection of Jesus, although our physical body is buried, our soul and spirit have an eternal afterlife the moment we take our last physical breath. This should erase any doubt or the fear of death.

The believers in the second camp may not fear death because of their steadfast belief in the afterlife, yet they do fear how the process of dying will play out. If you ask most people, believers and non-believers alike, how they would like to die, the common answer is "quick and painless." Although that happens to many who face death, it's not always the case. The thought of a slow and lingering death can cause immense fear for some and in turn cause their homecoming into eternal life to be secondary to the perceived pain and suffering of the act of dying.

The only way to alleviate this type of fear is to trust in God's promise in Philippians 4:13,

> *I can do all things [which He has called me to do] through Him who strengthens and empowers me [to fulfill His purpose—I am self-sufficient in Christ's sufficiency; I am ready for anything and equal to anything through Him who infuses me with inner strength and confident peace.]*

When it comes to those we love, I clearly understand that is easier said than done. There is no simple answer for why some have to experience suffering and others are spared. All I know is His grace is sufficient even during physical or mental suffering. I am reminded of the pain and suffering Jesus endured from the time of His arrest to His crucifixion. Although it took less time than a prolonged illness, Jesus had nothing to mitigate the pain. God gave Him the strength to accomplish His task, and He will do the same for any Christian who fears the process of dying.

This fear of death is irrational when we think of it in terms of being a distressing emotion aroused by impending danger, evil, pain, etc., whether the threat is real or imagined. Does going from a human bodily form to an eternal spiritual body that will live forever with the creator of the universe sound like something we should fear? Impending danger? Evil? Pain?

As with any fear, we must confront it head on in order to overcome it. If you have a fear of flying, the best thing to do is educate yourself on the safety statistics of aviation and then fly more to get over that fear. If a believer fears natural death, then the best remedy is to see what the Word says about death and confront it head on instead of avoiding the subject or *turning a blind eye*. Ministering to believers the absolute truth that, once they take their last breath, they will be at the feet of Jesus in a new body that lasts forever is a message of hope and comfort. Paul said in Philippians 3:20-21,

> *But [we are different, because] our citizenship is in heaven. And from there we eagerly await [the coming of] the Savior, the Lord Jesus Christ; who, by exerting that power which enables Him even to subject everything to Himself, will [not only] transform [but completely refashion] our earthly bodies so that they will be like His glorious resurrected body.*

If physical death is our worst-case scenario, then we are in pretty good shape.

All fear, including the fear of death, is from Satan; so, if a person is honest about that fear and desires not to be a slave to it, fear can be turned into faith. Hebrews 11:1 (NASB) defines faith from a spiritual perspective: *"Now faith is the assurance of things hoped for, the conviction of things not seen."* Let's break this down.

First of all, what do we hope for? Let's name just a few things we hope for: eternal life, new resurrected bodies that will never die, freedom from pain, sorrow and sickness, worshipping God forever, eternal joy and happiness absent from any negative feelings or emotions, being reunited with our saved loved ones, reaping the rewards from our acts while on earth, the new eternal house Jesus promised us, meeting people we don't know that our lives impacted and who received eternal life, constant love, constant light, and singing for eternity. Obviously, there are many, many more promises.

The word *assurance* means "a positive declaration intended to give confidence; a promise."[3] We would all agree that the Bible gives us clear assurances that the list above is true and correct. *Hope* is defined in the *Oxford Dictionaries* as "a feeling of expectation and desire for a particular thing to happen."[4] The list above is what we hope for based on the promises of God as reflected in Scripture. *Conviction* is defined in *Merriam-Webster* as "a strong persuasion or belief."[5] As it relates to the fear of death, I choose to say that my *faith* gives me the *assurance* that the promises from God of the things I hope for are mine based on my strong belief in the written Word of God.

We need to know that this promise is no different than any other in the Bible. If Jesus said it, then we can count on Him to fulfill all things hoped for as it relates to this subject. When that time comes, just sit back and enjoy the ride because it will be a short one to the gates of Heaven. As 2 Corinthians 5:1 says, *"For we know that if the earthly tent [our physical body] which is our house is torn down [through death], we have a building from God, a house not made with hands, eternal in the heavens."*

REMOVING THE BLIND EYE

The devil wants us all to fear many things during our stay on earth, but nothing more than death. He knows if we fear death, we will never be able to fulfill the callings of God while in these earthly tents. If we fear death, then we really don't believe what we are preaching, and thus become disabled in our faith and witness.

When this subject comes up with other believers, and it's apparent they are not at peace with the prospect of death, then walk them through some of the Scriptures in this chapter and help put their hearts at rest. Those who do not know the Lord should fear death, but a born-again believer should have the full confidence of his or her destination when life on earth is over. Fear is totally unnecessary, and Jesus left us with these words in John 14:1-4 to remind us of that truth:

> Do not let your heart be troubled (afraid, cowardly). Believe [confidently] in God and trust in Him, [have faith, hold on to it, rely on it, keep going and] believe also in Me. In My Father's house are many dwelling places. If it were not so, I would have told you, because I am going there to prepare a place for you. And if I go and prepare a place for you, I will come back again and I will take you to Myself, so that where I am you may be also. And [to the place] where I am going, you know the way.

If we choose to believe the Word, our fear of death will be defeated.

CHAPTER 30

THE FORGOTTEN

But when the Son of Man comes in His glory and majesty and all the angels with Him, then He will sit on the throne of His glory. All the nations will be gathered before Him [for judgment]; and He will separate them from one another, as a shepherd separates his sheep from the goats; and He will put the sheep on His right [the place of honor], and the goats on His left [the place of rejection]. Then the King will say to those on His right, "Come, you blessed of My Father [you favored of God, appointed to eternal salvation], inherit the kingdom prepared for you from the foundation of the world. For I was hungry, and you gave Me something to eat; I was thirsty, and you gave Me something to drink; I was a stranger, and you invited Me in; I was naked, and you clothed Me; I was sick, and you visited Me [with help and ministering care]; I was in prison, and you came to Me [ignoring personal danger]." Then the righteous will answer Him, "Lord, when did we see You hungry, and feed You, or thirsty, and give You something to drink? And when did we see You as a stranger, and invite You in, or naked, and clothe You? And when did we see You sick, or in prison, and come to You?" The King will answer and say to them, "I assure you and most solemnly say to you, to the extent that you did it for one of these brothers of Mine, even the least of them, you did it for Me." Then He will say to those on His left,

206 | Turning a Blind Eye

"Leave Me, you cursed ones, into the eternal fire which has been prepared for the devil and his angels (demons); for I was hungry, and you gave Me nothing to eat; I was thirsty, and you gave Me nothing to drink; I was a stranger, and you did not invite Me in; naked, and you did not clothe Me; sick, and in prison, and you did not visit Me [with help and ministering care]." Then they also [in their turn] will answer, "Lord, when did we see You hungry, or thirsty, or as a stranger, or naked, or sick, or in prison, and did not minister to You?" Then He will reply to them, "I assure you and most solemnly say to you, to the extent that you did not do it for one of the least of these [my followers], you did not do it for Me." Then these [unbelieving people] will go away into eternal (unending) punishment, but those who are righteous and in right standing with God [will go, by His remarkable grace] into eternal (unending) life. (Matthew 25:31-46)

FORGOTTEN

Greek: from *léthé*—literally means *oblivion, forgetfulness, or conceal-ment*

Cambridge English: to forget (about) is to stop thinking about some-one or something, or to stop thinking about doing something

Dictionary.com: to omit or neglect unintentionally, to fail to think of; take no note of, to neglect willfully; disregard or slight

Merriam-Webster: to be unable to remember; to overlook or neglect something

THE HOMELESS
(HUNGRY, THIRSTY, NAKED AND A STRANGER)

I AM CERTAIN many ministries serve the homeless, care for the sick and visit those in prison because many Christians support them. With that being said, these organizations are usually tax exempt and organized for those specific purposes. God challenged me in my spirit one day with this question as I was stopped at a traffic light watching a homeless man ask for money: "Greg, what are you doing about it as an individual?" I wasn't sure how to answer because from time to time I gave homeless people money and went on my way when the light turned green. That day, I came to the understanding that giving money simply was not enough if I looked at them through the eyes of Jesus.

Austin has a large homeless population and, like most people, I would from time to time look straight ahead and hope the person at the traffic light looking for a handout didn't knock on my window; I'd pray the for the light to turn green as quickly as possible. When I felt really inconvenienced and wanted to make sure the person saw that I was busy, I would act like I was talking on my phone. That is one part of my life review with God that I will want to fast forward! I was essentially *turning a blind eye* to that person in need. Instead of being selfish and self-centered, I could have looked at every person as an opportunity to bless someone and store up another treasure in my heavenly account.

That doesn't mean I have to give money every time I see a homeless person. God directed me to Acts 3 where Peter healed the lame man.

And Peter along with John, fixed his gaze upon him and said, "LOOK AT US!" And he began to give them his attention, expecting to receive something from them. But Peter said, "I do not possess silver and gold, but what I do have I give to you: In the name of Jesus Christ the Nazarene, walk!" (Acts 3:1-6)

See, Peter chose to look at this man and demand that he look back. I am sure there were many things to look at as they walked up to the busy temple, but Peter chose this needy man. He could have just as easily looked at him out of the corner of his eye and decided to ignore his plight, but he didn't. He did not know how to *turn a blind eye* after Pentecost.

Think of the hope we would spread if we just rolled down our windows and acknowledged the beggars by the roadside; if we blessed, encouraged and lifted them up for the few minutes we're stuck at a traffic light; if we let them know with our words and actions that they are not forgotten despite their circumstances. That's what Jesus would have done. Therefore, any time I do not acknowledge someone in obvious need, I am *turning a blind eye* to the forgotten. I realized God expected more from me, so I decided to change; and that's when God did some amazing things in my heart.

I often stop at a coffee shop near a busy intersection where many homeless people ask for food or money. One day after getting my coffee and going out to the patio, I prayed and ask God to allow me to bless someone that day. Shortly thereafter, a homeless man in his late twenties approached me and asked if I would buy him a cup of hot coffee or a little bite to eat. I had many business issues on my mind that day, but instead of acting busy and throwing the guy a dollar while wishing him well, I decided to invite him to sit down so I could invest time into his life.

I did buy him coffee and food, but I also listened to his problems and the story of how he became homeless. His name was Jacob. He was filthy, and he smelled bad because he had not bathed for some time. He also had some medical issues due to using meth, and he openly admitted his addiction. I made a commitment to him that if he truly wanted to get clean and not be homeless, that I would be sitting in the same spot the next day at 10:00 a.m. I told him if he showed up and made that decision, that I would be happy to help him out. He did show up the next morning, which started a process of helping him live sober; he also got some clean clothes and food. God gave me the opportunity to provide four of six important provisions—not only to Jacob but also to Jesus. This all started with me being willing not to *turn a blind eye* to the forgotten. In my case, God gave me Jacob; with others, it might simply be giving a kind word to the person who needs it today.

THE SICK

Unfortunately, many people in our communities, churches and places of business are sick. So, as I examine my circle of influence, I need to consider how I respond when a friend or business associate or my pastor is the one who is ill. Sadly, I often say to myself, "Surely someone is taking care of them, so they will be all right." What I am really saying is that I don't have the time to go by or at least call to let them know I am thinking about them. That's *turning a blind eye.*

When one of my children was sick, I would call my wife several times during the day asking how that child was doing. I believe God feels that same way for all His children, and since His resurrection, He has left it to us to represent Him and comfort His children as we would our own. Everyone can think of someone we know who is sick, but we never bother to call and check up on them and lift their spirits. What if we all took the time to go visit just one person in the hospital to offer a bit of hope? In nursing homes all across our land, many elderly patients stay in those rooms all by themselves because they have nobody in their lives. What if we made a commitment to visit a local hospice to comfort people whose remaining time on this earth is brief? I am convinced that is exactly what Jesus would have done, so I believe He expects us to do it in His place until He returns.

PRISON INMATES

It's not often that you hear fellow believers talking about reaching out to those who are incarcerated. It was obviously important to Jesus, otherwise he would not have mentioned it in the parable. Many

churches and ministries are dedicated to reaching prisoners, but rela-
tively few Christians, including me, have thought about how to bring
hope and encouragement to inmates. It's often a case of out of sight,
out of mind, but that is just a convenient way of *turning a blind eye.*
According to the U.S. Bureau of Justice Statistics the United States
prison population at the end of 2017 was 1,489,363.[1] Those lives can
be touched if we will simply reach out—and we would also be sharing
some of the burden of caring for these inmates with ministries who are
already helping them.

REMOVING THE BLIND EYE

THE HOMELESS

As an individual in this country, we have ample opportunity to
bless someone who is homeless and unfairly considered an outcast in
our society. Jesus said in Matthew 26:11, *"For you always have the poor
with you; but you will not always have Me."* All of us have the privilege
of practicing not *turning a blind eye* to the hopeless as we live our daily
lives. It's as simple as acknowledging that person holding a sign on a
street corner to let them know they are loved. At every opportunity
that I am given by God, I roll down my window and say, "Just wanted
you to know that God loves you, Jesus loves you and I love you in spite
of your circumstances. Just know there is hope." I will often give the
person money or else just try to say an encouraging word.

Many people will say that "these people" asking for money to buy
food are nothing more than drug addicts looking for a score. I'm sure
that is the case with many of them, but regardless, God looks at our
heart and our desire to bless someone else—not the motive of the
person in need. Many homeless camps have their own barter system
where they can trade cash or goods for food, clothes or hygiene prod-
ucts. I know from firsthand experience that not all of them are buying
drugs. These folks have the same needs we do and, given the right opportunity through our kindness, many could break out of their cir-

cumstances. That "person" is someone's daughter, son, mother, father, brother or sister. Just because they are not our relatives does not mean we have license to ignore them. By the grace of God, one of my children beat a very serious heroin addiction—but it could have been him on the street. So, don't worry about what the sign says or what people will do with the money you give them. Just encourage them with your words, give resources if you feel led, and leave the rest to God.

Perhaps you could carry bottled water in your car to share with a homeless person. Many retail establishments will not allow the homeless community to get water from their stores. Grab an extra sandwich while you're at lunch and give it away at the traffic light on the way back to work. Perhaps put one pair of the countless shoes and socks we all have in our closets into your car to give away. You could carry something with the address of your church on it and invite a homeless person to join you for an upcoming service. Some people take shower trailers to the homeless camps in their communities and offer free showers every Saturday.

Whether you reach out individually, through your local church homeless outreach, or through some other organization, you never know what will happen until you take that first step of contributing your time and/or your financial resources to reach these people in need. Can you imagine how many souls could be reached if every Christian ministered to every homeless person they encountered? Just as Jesus said in the parable of the lost sheep in Luke 15:4 and 7:

> *What man among you, if he has a hundred sheep and loses one of them, does not leave the ninety-nine in the wilderness and go after the one which is lost, [searching] until he finds it?...I tell you, in the same way there will be more joy in heaven over one sinner who repents than over ninety-nine righteous people who have no need of repentance.*

This verse is speaking about salvation, but there is likely just as much joy when God sees us blessing one of His children in need of encour-agement. Remember that Jesus told us, *"I assure you and most solemnly say to you, to the extent that you did not do it for one of the least of these [my followers], you did not do it for Me."* (v. 45)

Do you realize that when you show kindness to a stranger that it might actually be an angel of God? Hebrews 13:2 says,

> *Do not neglect to extend hospitality to strangers [especially among the family of believers—being friendly, cordial, and gra-cious, sharing the comforts of your home and doing your part generously], for by this some have entertained angels without knowing it.*

God uses angels throughout the pages of the Bible, so who is to say that one of these homeless individuals is not an angel sent to test our heart and generosity? Just open your eyes and, trust me, you will see someone in need, and it might even be an angel.

THE SICK

We can find sick people in homes, hospitals, hospice care facilities, nursing homes, assisted living homes and even on the streets. It was important to Jesus that these people be seen and, when He saw them, He healed them all. He gave us the example to follow in Mark 1:29-31 when He went to Peter's mother-in-law's house.

> *And immediately they left the synagogue and went into the house of Simon [Peter] and Andrew, accompanied by James and John. Now Simon's mother-in-law was lying sick with a fever; and immediately they told Him about her. Jesus went to her, and taking her by the hand, raised her up; and the fever left her, and she began to serve them [as her guests].*

This passage contains a couple of interesting points that can help us become more active in visiting the sick. First, this woman only had a fever. Many of Jesus' healings were miraculous and lifesaving, yet He took the time to go heal this woman who just had a fever. Secondly, this woman was related to Jesus' friends. He desired to heal her because she was ill, but I also believe it had to do with his love for Simon, Andrew, James and John. He took the time out of His day to help not just the woman, but also His closest friends.

We should all take the time to visit people who are sick or even dying, especially those people who have no loved ones around them. We can volunteer at hospitals, hospice facilities and nursing homes for an hour a week and simply keep lonely people encouraged. If we have a sick friend, relative or co-worker, an in-person visit or at least a call, text or email letting them know we are praying is the least we can do. We tend to tell ourselves that someone else has likely reached out, so there is no need to bother the sick person, but when I was receiving treatment for leukemia, it made my day when someone reached out to check on me. Sadly, it didn't happen that often—and I don't believe it was because people didn't care. Instead, it was a case of *turning a blind eye* due to busy lifestyles. If you know people are sick, then reach out and lift their spirits. If you're led to take it to another level, investigate volunteering at a local hospital, nursing home, hospice care or assisted living facility. Reaching out to the sick will get us focused on the needs of others who desperately need encouragement instead of ourselves.

INMATES

Visiting those who are incarcerated can be a difficult process without the support of a ministry that specifically works in this field. Many such organizations would appreciate having more volunteers to go to the prisons throughout our country and bring the Word of God, hope, healing and friendship. Some folks are afraid to go behind bars, and that's understandable; but as Christians, we are called to reach out to these inmates. Such fear is addressed in 2 Timothy 1:7, which says,

For God did not give us a spirit of timidity or cowardice or fear, but [He has given us a spirit] of power and of love and of sound judgment and personal discipline [abilities that result in a calm, well-balanced mind and self-control].

If we can't go ourselves, then sending regular financial gifts to organizations that minister to these people groups is another way to participate and will address what Jesus spoke about in Matthew 25:31-46.

CHAPTER 31

CARING FOR BELIEVERS

I have manifested Your name [and revealed Your very self, your real self] to the people whom You have given Me out of the world; they were Yours and You gave them to Me, and they have kept and obeyed Your word. Now [at last] they know [with confident assurance] that all You have given Me is from You [it is really and truly Yours]. For the words which You gave Me I have given them; and they received and accepted them and truly understood [with confident assurance] that I came from You [from Your presence], and they believed [without any doubt] that You sent Me. I pray for them; I do not pray for the world, but for those You have given Me, because they belong to You; and all things that are Mine are Yours, and [all things that are] Yours are Mine; and I am glorified in them. I am no longer in the world; yet they are still in the world, and I am coming to You. Holy Father keep them in Your name, the name which You have given Me, so that they may be one just as We are. While I was with them, I was keeping them in Your name which You have given Me; and I guarded them and protected them, and not one of them was lost except the son of destruction, so that the Scripture would be fulfilled. But now I am coming to You; and I say these things [while I am still] in the world so that they may experience My joy made full and complete and perfect within them [filling their hearts with My delight]. I have given to them Your word [the message You gave Me]; and the world has hated them because they are not of the world and do not belong to the world, just as I am not of the world and do not belong to it. I do not ask You to take them out of the world, but that You keep them and protect them from the evil one. (John 17:6-15)

CARING

Greek: from *episkopeo*—to look upon, to care for

Cambridge English: a caring person is kind and gives emotional support to others

Dictionary.com: to be concerned or solicitous; have thought or regard

Merriam-Webster: feeling or showing concern for other people

JESUS WAS deeply concerned about His disciples as He knew the time was near to go to the cross. In fact, He prayed the verses above just prior to going to the garden of Gethsemane and His arrest shortly thereafter. We know this because in John 18:1 says, *"Having said these things, Jesus left with His disciples and went across the ravine of the Kidron. There was a garden there, which He and His disciples entered."* I try to put myself in Jesus' shoes that day and think how I would have handled the situation. He knew that He would soon be arrested, beaten, scourged, spat upon, and have a crown with one- to three-inch thorns smashed on His head. He knew He would be repeatedly beaten in the face, have His beard pulled out, and according to Roman custom, be stripped naked, be mocked and blindfolded, then forced to walk to His own execution carrying a hundred-pound crossbeam. He knew His hands and feet would be nailed to the cross. He knew that cross would be dropped upright into a hole and that He would hang naked in the hot sun for all to view from nine in the morning until three in the afternoon before dying. Yet, knowing all this, He was more concerned over the men with whom He walked than He was with Himself.

Most of us will never face that kind of pressure, pain and suffering; but what Jesus showed us through this is how important the family of God is to Him and how important it should be to us. How often do we *turn a blind eye* to the needs of our fellow brothers and sisters? It could be financially, spiritually, emotionally or relationally—and it is usually caused by our self-centeredness and a lack of knowledge of the bar Jesus set regarding the importance of our spiritual family. The apostle Paul understood this, as reflected in Galatians 6:10:

> *So then, while we [as individual believers] have the opportunity, let us do good to all people [not only being helpful, but also doing that which promotes their spiritual well-being], and especially [be a blessing] to those of the household of faith (born-again believers).*

Then in Philippians 2:4 we see, "*Do not merely look out for your own personal interests, but also for the interests of others.*" But my favorite example is found in 2 Corinthians 11:22-28, which says,

> *Are they Hebrews? So am I. Are they Israelites? So am I. Are they descendants of Abraham? So am I. Are they [self-proclaimed] servants of Christ? —I am speaking as if I were out of my mind— I am more so [for I exceed them]; with far more labors, with far more imprisonments, beaten times without number, and often in danger of death. Five times I received from the Jews thirty-nine lashes. Three times I was beaten with rods, once I was stoned. Three times I was shipwrecked, a night and a day I have spent adrift on the sea; many times on journeys, [exposed to] danger from rivers, danger from bandits, danger from my own coun- trymen, danger from the Gentiles, danger in the city, danger in*

the wilderness, danger on the sea, danger among those posing as believers; in labor and hardship, often unable to sleep, in hunger and thirst, often [driven to] fasting [for lack of food], in cold and exposure [without adequate clothing]. Besides those external things, there is the daily [inescapable] pressure of my concern for all the churches.

Paul said, *"Besides those external things"*? Are you kidding me? That's quite an understatement. After all that, his only concern was for the church and its people. We are called to love everyone and treat others as we want to be treated, but there is something special about those in the "household of faith" that is important to God. Still, *turning a blind eye* to the welfare of believers is all too common in today's world.

Paul said in Galatians 6:2, *"Carry one another's burdens and in this way you will fulfill the requirements of the law of Christ [that is, the law of Christian love]."* Look for the opportunity to ask a fellow brother or sister in the Lord whether there is anything you can do for them. Please be careful about asking, "How are you doing?" when you don't really want to know. I can't count how many times I have heard in a church setting, "How are you doing, Greg? Good to see you." I have even said the very same thing when I had no legitimate reason why is was good to see that person. If you're going to tell someone it's good to see them, then tell them why. If you're going to ask how someone is doing, be prepared to listen, then offer encouragement.

I try hard to say good morning, good afternoon or good evening with a "hope all is well," because I really mean that. I am speaking a blessing. I like to save the "how are you doing" question for when I am in a private moment looking a person directly in the eye.

Even when we do ask sincerely about someone's welfare, we usually get the standard, "Doing great, thank you." That's when we should ask again, "How are you *really* doing, and can I do anything for you?" Perhaps they need resources for food, prayer for their children who are rebelling, physical healing, an encouraging word or their faith built up. If they truly are doing well and don't need anything, then praise God; but if they do have needs and you take the time to ask and perhaps meet some need, God sees it and will reward you. **Most people will not just walk up and share their needs, so we won't know unless we ask.** But if we are constantly looking for an opportunity to care for a fellow believer, God will put people in our path who need our help.

Financial needs are where the rubber meets the road. 1 John 3:16-17 says the following:

> *By this we know [and have come to understand the depth and essence of His precious] love: that He [willingly] laid down His life for us [because He loved us]. And we ought to lay down our lives for the believers. **But whoever has the world's goods (adequate resources), and sees his brother in need, but has no compassion for him, how does the love of God live in him?***

This Scripture is clear that those of us who have any of the world's goods should never refuse to help a brother or sister in need. It doesn't matter how much we give, but the act of helping at all shows that we have the love of God in us and not the love of the world.

I know many very wealthy men who profess to be Christians yet would not give even a nickel to help others, not even a believer. We are talking about men who are worth millions of dollars and have more money than they could possibly spend in multiple lifetimes. Paul described such people in Philippians 2:21, "*For the others [who deserted me after my arrest] all seek [to advance] their own interests, not those of Jesus Christ.*" We should all seek not to be the type of Christian Paul is describing here.

REMOVING THE BLIND EYE

Caring for the spiritual needs of fellow believers was something the apostle Paul endeavored to accomplish during his ministry. His deep concern is evident throughout all his writings. It seems so uncommon in today's church world to hear a person inquire about the spiritual condition of a friend, a friend's family, a member of their local church or, heaven forbid, a total stranger. How do we know what others need unless we are genuinely concerned and take the time and effort to ask them?

It's so easy to *turn a blind eye* to the spiritual needs of others because it's easier to assume everyone is okay; we convince ourselves that we don't have the time to find out. Many believers struggle with fear, faith, doubt, demonic attacks and strongholds—just to give a few examples. They need encouragement, prayer and the knowledge that someone besides the pastor is concerned about their walk with the Lord. Take the time before or after church services to reach out to ask if others have a need. It could be somebody you know well, an acquaintance, or even someone you have never met before. Simply ask if there are any spiritual needs that you can pray about in their lives. You will be surprised how many folks will respond, "Yes, there is, and thank you for asking." If you follow up and continue to check on that spiritual need, you will likely discover that you feel far more blessed than the person you are helping.

Caring for the emotional needs of a fellow believer requires a deeper dive into that person's life. In this world, the church is full of Jesus-loving folks who battle depression, addiction, or low self-esteem; have shaky marriages; have children acting out in a negative way; are grieving the loss of a loved one; suffer from some illness; or have some other difficulty impacting their lives. Lost people suffer from the same problems, but the difference is that we are supposed to take care of the needs of our own. Paul said in Romans 15:1, *"Now we who are strong [in our convictions and faith] ought to [patiently] put up with the weaknesses of those who are not strong, and not just please ourselves."*

All of us will have highs and lows in life where we need someone to press through in faith and stand alongside us to see us through to the other side. During some of my personal darkest days, I wish someone had inquired about my emotional needs. If they had, I would have opened up like a dam that had collapsed and shared my heart in hopes of being comforted. Many feel that sharing emotional needs is a sign of weakness but, quite the contrary, it's a sign of strength. Just be sensitive to the Holy Spirit and look for opportunities to show you care about others' well-being and not just your own.

Caring for the needs of fellow believers financially is not just a suggestion; all believers should consider it a requirement. The early church depended on each other to meet the needs of the entire Christian community. Unfortunately, many Christians not only *turn a blind eye* to the financial needs of others but also purposely run in the other direction. If you doubt the truth of that statement, look at the *gofundme.com* website and see how many campaigns are by believers looking for monetary help. They are going to the world because the body of believers has failed them, though in some cases you'll see a believer use such sites to reach more Christians to help with a particular need. That should be commended and serve as an example to all of us. When was the last time you asked any follower of Jesus about a financial need that you could either help with or at the very least agree in prayer asking that God meet that need?

In order to remove this *blind eye*, we must begin to look at our accumulated temporal material possessions as obstacles to helping those in real need. In other words, is there anything we can live without in order to potentially help others? If every believer would consider this prior to making any purchase, our churches would be able to take care of their own. We all need to be willing to allow God to use us to financially bless others when it's within our power to do so. All we have to do is look or ask!

CHAPTER 32

OUR PASTORS

Stay in that house, eating and drinking what they provide, for the laborer is worthy of his wages. Do not move from house to house. (Luke 10:7)

WORTHY

Greek: from *axioó*—to reckon as *worthy, matching value* to actual substance—i.e., worth as it corresponds to reality

Cambridge English: deserving respect, admiration, or support

Dictionary.com: a person of eminent worth, merit, or position

Merriam-Webster: Having worth or value, having sufficient worth or importance

I AM GOING to be brutally honest—when I read these four definitions, not one of them seems to match how full-time pastors are treated in this country today. Many believers take these full-time saints for granted and treat them more like emergency services personnel. We think about them or call them only when there is some emergency or urgent need; otherwise, they are out of sight and out of mind—until Sunday. What we all must remember is that full-time pastors have families, goals and aspirations, needs and wants, and most importantly feelings—just like those of us who are not in full-time ministry.

According to *Indeed.com* the average salary for a full-time pastor in the United States is $39,087, which was based on 479 salaries submitted anonymously to the organization.[1] *Indeed* also states that the average tenure is three to five years. We all know that many renowned pastors make more than the national average and others overseeing what are called mega-churches who are compensated on a more "worthy" level, as they should be, due to the sheer size of the ministry and the resulting level of responsibility they carry. What most people don't know is that the median church in the Unites States has seventy-five regular participants in worship on Sunday mornings.[2]

Let's compare the situation using the average size church versus a business of the same size. A pastor's typical duties for a congregation of seventy-five people include teaching, counseling, performing marriages, conducting funerals and being prepared to preach every Sunday. The pastor must also oversee the church business and handle any of the community services. He can get called any time of the day or night to deal with someone's personal emergencies. Now, consider a man or woman who heads up a mid-sized company with seventy-five employees and must meet those employees' needs to make that company successful. Let's say that person has the same business responsibilities, the same personal responsibility and perhaps the same community responsibilities—but gets weekends off and is not required to be on call 24/7. I don't think any qualified person would take that secular job for $39,087 per year.

The fact is that many Christians feel that since pastors choose the ministry, they are not entitled to the same or even close to the same compensation as those in secular occupations. This attitude permeates most churches, and it needs to change. I have a very big heart for full-time ministers because I have seen them up close and personal in my own life. They sacrifice time from their marriage and with their children to do their job, and they struggle constantly to keep their family afloat financially. A double standard should not exist between ministry and secular work in terms of compensation. 1 Timothy 5:17-18 says:

> *The elders who perform their leadership duties well are to be considered worthy of double honor (financial support), especially those who work hard at preaching and teaching [the Word of God concerning eternal salvation through Christ]. For the Scripture says, "You shall not muzzle the ox while it is treading out the grain [to keep it from eating]," and, "The worker is worthy of his wages [he deserves fair compensation]."*

If most believers were honest, they apply this Scripture to themselves but not to their pastor. Why don't we consider the plight of those in full-time ministry the same as our own? Look at what 3 John 5-8 says.

> *Beloved, you are acting faithfully in what you are providing for the brothers, and especially when they are strangers; and they have testified before the church of your love and friendship. You will do well to [assist them and] send them on their way in a manner worthy of God. For these [traveling missionaries] went out for the sake of the Name [of Christ], accepting nothing [in the way of assistance] from the Gentiles. So we ought to support such people [welcoming them as guests and providing for them], so that we may be fellow workers for the truth [that is, for the gospel message of salvation].*

That was the way the early church "pastored," but even though most pastors today minister in only one place, the obligation of those of us who receive from them still applies today.

Pastors are worthy not only of financial benefits but also of appreciation for their service in our lives. 1 Thessalonians 5:12-13 says,

> *Now we ask you, brothers and sisters, to appreciate those who diligently work among you [recognize, acknowledge, and respect*

your leaders], who are in charge over you in the Lord and who give you instruction, and [we ask that you appreciate them and] hold them in the highest esteem in love because of their work [on your behalf]. Live in peace with one another.

According to Philippians 2:4, we are called to put the interests of others before our own, and that should start with those who are the shepherds of the flock: "*Do not merely look out for your own personal interests, but also for the interests of others.*" A great place to start is with your local pastor!

REMOVING THE BLIND EYE

In many congregations today, the giving and receiving usually goes only one way—that's the pastor asking whether his flock needs prayer, assistance in life's daily struggles, or help in their families. We generally answer the pastor's questions and don't think twice about the need to reciprocate because we feel it is the pastor's "job" to serve us. We really feel a sense of entitlement on any given Sunday. But even though we are at church to get fed spiritually, we should think about sharing the same meal with our pastor.

After the next Sunday service, just stop and engage your pastor and ask after his welfare. Does he need anything? Ask what you can pray for specifically in his life and family. During the week, send an encouraging email about how grateful you are for your pastor's love and sacrifice to your spiritual soul. And it's important that your concern is not just an act, but something genuine that comes from your heart. I realize that some churches are too large to have this kind of personal interaction, but an email would lift the spirits of any pastor regardless of the church size. Let these unsung spiritual heroes know that you care. Try it and see what blessings God will pour out in your own life as you extend love and care to His appointed ministers.

CHAPTER 33

OUR TONGUE

It is not what goes into the mouth of a man that defiles and dishonors him, but what comes out of the mouth, this defiles and dishonors him. (Matthew 15:11)

DEFILE

Greek: from *spilos*—defile, spot, stain, soil

Cambridge English: to spoil the goodness or beauty of something

Dictionary.com: to make foul, dirty, or unclean; pollute; taint; debase

Merriam-Webster: to make unclean or impure

IF CHRISTIANS understood the importance of the words we speak, I have no doubt that we would be better off as a body of believers. Prior to receiving this revelation, I would utter any negative word that came to my mind to describe my circumstances; and usually it did more harm than good.

Think about how God created the world. Every time He formed something, Genesis 1 states that, *"Then God said."* He spoke it first, then the result He desired was formed. We see that when Jesus was tempted by the devil in Matthew 4:1-11, He defeated the devil by speaking Scripture to him. As Christians we have no issue believing the many miracles

Jesus performed during His earthly ministry, yet we discount the importance and the power of the words we speak. That does not mean we have the power through our words to form material things like God did, for only He has the power to create. Still, the mind God gave us is very powerful—although we use only about ten percent of its capacity.

A psychosomatic illness happens when a person thinks and talks about being sick so much that their mind interprets it as reality, which causes their body to produce the symptoms of that illness. That's how powerful the mind is, and when the devil hears us constantly saying these things, then he springs into action to marginalize our faith in God. People often speak the very thing they don't desire, so it's important to control our tongues and keep watch over our words.

I believe James summed it up best. James 3:3-12 says:

*Now if we put bits into the horses' mouths to make them obey us, we guide their whole body as well. And look at the ships. Even though they are so large and are driven by strong winds, they are still directed by a very small rudder wherever the impulse of the helmsman determines. In the same sense, the tongue is a small part of the body, and yet it boasts of great things. See [by comparison] how great a forest is set on fire by a small spark! And the tongue is [in a sense] a fire, the very world of injustice and unrighteousness; the tongue is set among our members as that which contaminates the entire body and sets on fire the course of our life [the cycle of man's existence] and is itself set on fire by hell (Gehenna). For every species of beasts and birds, of reptiles and sea creatures, is tamed and has been tamed by the human race. But no one can tame the human tongue; it is a restless evil [undisciplined, unstable], full of deadly poison. **With it we bless our Lord and Father, and with it we curse men, who have been made in the likeness of God.** Out of the same mouth come both blessing and cursing. These things, my brothers, should not be* *this way [for we have a moral obligation to speak in a manner that reflects our fear of God and profound respect for His precepts]. Does a spring send out from the same opening both fresh and bitter water? Can a fig tree, my brothers, produce olives, or a grapevine produce figs? Nor can salt water produce fresh.*

The bolded verse (v. 9) of this passage stopped me in my tracks: "*With it we bless our Lord Father, and with it we curse men, who have been made in the likeness of God.*" **How could I praise God on one hand then speak derogatorily about another person with the same tongue?** The bottom line is that it should not happen. James says our words "*set on fire the course of our life,*" which means that our words have an effect that is either beneficial or detrimental. Proverbs 18:20-21 says,

A man's stomach will be satisfied with the fruit of his mouth; He will be satisfied with the consequence of his words. Death and life are in the power of the tongue, And those who love it and indulge it will eat its fruit and bear the consequences of their words.

I am totally perplexed how Christians can read this Scripture and fail to believe that the words they speak could have bearing on the outcome of their lives.

REMOVING THE BLIND EYE

Psalm 39:1 says, "*I said, I will guard my ways that I may not sin with my tongue; I will muzzle my mouth while the wicked are in my presence.*" It's critical to acknowledge deep in our soul that we must guard our mouths and watch what words we speak. James said that no human can tame the tongue, but I know from experience that the Holy Spirit can and will, if sought. The next time you think about saying anything negative, close your mouth! This is not the power of positive thinking but just common sense for those who follow Christ and believe in His Word.

CHAPTER 34

FOUL-MOUTHED BELIEVERS

But I tell you, on the day of judgment people will have to give an accounting for every careless or useless word they speak. (Matthew 12:36)

FOUL-MOUTHED

Greek: from *aischros* and *logos*—vile conversation, filthy communication

Cambridge English: if someone is foul-mouthed, they use offensive language

Dictionary.com: using obscene, profane or scurrilous language; given to filthy or abusive speech

Merriam-Webster: given to the use of obscene, profane, or abusive language

I F EVERY true Christian believed Matthew 12:36, then I think most would think twice about the words that come out of their mouths, especially foul ones. I realize this topic will likely cause a reaction from some readers, but it must be addressed for so many reasons.

Most would have to agree that obscene, profane, vile, offensive or abusive language—which includes cursing—qualifies as careless or useless words. Those who don't agree must be reading a different Bible than mine. True to the entire principle of this book and focusing on what Jesus said to be the absolute truth, He made it clear to us in Mark 7:20-22:

> *And He said,* "*Whatever comes from [the heart of] a man, that is what defiles and dishonors him. For from within, [that is] out the heart of men, come base and malevolent thoughts and schemes, acts of sexual immorality, thefts, murders, adulteries, acts of greed and covetousness, wickedness, deceit, unrestrained conduct, envy and jealousy, slander and* **profanity**, *arrogance and self-righteousness and foolishness (poor judgment)*."

As Jesus pointed out, this type of language starts in the heart. As discussed in a previous chapter, the heart is part of a person's spiritual DNA. All emotions, desires and motives begin in the spiritual heart, which then determine the actions we take that drive our behavior. Jesus said these words defile us and dishonor us, yet the use of foul language is as common among believers as rain is in Seattle. I've heard many men say that they have always cussed, and it's just ingrained into their minds—that it's just a "bad habit." But that excuse will not fly. Paul said in Ephesians 5:3-5,

> *But sexual immorality and all [moral] impurity [indecent, offensive behavior] or greed must not even be hinted at among you, as is proper among saints [for as believers our way of life, whether in public or in private, reflects the validity of our faith]. Let there be* **no filthiness and silly talk, or coarse [obscene or vulgar] joking, because such things are not appropriate [for believers];** *but instead speak of your thankfulness [to God]. For be sure of this: no immoral, impure, or greedy person—for that one is [in effect]*

an idolater—has any inheritance in the kingdom of Christ and
God [for such a person places a higher value on something other
than God].

How can any true believer read this Scripture and not realize that a
foul mouth is not appropriate for those who walk with the Lord? A
foul mouth is a detriment to our witness, our families, our friends
and ourselves. I used to cuss before I was saved; but once I was filled
to the brim with the Holy Spirit, He took that desire away from me
immediately.

When it comes to actions straight from the heart, profanity is right
up there with "base and malevolent thoughts and schemes, sexual immorality, thefts, murders, adulteries, greed, covetousness, wickedness,
deceit, unrestrained conduct, envy, jealousy, slander, arrogance, self-
righteousness and foolishness" according to Jesus. I purposely listed
these again not to be repetitious but to put profanity in the proper
perspective. Say it out loud, and I promise it will get into your spirit.

Paul said the following in Ephesians 4:29:

*Do not let unwholesome [**foul, profane, worthless, vulgar**]*
words ever come out of your mouth, but only such speech as is
good for building up others, according to the need and the occa-
sion, so that it will be a blessing to those who hear [you speak].

It's my guess that before Paul's encounter with Jesus on the road to Da-
mascus, he likely used all sorts of foul, profane and vulgar words as he
persecuted Christians. Again, he says in Colossians 3:8, "*But now rid*
yourselves [completely] of all these things: anger, rage, malice, slander,
*and **obscene (abusive, filthy, vulgar) language from your mouth**.*"

The evidence is clear that we cannot *turn a blind eye* in the church
to foul-mouthed believers, and the only way to begin to see progress
toward godly speech is to hold one another accountable by calling it
out when we hear it.

REMOVING THE BLIND EYE

Have you ever heard someone say, "Hey, watch your language; the kids are here"? I know that I have on many occasions. What a person is really trying to say is, don't use obscene, profane, filthy or abusive speech because my children could hear it and then use that same speech themselves, which would have consequences down the road. I believe that's exactly what Jesus was saying to us when He said, *"But I tell you, on the day of judgment people will have to give an accounting for every careless or useless word they speak."* (Matthew 12:36) The difference is earthly consequences we can understand because we realize the negative effect it can have in this life as human beings. If little Johnny goes to school and throws out the vilest word in today's English vocabulary that he heard you or your guest say or repeats a vile comment he heard about sexuality, then you're likely going to be invited to pay a visit to the school's principal.

Jesus was saying the same thing, but in a spiritual paradigm. When we face judgment, we will be held accountable for every careless or useless word we speak while on this earth. If you believe this to be the case, then it likely has opened your eyes and you can see this "bad habit" in a whole different light. When you find yourself wanting to cuss, stop; pause before you say it and think of another way to express yourself. If you're thinking about telling a filthy joke or making some sexual innuendo, stop yourself and don't say it! If you slip up, then repent and ask the Holy Spirit to change your heart in this area of your life. It's like any other stronghold that believers face in their daily lives. You have to recognize it first, then make a conscious and deliberate decision to change that part of your life.

We owe it to God, our families, our friends and our witness to the world to tame our tongue. Anyone can do it, if you allow God to help you!

CHAPTER 35

BLESSING MEALS

Now as they were eating Jesus took bread, and after blessing it, He broke it and gave it to the disciples, and said, "Take, eat; this is My body." (Matthew 26:26)

BLESSING

Greek: from *eulogia*—adulation, praise, blessing, gift

Cambridge English: a blessing also means the approval to do something

Dictionary.com: a special favor, mercy, or benefit

Merriam-Webster: the act or words of one that blesses

*T*URNING *A blind eye* in this area is widespread. All too often, we take for granted the fact that we have food in adequate supply. At times, I am way too focused on my food in my desire to eat quickly. Every time I choose not to bless the food that God provided, I am making an unconscious decision to be ungrateful for God's provision for me. That is certainly not my intention, but I have come to the realization that ingratitude is all too common among believers.

Jesus took the bread and immediately blessed it. He didn't take a bite or ask someone at the table to take a bite to test the flavor. He thanked God first, because He knew it was a true gift to have food. We can feel intimidated about blessing our food when there are people all around us, like in a restaurant, for example. That should never be the case because if our hearts are full of gratitude, we should always take the opportunity to lift our voices in thanks to our Father.

While blessing our food may seem to be a trivial way we *turn a blind eye*, keep in mind that it was important enough to God that His Son taught us what to do by example. Jesus thanked the Father before He fed 5,000 people with five loaves and two fish. Matthew 14:19-20 says,

> *Then He ordered the crowds to sit down on the grass, and He took the five loaves and the two fish and, looking up toward heaven, He blessed and broke the loaves and gave them to the disciples, and the disciples gave them to the people, and they all ate and were satisfied. They picked up twelve full baskets of the leftover broken pieces.*

I love this Scripture because it states that Jesus looked up toward Heaven first, then blessed the food. I can picture in my mind Jesus looking up at His Father in deep gratitude for what He was about to do in multiplying the provision so everyone could eat. He did the same when He fed the 4,000. Matthew 15:36-37 has the following account:

> *And He took the seven loaves and the fish; and when He had given thanks, He broke them and started giving them to the disciples, and the disciples [gave them] to the people. And they all ate and were satisfied, and they gathered up seven full baskets of the broken pieces that were left over.*

Jesus set the standard when He practiced giving thanks Himself, so we should never take our provision of food for granted. By thanking God, we practice the habit of gratitude.

REMOVING THE BLIND EYE

This problem is a simple one to overcome. After reading this chapter, simply stop before you eat at your next meal and thank God for the food He places before you. If you're with your family, then have them join in so your children see the same pattern set for them that Jesus set for us. If you're out in public, do the same. Remember it's not how loud you pray or how many words you use; it's just a heartfelt acknowledgment of your thankfulness.

CHAPTER 36

FAITHFUL FRIENDSHIPS

No one has greater love [nor stronger commitment] than to lay down his own life for his friends. (John 15:13)

FAITHFUL

Greek: from *pistos*—faithful, reliable

Cambridge English: firm and not changing in your friendship with or support for a person or an organization, or in your belief in your principles

Dictionary.com: steady in allegiance or affection; loyal; constant.

Merriam-Webster: loyal, conscientious, accurate, reliable

I T'S ALL too common to hear people in the secular world say, "I thought he or she was my friend." I'm sure King David felt the same way when he said in Psalm 55:12-14,

For it is not an enemy who taunts me—Then I could bear it; Nor is it one who has hated me who insolently exalts himself against me—Then I could hide from him. But it is you, a man my equal and my counsel, My companion and my familiar friend; We who had sweet fellowship together, who walked to the house of God in company.

Like King David, when this happens, an individual can feel betrayed—whether real or imagined—and they are hurt emotionally. Such betrayal is very common in the business arena where money, position and power always seem to trump friendships.

Unfortunately, such betrayals can happen among believers just as they do in the world. Jesus set the bar very high based on this Scripture and gave us a footprint for the level of commitment required to be a true friend. It's unlikely that most of us will ever be required to lay down our lives for a friend, but we can certainly learn from this exhortation and understand that loyalty, sacrifice and being true to your word is what separates Christian friendships from friendships among the unsaved.

I, too, have experienced those that I thought cared deeply for me simply *turning a blind eye*. God healed my heart of those hurts, but as God always does in my life, He revealed through my own personal pain that I have not been a true friend to others on many occasions.

In the church today, it can be something as simple as a negative comment behind your friend's back or not standing up for a friend when someone else does the same and *turning a blind eye* to loyalty. It happens when we are too busy to help a friend in need or simply communicate on a regular basis, *turning a blind eye* to the sacrifices required in friendship. Being an unfaithful friend is making a promise to a friend and not fulfilling your word.

I really love how Paul described a true friend and fellow believer. In Colossians 4:7-9, he says,

As to all my affairs, Tychicus, who is a much-loved brother and faithful assistant and fellow bond-servant in the Lord, will give you all the information. I have sent him to you for this very purpose, that you may know how we are doing and that he may encourage your hearts; and with him is Onesimus, our faithful and beloved brother, who is one of you. They will let you know everything about the situation here [in Rome].

Onesimus was a runaway slave hiding out in Rome who, while visiting Paul in prison, became a believer then committed to serve Paul and the church. It's believed that Onesimus stole property from Philemon his master. Based on Roman law, Philemon had the right to apply any form of punishment, including death. Due to Paul's deep love for Onesimus, he wrote a letter to make a request of Philemon, his co-worker and likely someone he had led to Christ based on Philemon 1:10-19, when Paul says,

> *I appeal to you for my [own spiritual] child Onesimus, whom I have fathered [in the faith] while a captive in these chains. Once he was useless to you, but now he is indeed useful to you as well as to me. I have sent him back to you in person, that is, like sending my very heart. I would have chosen to keep him with me, so that he might minister to me on your behalf during my imprisonment for the gospel; but I did not want to do anything without first getting your consent, so that your goodness would not be, in effect, by compulsion but of your own free will. Perhaps it was for this reason that he was separated from you for a while, so that you would have him back forever, no longer as a slave, but [as someone] more than a slave, as a brother [in Christ], especially dear to me, but how much more to you, both in the flesh [as a servant] and in the Lord [as a fellow believer]. So if you consider me a partner, welcome and accept him as you would me. But if he has wronged you in any way or owes you anything, charge that to my account; I, Paul, write this with my own hand, I will repay it in full (not to mention to you that you owe to me even your own self as well).*

Now that's a faithful friend! Can we apply these definitions to how we view and interact in our godly friendships as Paul did? If not, then we are all *turning a blind eye*.

If we're going to enter this covenant relationship as a friend, just like in a marriage, we need to understand that we must maintain certain requirements in order to have that level of trust. Once there is trust and commitment, then loyalty, sacrifice and honesty follow. Proverbs 18:24 gives us a template to follow as it relates to our covenant relationships outside of biological families: *The man of too many friends [chosen indiscriminately] will be broken in pieces and come to ruin, but there is a [true, loving] friend who [is reliable and] sticks closer than a brother.*

When it comes to family, nobody loves their blood family any more than I do. I am certain many people feel the same way. Family is important to God, but sometimes friendships get thrown under the proverbial bus when people are forced to choose between family and friends. That's likely where the phrase, "Blood is thicker than water" came into being. What I find interesting is Jesus' perspective on our earthly families in Luke 8:19-21 when He said,

> *Then Jesus' mother and His brothers came up toward Him, but they could not reach Him because of the crowd. And He was told, "Your mother and Your brothers are standing outside, asking to see You." But He answered, "My mother and My brothers are these who listen to the Word of God and do it!"*

Most of us in that situation would without a doubt have shown favoritism to our blood family and had someone go out and get them. Jesus basically said, "My real family is everyone who hears God's Word and then obeys it." He went as far as saying in Matthew 10:37, *"He who loves father or mother more than Me is not worthy of Me; and he who loves son or daughter more than Me is not worthy of Me."* Jesus was not encouraging us to love our earthly families less but to love Him more and to see them from an eternal perspective instead of just an earthly one.

The fact that Jesus said that laying down your life for a friend is the greatest form of love reflects the importance of lifelong friends.

JOHN 15:12-15, *"This is My commandment, that you love and unselfishly seek the best for one another, just as I have loved you.*

No one has greater love [nor stronger commitment] than to lay down his own life for his friends. You are my friends if you keep on doing what I command you. I do not call you servants any longer, for the servant does not know what his master is doing; but I have called you [My] friends, because I have revealed to you everything that I have heard from My Father."

Jesus believed so intently in friendships that, as He hung on the cross, He instructed John—who is thought to be the disciple whom He loved—to care for His mother instead of asking a blood relative. John 19:26 tells us, *So Jesus, seeing His mother, and the disciple whom He loved (esteemed) standing near, said to His mother, "[Dear] woman, look, [here is] your son!"*

REMOVING THE BLIND EYE

You will sometimes hear people say, "You can count your true friends on one hand." I think that attitude is wrong and robs us of all the real and life-changing benefits friends can provide. Jesus had twelve "true" friends (minus Judas) when He addressed His disciples in John 15:12-15. I believe that Jesus' disciples were not His only friends because we know from Scripture that He had other deep relationships like those with Mary, Martha and Lazarus that we see in John 11:1-4:

Now a certain man named Lazarus was sick. He was from Bethany, the village where Mary and her sister Martha lived. It was the Mary who anointed the Lord with perfume and wiped His feet with her hair, whose brother Lazarus was sick. So the sisters sent word to Him, saying, "Lord, he [our brother and Your friend] whom You love is sick." When Jesus heard this, He said, "This sickness will not end in death; but [on the contrary it is] for the glory and honor of God, so that the Son of God may be glorified by it."

He loved these three siblings, so He obviously counted them as friends.

Jesus traveled all the way to Judea just to raise Lazarus from the dead! Now that is a true friend. We should treat all close friends "like family"—whether they need a shoulder to lean on, a confidant to share those deepest secrets, someone to stand up for them with others, financial assistance or comfort in a time of grieving.

I have one friend who answered the call in one of my greatest times of distress. I had just dropped off one of my children who had a heroin addiction at a local twelve-step recovery club and basically told him he was on his own. My wife and I had no idea what else to do at that time, and "tough love" seemed to be our only remaining option. It was one of the hardest things I ever had to do in my life.

I remember calling my friend Allen in the middle of his workday and telling him I needed to come by his office right then. When I arrived, he greeted me in the parking lot and jumped in my car. I cried like never before and just poured out my heart to him. He could do nothing to take away the pain except be there for me and allow me a safe place to let go, but he was a great help to me that day.

I knew I could count on Allen because he always stayed in touch and asked how I was doing, and I believe that's where a lot of us miss it. We need to consciously think about the needs of our friends and not be so self-centered—and we need to express our concern to them verbally.

Go the extra mile when asked, be available at a moment's notice, remember birthdays for their entire family, and let them know you are there for them 24/7. These acts of love and others should be easy in comparison to laying down your life and treating your friends with such care will allow you to build true and lasting friendships.

CHAPTER 37

THE PATHWAY
TO GOD

Again Jesus began to teach beside the sea [of Galilee]. And a very large crowd gathered around Him, so He got into a boat [anchoring it a short distance out] on the sea and sat down; and the whole crowd was by the sea on the shore. And He taught them many things in parables, and in His teaching He said to them, "Listen! A sower went out to sow seed; and as he was sowing, some seed fell by the road, and the birds came and ate it up. Other seed fell on rocks where there was not much soil; and immediately a plant sprang up because the soil had no depth. And when the sun came up, the plant was scorched; and because it had no root, it dried up and withered away. Other seed fell among thorns, and the thorns came up and choked it, and it yielded no grain. And other seed fell into good soil, and as the plants grew and increased, they yielded a crop and produced thirty, sixty, and a hundred times *[as much as had been sown]."* *And He said,* "He who has ears to hear, let him hear and heed My words." *As soon as He was alone, those who were around Him, together with the twelve [disciples], began asking Him about [the interpretation of] the parables. He said to them,* "The *mystery of the kingdom of God has been given to you* **[who have teachable hearts]***, but those who are outside* **[the unbelievers, the spiritually blind]** *get everything in parables, so that* THEY WILL CONTINUALLY LOOK BUT NOT SEE, AND THEY WILL CONTINUALLY HEAR BUT NOT UNDERSTAND, OTHERWISE THEY MIGHT TURN **[from their rejection of the truth]** AND BE FORGIVEN." **Then He said to them,** *"Do you not understand this parable? How will you understand and grasp the meaning of all the parables? The sower sows the word* **[of God, the good news regarding the way of salvation]***. These* **[in the first group]** *are the ones along the road where the word is sown; but when they hear, Satan immediately comes and takes away the word which has been sown in them. In a similar way these* **[in the second group]** *are the ones on whom seed was sown on rocky ground, who, when they hear the word, immediately receive it with joy* **[but accept it only superficially]***; and they have no real root in themselves, so they endure only for a little while; then, when trouble or persecution comes because of the word, immediately they* **[are offended and displeased at being associated with Me and]** *stumble and fall away. And others are the ones on whom seed was sown among the thorns; these are the ones who have heard the word, but the worries and cares of the world* **[the distractions of this age with its worldly pleasures]** *and the deceitfulness* **[and the false security or glamour]** *of wealth [or fame], and the passionate desires for all the other things creep in and choke out the word, and it becomes unfruitful. And those* **[in the last group]** *are the ones on whom seed was sown on the good soil; and they hear the word* **[of God, the good news regarding the way of salvation]** *and accept it and bear fruit—thirty, sixty, and a hundred times as much* **[as was sown]***."* (Mark 4:1-20)

PATH

Greek: from *hodos*—a way, road, journey, path

Cambridge English: set of actions that you take in life

Dictionary.com: a path, course, route, or way

Merriam-Webster: a line of movement, a course of conduct or thought

I HAVE READ this Scripture so, so many times over the years, yet I never before pondered the significance of the statement when Jesus asked His disciples, *"Do you not understand this parable? How will you understand and grasp the meaning of all the parables?"* Jesus told thirty-nine parables in the New Testament. He said if we don't understand and grasp the meaning of this one, then we will likely not understand all the others. I asked myself first why it was so important to Jesus that He would ask His disciples the question and second the significance of how clearly He laid out the four paths people take when they hear the Word of God. I concluded that there were four paths over 2,000 years ago and still four paths now, but still only one right road. Below is a summary for each path and its consequences.

Seed (or Word):	*Sown on the road*
Reaction:	*Hear the Word*
Parable Results:	*The birds eat it.*
Plain English Results:	*Satan immediately takes away the Word*
End Result:	*Hell*

Seed (or Word):	*Sown on rocky places*
Reaction:	*Hear the Word and receive it with joy*
Parable Results:	*Scorched by sun and withered*
Plain English Results:	*No firm root, temporary; persecution and affliction come; they fall away*
End Result:	*Hell*

Seed (or Word):	*Sown among the thorns*
Reaction:	*Hear the Word*
Parable Results:	*Thorns choke it; yields nothing*
Plain English Results:	*Worries of the world; deceitfulness of riches; desire for other things choke the Word; becomes unfruitful*
End Result:	*Hell*

Seed (or Word):	*Sown in good soil*
Reaction:	*Hear the Word*
Parable Results:	*Grew and increased; produced crop*
Plain English Results:	*Accepted it; bear fruit of 30, 60, 100 times*
End Result:	*Eternal life*

My understanding of this Scripture is that each of the four paths all heard the Word, meaning a pastor, a minister, an evangelist, a Sunday school teacher or any other person preached the good news of Jesus Christ to them. The listeners all hear what is required to have eternal life—repent of your sins, believe that Jesus Christ died and rose on the third day and sits at the right hand of the Father, accept Jesus as the Lord of your life, and then produce fruit based on that belief.

So, let's look at each path, and put some modern-day examples by each one.

WORD SOWN ON THE ROAD

You're preaching to someone at the coffee bar at your office. You only have a few minutes but it's enough to get the message across. Before that person can even take a sip of his coffee, the devil immediately steals the Word from his heart. In other words, maybe for a brief second he contemplated the good news; but after the devil stole the seed, he thanked you and walked back to his cubical "to get back to work."

The bottom line is that the devil stole the Word so quickly, that person never had a chance to gain eternal life.

WORD SOWN ON THE ROCKY PLACES

You're back at the coffee bar sharing the good news of Jesus Christ. This individual hears and immediately receives it with joy. A big smile comes across his face, and you can see that he is excited. You tell him that when he is ready you would be happy to grab your Bible to sit down and go through the Word together. You try for days to reconnect with him, but you can't seem to find him anywhere or, in some cases, he seems like he is avoiding you altogether.

One day you corner this person at the snack machine and ask him if he thought any more about your discussion and if he would like to get together again and crack open the Bible. He gives you a strange look and seems a little embarrassed, so you sense something is not right. You ask him what is wrong, and he begins to tell you that he has not had time to think about it and that after sharing your conversation, he is catching grief from his friends, his girlfriend and even his family. He tells you his other coworkers have made him the butt of jokes and are talking behind his back after seeing him talking to "that Jesus freak." He politely states he is grateful for the time you spent with him, but "this Jesus thing" is probably not for him at this time in his life.

The bottom line is that he heard the truth and even became excited about it, but he simply fell away once persecution and affliction came on the scene; without a firm root, he had no defense against the devil and his attacks.

WORD SOWN AMONG THE THORNS

Back to the coffee bar! You're preaching the good news to a gentleman who is a big hitter at your firm and is in fact a partner with all the trappings of earthly success. He hears it, receives it and seems excited that he now has a way to fill a void in his life that he has worked so hard to fill through accomplishments. You finish up by telling him that when he is ready, you would be happy to grab your Bible and sit down and go through the Word together. Soon after, you run into this guy at

Starbucks and mention your conversation. This guy is a type A alpha male, so he has no issue telling you how he feels about things. He says he was grateful for the awesome information and is certainly open to learning more, but he has a gigantic deal he is worried about that he must close because it will make him a ton more money that he will need when he upgrades his home. He also shares that he just doesn't have the time right now to focus on this "Bible stuff" because he is so close to his goal of becoming managing partner of the company, which is something he has wanted ever since he joined the firm. You both pay for your coffee and part ways, and you know in your heart he will never follow up.

The bottom line is that he heard the Word, but it was choked due to other worldly ambitions.

Word Sown on the Good Soil

You have another encounter with one of your peers while grabbing a bite to eat in the break room. You have your Bible out and you are reading the book of John. Your co-worker asks what you're reading, though it's clear you're reading the Bible. You respond that you're reading the book of John, which is one of your favorite books in the New Testament because it reveals just how much God loves us.

To your surprise, he wants to know more, so you begin to walk him through the plan of salvation and explain why we need Jesus in our lives. Although his countenance looks like a deer in the headlights, you sense that every Scripture seems to penetrate deep into his soul. You finish, then ask him what he thinks about what you've said and whether he is sure he will live eternally with God when he takes his last breath. He sheepishly admits that his parents dedicated him to the Lord at church at a young age, and that he has always thought of himself as a good person. In fact, he tells you he doesn't drink alcohol, does a ton of community work and never has cheated on his wife. Then you sense the moment when it suddenly hits him like a ton of bricks that

248 | *Turning a Blind Eye*

he is likely missing the mark based on what you just shared because no one has ever taken the time to open the Bible and show him exactly who Jesus really is and why God sent Him to earth. You then ask if he is ready to accept the Lord as His Savior so he can be a hundred percent certain that he will live forever. He agrees that he is indeed ready, and you lead him to the Lord. You run into him again some months later, and he tells you that he is part of a local church, participating in a men's Bible study, reading the Word daily and sharing the good news whenever he has the opportunity.

The bottom line in this case is that he heard the Word and accepted it and gained eternal life. He produced twice as much fruit in his life as he ever dreamed possible.

People turn away from God in multiple ways and for a multitude of reasons—and in many cases, you will never be able to get to a point of even discussing God's Word because the person is Atheist, Agnostic, Jewish, Muslim, Hindu, Buddhist, Unitarian or—what is worst of all in my opinion—a "religious" person who follows American church traditions and sees no need to hear what the Bible actually says about salvation. With that being said, Hebrew 4:12 (NASB) says the following:

> *For the Word of God is living and active and sharper than any two-edged sword and piercing as far as the division of the soul and spirit, of both joints and marrow, and able to judge the thoughts and intentions of the heart.*

This Scripture reminds me of when I had a bone marrow biopsy to confirm my diagnosis of leukemia. The doctor jammed a giant needle so far into my hip that it literally pierced the bone to get to my marrow. My wife said the doctor had to stand on his tiptoes to get enough weight behind the needle to pierce the bone so he could obtain the tissue. I will never forget that experience, so when I think of the Word of God and its ability to pierce both joints and marrow, I have a personal understanding of how deep that is. I have also personally experienced the effect of the Word of God and how deep it got into my heart, soul and spirit on April 29, 1990, when I was saved. So, what I am saying is, always preach the Word regardless of someone's position because if it can go that deep into a person, it will produce one day.

Think about Mark 4:1-20 in terms of odds. Of the four paths, only one choice is the right one. After each of the first three examples, Jesus clearly states that the Word *"is taken away"* (road), that it *"immediately fell away"* (rocky places) or *"the world chokes the Word and it becomes unfruitful"* (thorns). Does that sound like any who chose those three paths have eternal life? I have so often seen professing Christians who have little to no fruit to reflect that commitment according to the Word of God. John the Baptist said in Matthew 3:8, *"So produce fruit that is consistent with repentance [demonstrating new behavior that proves a change of heart, and a conscious decision to turn away from sin]."* Since 1990 when I began walking with the Lord, I have run across those where the seed was sown on the road, in rocky places, among thorns and in good soil. As I look back, I realize that I have on occasion *turned a blind eye* to the first three Jesus described when I failed to take the opportunity to minister and show a person the truth of Scripture. Now I have to ask myself what if that one person I failed to minister to died the next day without eternal life?

In the United States, 1 person dies every 11.59 seconds; that's 311 people per hour. That means 7,464 people face eternity and judgment before God every day in America alone.[1] If you include the entire world, 1 person dies every 2 seconds; that's 1,800 people each hour, or 43,200 every day that face eternity and judgment before God.[2] Hebrews 9:27 says, *"And just as it is appointed and destined for all men to die once and after this [comes certain] judgment."*

It's wonderful when you share the gospel and the Word convicts a person who then gives his or her life to Jesus. It's even better when you see that person grow in the Lord and keep bringing forth fruit of genuine repentance. Those are the folks you know you will see in Heaven when the time comes. But what about the other three groups Jesus mentioned who potentially chose the wrong path? How much effort do we put into reaching those who casually claim to be Christians? I am thankful someone didn't accept that claim from my wife and me. In our case, the Word was sown among the thorns and became unfruitful. When we met with a childhood friend who was an evangelist, we professed to be Christians and believed that to be true based on our limited knowledge and what religion taught us. It was not until our friend opened the Word and gently walked us through our beliefs and compared them to what the Word says that we truly understood that neither of us would have known the true Christ even if He had been sitting in our laps! This friend made the decision to avoid *turning a blind eye* to our true condition and to invest the time necessary to share God's Word so the Holy Spirit could convict us.

We will talk about this in a later chapter, but I am convinced God had a reason for revealing to John the size of Heaven while the size of Hell is described only as bottomless. Hell must be big enough to hold all the people where the Word was sown on the road, in rocky places and among thorns. Heaven's size is confirmed in Revelation 21:15-16 which says the following:

> *The one who was speaking with me had a gold measuring rod to measure the city, and its gates and its wall. The city is laid out as a square, its length being the same as its width; and he measured the city with his rod—twelve thousand stadia (about 1,400 miles); its length and width and height are equal.*

Hell is described in Luke 8:30-31 which says, *Then Jesus asked him, "What is your name?" And he said, "Legion"; because many demons had entered him. They continually begged Him not to command them to go into the abyss.*

It's only by the grace of God that He is patient with us, as 2 Peter 3:9 relates, "*The Lord does not delay [as though He were unable to act] and is not slow about His promise, as some count slowness, but is [extraor-dinarily] patient toward you, not wishing for any to perish but for all to come to repentance."* I think about those 7,464 people who die each day in our nation and wonder how many of them fall into the first three categories. I also often wonder what impact we could have on that out-come, if we would only take the time to ask.

REMOVING THE BLIND EYE

It is actually very easy to take the road less traveled when discuss-ing a person's earthly life choices that could have catastrophic con-sequences for eternity. The way to frame such a conversation is not by talking theoretically or giving your opinion, but by taking them straight to Mark 4:1-20 and having them read it for themselves. Get-ting someone into a setting where the Bible can be opened depends on each person's unique anointing. Some people, like me, mistakenly believed they had chosen the right path and have no idea what the Word says about the subject. Others have never even considered their eternal destiny, so you're working with a clean slate. In either case, if the person reads the Scripture passage and can honestly assess their condition by realizing perhaps they chose the wrong path, then walk-ing that individual through the plan of salvation that brings about a saving faith should be easy.

I believe the key to piquing someone's interest in considering the one and only right path is to simply ask. Many of us too readily accept a profession to be a Christian because we are concerned about offend-ing someone. However, we're talking about a one-time deal here, and once someone dies, it's too late. Ask God to open doors for you to have the opportunity to discuss the four pathways Jesus spoke about and be prepared to deliver the truth with confidence but also in love. Thousands die every single day who may never see the gates of Heaven unless someone asks the tough questions.

CHAPTER 38

SAVING FAITH

Enter through the narrow gate. For wide is the gate and broad and easy to travel is the path that leads the way to destruction and eternal loss, and there are many who enter through it. But small is the gate and narrow and difficult to travel is the path that leads the way to [everlasting] life, and there are few who find it. (Matthew 7:13-14)

BELIEVE

Greek: from *pisteuo*—to believe, entrust

Cambridge English: to think that something is true, correct, or real

Dictionary.com: to have confidence in the truth, the existence, or the reliability of something, although without absolute proof that one is right in doing so

Merriam-Webster: to have a firm or wholehearted religious conviction or persuasion, to regard the existence of God as a fact, to accept the word or evidence of

T HE LEGENDARY Billy Sunday who played in the National Baseball League then became one of the most widely known evangelists in the late 1800s and early 1900s said, "Going to church doesn't make you a Christian any more than going to a garage makes you an automobile."[1] That statement certainly applied to me. I would like to say this for the record and before anyone who is reading this book gets bent out of shape and labels me a heretic. I believe in Romans 10:8-10, which says,

> *But what does it say? "THE WORD IS NEAR YOU, IN YOUR MOUTH AND IN YOUR HEART"—that is, the word [the message, the basis] of faith which we preach—because if you acknowledge and confess with your mouth that Jesus is Lord [recognizing His power, authority, and majesty as God], and believe in your heart that God raised Him from the dead, you will be saved. For with the heart a person believes [in Christ as Savior] resulting in his justification [that is, being made righteous—being freed of the guilt of sin and made acceptable to God]; and with the mouth he acknowledges and confesses [his faith openly], resulting in and confirming [his] salvation.*

I also believe we are saved by grace as reflected in Ephesians 2:8,

> *For it is by grace [God's remarkable compassion and favor drawing you to Christ] that you have been saved [actually delivered from judgment and given eternal life] through faith. And this [salvation] is not of yourselves [not through your own effort], but it is the [undeserved, gracious] gift of God.*

As a believer, I have always focused on how to get into Heaven, but I have rarely thought about how we can miss Heaven. You might wonder if that is even possible. I can speak only from my own personal experience—and in my case, it was not only a possibility, but a reality. Before I was saved, I never had the saving faith to gain salvation in the first place. I followed tradition and went through all the right motions but doing all of that never was a life-changing experience until I reached the age of thirty. Until that time, I knew *of* Jesus, but I never *met* Jesus. If you "know of" someone yet have never met that person or gotten to know them, then you have no relationship with that individual. You could even tell others what you have learned about that person through various methods, but you still don't really know that individual. The same is true of Jesus.

We have to ask ourselves the tough and uncomfortable questions.

- Can a person give his life to Jesus with his lips then go on living like the rest of the world?

- What about the person who makes an idol of materialism and rarely gives God a second thought?

- What about the guy like me that professes to be a Christian without a true change of heart?

- Do any of these people have a saving faith?

I believe we risk making a big mistake in believing people are saved simply because they make a verbal profession of faith when there is no true change of heart followed by a deep desire to know God. Religious requirements or empty words can't save anyone; salvation is based on a personal and deep relationship with Jesus Christ. Paul said in Romans 10:10 that man believes with the heart and confesses with the mouth. John said in 2 John 9:

> *Anyone who runs on ahead and does not remain in the doctrine of Christ [that is, one who is not content with what He taught], does not have God; but the one who continues to remain in the teaching [of Christ does have God], he has both the Father and the Son.*

He said we must remain in the teachings of Christ. What if someone never received that teaching after confessing Christ or did receive it for a short period of time then ran for what the world has to offer?

Since I confessed Jesus as Lord, but it never really got into my heart, how could I be saved? I never took the steps the Bible points out to gain a personal relationship with Him through reading the Word, praying and participating in fellowship. Yes, I told anyone who asked me that I was a Christian and people accepted it at face value. Perhaps though this is why Jesus made the following statement in Matthew 7:14, *"But small is the gate and narrow and difficult to travel is the path that leads the way to [everlasting] life, and there are few who find it."*

I've read estimates that 100.8 billion people have died over the course of human history.[2] If billions and billions of people over that period of time have "called on the name of the Lord," then why will only a few find eternal life? What did Jesus mean when He said this? He goes on to say in Matthew 7:21-23,

> *Not everyone who says to Me, "Lord, Lord," will enter the kingdom of heaven, but only he who does the will of My Father who is in heaven. Many will say to Me on that day [when I judge them], "Lord, Lord, have we not prophesied in Your name, and driven out demons in Your name, and done many miracles in Your name?" And then I will declare to them publicly, "I never knew you; DEPART FROM ME [you are banished from My presence], YOU WHO ACT WICKEDLY [disregarding My commands]."*

This Scripture seems to be addressing those believers who have manifested some of the gifts of the Spirit as well as the power of the Holy Spirit. Who are they talking about in these Scriptures if they were not addressing followers?

In my case, I did go to church from time to time, and I repeated the words someone gave me to say when I "dedicated" my life to Christ. I did get the "confess-with-your-mouth" part right, but I didn't have the "believe-with-all-your-heart" part sewn up. Matthew 15:8 and 9 applied to me: "THIS PEOPLE HONORS ME WITH THEIR LIPS, BUT THEIR HEART IS FAR AWAY FROM ME. BUT IN VAIN DO THEY WORSHIP ME, FOR THEY TEACH AS DOCTRINES THE PRECEPTS OF MEN." In my study I found the meaning of the word *vain* described as ineffectual, having no real value, idle or worthless. I realized my worship of God was vain because I was following the traditions of man.

Prior to my thirtieth birthday, I looked the part of a Christian—I had a family and a good job, and I attended church on Christmas Eve and Easter Sunday. The depth of my belief was in reality no different than my belief regarding which NFL football team would win the Super Bowl each year. Sure, I believed a certain team would win, but I had no idea if that was the truth. That belief was similar to my experience with salvation. Did I "believe" Jesus was God's Son? That He died and rose on the third day? That if I made Him Lord of my life, I could have eternal life? Yes, because that's what was on the card I read when I made my statement of faith. I heard all these things, but I was never shown the truth in God's Word or even desired to seek what it really meant to have saving faith.

I was never taught that sin is a condition like any hereditary illness—one that we are literally born with instead of just a behavior we exhibit in our lives. This sinful condition is why some humans commit such evil, wicked acts. And that very same sinful condition means that many today will not carry out a despicable act *per se,* but they have become totally self-sufficient, failing to recognize their need for God. These people may claim to know God, but their behavior is far from reflecting any hint of sanctification in regard to justification.

I am sure many people in the denominational church I attended while growing up and as an adult truly loved and knew Jesus. However, no one in that church ever introduced Him to me. I recall that our minister's response when he was asked whether there was really a Hell was, "I sure hope not." So, in my case, if I had died before the age of thirty, I am certain that I would have gone to Hell—because I certainly did not possess eternal life.

In the movie *Billy Graham: An Extraordinary Journey,* Graham told a story that really resonated with me. He was a young man raised by God-fearing parents who was focused on baseball and girls and attended church on a regular basis. An evangelist named Mordecai Ham came to Charlotte, North Carolina, for an old-fashioned tent revival, but Billy Graham wanted nothing to do with it. He even stated he thought it would be like a circus show. However, curiosity got the best of him, and he decided to go with some of his buddies. During the revival meeting, he came to the understanding that, despite being a church member, he knew he lacked something and that he too was a sinner in need of redemption.[3] **What he lacked was a personal relationship with Jesus Christ, so he gave his life to Jesus, and the rest is history.**

Many people believe in the historical reality of Jesus; in fact, Scripture tells us that even the demons believe He is real. But that's not enough to gain eternal life—that requires accepting Jesus' sacrificial atonement for justification in every fiber of our being, so that we desire to build that personal relationship with Him, which leads to sanctification. A real relationship with Jesus Christ is similar to falling in love with someone here on earth. When you're smitten with another person, you have a desire to show how much you care and how grateful you are the person is in your life; you endlessly want to seek a deeper and more meaningful relationship with that individual. That is exactly what justification looks like when we accept Jesus' personal atonement for our sins. It starts with a "spark" and continues to grow as we work out our salvation through sanctification.

How many times, out of fear that we will offend, do we *turn a blind eye* to a person who seems to have all the answers when asked about eternal destiny? I have heard, "Oh, yes, I am a member of this denomination," or "I was baptized and sprinkled as a baby," or "I was dedicated as a child by my parents," or "I have gone to church all my life," or "I believe in God." But there is no mention of Jesus. What if people all over the world are trusting in their religion instead of a saving faith in Christ to gain eternal life?

Saying I believe it will rain today is not the same as saying I believe in Christ. Whether or not it rains, I will go on with my day without changing anything; but if I believe in Christ, then my whole life—including my words and actions—reflect that belief, in spite of my faults. John the Baptist said to the Pharisees and Sadducees who came to witness his baptisms in Matthew 3:8, "*So produce fruit that is consistent with repentance [demonstrating new behavior that **proves** a change of heart, and a conscious decision to turn away from sin].*" In the *New American Commentary*, author Craig L. Blomberg says, "A fruitless Christian is not a Christian at all."[4]

Perhaps the lack of fruit prompted the disciples' question to Jesus on the way to Jerusalem in Luke 13:23-30:

> *And someone asked Him, "Lord, will only a few be saved [from the penalties of the last judgment]?" And He said to them, "Strive to enter through the narrow door [force aside unbelief and the attractions of sin]; for many, I tell you, will try to enter [by their own works] and will not be able. Once the head of the house gets up and closes the door, and you begin to stand outside and knock on the door [again and again], saying, 'Lord, open to us!' then He will answer you, 'I do not know where you are from [for you are not of My household].' Then you will begin to say, 'We ate and drank in Your presence, and You taught in our streets'; but He will say to you, 'I do not know where you are from;* DEPART FROM ME, ALL YOU EVILDOERS!' *In that place there will be weeping [in sorrow and pain] and grinding of teeth [in distress and anger] when you see Abraham and Isaac and Jacob and all the prophets in the kingdom of God, but yourselves being thrown out and driven away. And people will come from east and west, and from north and south, and they will sit down [and feast at the table] in the kingdom of God. And behold, some are last who will be first, and some are first who will be last."*

True saving faith will produce a way of living and behavior that demonstrates a changed heart, which will produce the same character of Jesus. Colossians 2:6-7 tells us,

> *Therefore as you have received Christ Jesus the Lord, walk in [union with] Him [reflecting His character in the things you do and say—living lives that lead others away from sin], having been deeply rooted [in Him] and now being continually built up in Him and [becoming increasingly more] established in your faith, just as you were taught, and overflowing in it with gratitude.*

Actions demonstrate a saving faith. Titus 1:16 says, **They profess to know God [to recognize and be acquainted with Him], but by their actions they deny and disown Him.** *They are detestable and disobedient and worthless for good work of any kind.* Paul said in 1 Corinthians 15:34,

> *Be sober-minded [be sensible, wake up from your spiritual stupor] as you ought, and stop sinning; for some [of you] have no knowledge of God [you are disgracefully ignorant of Him, and ignore His truths]. I say this to your shame.*

The uncomfortable reality that the church won't accept is that a faith that does not produce change is not a saving faith at all. The outside of that person may change, but the inner being is unchanged.

Another touchy question that is rarely brought up is, what about true believers who fall away? Some people believe the doctrine of eternal security—or "once saved, always saved." I believe that no one can know a person's heart except God. With that being said, we must ask ourselves why Scripture addresses this issue and what is the outcome for those who fall into this category. Hebrews 10:26-27 says,

> *For if we go on willfully and deliberately sinning after receiving the knowledge of the truth, there no longer remains a sacrifice [to atone] for our sins [that is, no further offering to anticipate], but a kind of awful and terrifying expectation of [divine]*

judgment and THE FURY OF A FIRE *and* BURNING WRATH WHICH WILL CONSUME THE ADVERSARIES *[those who put themselves in opposition to God].*

This passage seems to imply the author is talking about an existing believer. The same author said in Hebrews 6:4-6:

For [it is impossible to restore to repentance] those who have once been enlightened [spiritually] and who have tasted and consciously experienced the heavenly gift and have shared in the Holy Spirit, and have tasted and consciously experienced the good Word of God and the powers of the age (world) to come, and then have fallen away—it is impossible to bring them back again to repentance, since they again nail the Son of God on the cross [for as far as they are concerned, they are treating the death of Christ as if they were not saved by it], and are holding Him up again to public disgrace.

Let's consider how this Scripture compares to Ephesians 2:8, *"For it is by grace [God's remarkable compassion and favor drawing you to Christ] that you have been saved [actually delivered from judgment and given eternal life] through faith."* It appears to me that a valid argument can be made that if a Christian knowingly continues to sin against God, then grace is nullified until true repentance occurs once again.

The greatest sin against God is turning our backs on Him and living for ourselves. Does the person who only acknowledges God with his lips and then lives a life that reflects the opposite fall into this category? A good comparison is my marriage. How can I say I love my wife and will be dedicated to exemplifying that love in my daily affairs, then never want to spend time with her? If all I do is work all the time and then play golf, hunt, fish or do other recreational activities with my buddies in my spare time, would others see that I was in love with my wife? They would likely say that I was in love with the **idea** of being

in love, but that my actions did not reflect that I was in love with her. It's the same principle with our love for God, but then knowingly sinning is added to the mix. These believers had been enlightened spiritually, tasted and experienced the heavenly gift, shared in the Holy Spirit, knew the Word of God and understood this life was temporal; yet they fell away, and there was little hope to bring them back to repentance. We see this same idea again in Hebrews 3:12, which says, "*Take care, **brothers and sisters,** that there not be in any one of you a wicked, unbelieving heart [which refuses to trust and rely on the Lord, a heart] **that turns away from the living God.**"* Jesus made it very clear that some will call Him Lord then not enter the kingdom of Heaven. The Scriptures in Hebrews say something very similar to Matthew 7:21-23, just in different way.

We must also consider what Paul said in 1 Timothy 1:18-19:

*This command I entrust to you, Timothy, my son, in accordance with the prophecies previously made concerning you, so that [inspired and aided] by them you may fight the good fight [in contending with false teachers], keeping your faith [leaning completely on God with absolute trust and confidence in His guidance] and having a good conscience; **for some [people] have rejected [their moral compass] and have made a shipwreck of their faith.***

To make a shipwreck of faith implies it's totally ruined and useless. Paul said some rejected and suffered shipwreck in regard to their faith—not their unbelief. Hebrews 11:1 defines faith for us with laser accuracy. "*Now faith is the assurance (title deed, confirmation) of things hoped for (divinely guaranteed), and the evidence of things not seen [the conviction of their reality—faith comprehends as fact what cannot be experienced by the physical senses].*" In order to shipwreck faith, one must have possessed it in the first place.

Discussing a saving faith and addressing believers who fall away will likely prompt the same reaction Martin Luther received when he nailed the *95 Theses* to the church door in Germany during the sixteenth century—an action that ushered in the Protestant Reformation. That is certainly not my intent, but is it so wrong to encourage all of us believers to search our hearts, to challenge all of us to examine our conversion experience to determine if it was biblical, real and life changing? I believe this subject is the 800-pound elephant in the sanctuary that nobody wants to discuss. The apostle Paul had similar concerns when he said in 2 Corinthians 13:5,

> *Test and evaluate yourselves to see whether you are in the faith and living your lives as [committed] believers. Examine yourselves [not me]! Or do you not recognize this about yourselves [by an ongoing experience] that Jesus Christ is in you—**unless indeed you fail the test and are rejected as counterfeit?***

Paul said to test ourselves—and we cannot ignore this Scriptural admonition. Paul was not saying that salvation entailed additional requirements, but he did plainly say that Jesus Christ must be in us. If He is not in us, then how can we possess saving faith—regardless of whether we are accepting Jesus for the first time or accepted Him years earlier and fell away? That's not a faith based on works or other external factors, but rather an internal faith based on the love of Jesus in us.

We all know people who claim they were converted in their youth, yet their lives and actions reflect otherwise. They love the world and everything it has to offer, and the God of the Bible is only part of their lives in theory without any fruit whatsoever. These are the folks who pull out their "Christian card" when it suits them and get very offended when they are challenged. These people are having a love affair with the world as their mistress. The Bible says that we have been separated and alienated from God because we have willfully turned our backs on Him and decided to run our lives without Him. That's the single issue that prohibits so many from having eternal life. People who are born again will continue to sin because we are human, but because Jesus is in us, we know God's grace is sufficient if we simply repent and turn back to God. 1 John 1:6-10 says,

> *If we say that we have fellowship with Him and yet walk in the darkness [of sin], we lie and do not practice the truth; but if we [really] walk in the Light [that is, live each and every day in conformity with the precepts of God], as He Himself is in the Light, we have [true, unbroken] fellowship with one another [He with us, and we with Him], and the blood of Jesus His Son cleanses us from all sin [by erasing the stain of sin, keeping us cleansed from sin in all its forms and manifestations]. If we say we have no sin [refusing to admit that we are sinners], we delude ourselves and the truth is not in us. [His word does not live in our hearts.] If we [freely] admit that we have sinned and confess our sins, He is faithful and just [true to His own nature and promises] and will forgive our sins and cleanse us continually from all unrighteousness [our wrongdoing, everything not in conformity with His will and purpose]. If we say that we have not sinned [refusing to admit acts of sin], we make Him [out to be] a liar [by contradicting Him] and His word is not in us.*

John wrote this passage to believers in the Asian churches that he was likely overseeing.

> JAMES 5:19-20 says, *My brothers and sisters, if anyone among you strays from the truth and falls into error and [another] one turns him back [to God], let the [latter] one know that the one who has turned a sinning believer from the error of his way will* **save that one's soul from death** *and cover a multitude of sins [that is, obtain the pardon of the many sins committed by the one who has been restored].*

James is telling believers that if we turn the sinner who strays from the error of his way, we will save his soul from death. Peter put it even more strongly than James in 2 Peter 2:20-22 when he wrote:

> *For if, after they have escaped the pollutions of the world by [personal] knowledge of our Lord and Savior Jesus Christ, they are again entangled in them and are overcome, their last condition has become worse for them than the first. **For it would have been better for them not to have [personally] known the way of righteousness, than to have known it and then to have turned back from the holy commandment [verbally] handed on to them.** The thing spoken of in the true proverb has happened to them, "THE DOG RETURNS TO HIS OWN VOMIT," and, "A sow is washed only to wallow [again] in the mire."*

There are no mulligans or do-overs once we die and face the judgment seat of God. That sounds so harsh, but it's the reality. Hebrews 9:27 says, *"And just as it is appointed and destined for all men to die once and after this [comes certain] judgment."*

My purpose in this chapter is not to make a determination but rather to make the reader aware of Scripture that could challenge ingrained religious traditions and allow each individual to make an informed decision either for yourself or someone you know. The focus of this chapter is one key question: **are you born again?** To be born again is so much more than citing religious creeds. It's a life-changing experience that follows a belief that is evidenced in how we live after making the confession that Jesus is Lord. Luke described what a born-again believer is like in God's eyes in Luke 15:10, which says,

> *In the same way, I tell you, there is joy in the presence of the angels of God over one sinner who repents **[that is, changes his inner self—his old way of thinking, regrets past sins, lives his life in a way that proves repentance; and seeks God's purpose for his life].***

Nicodemus, a Pharisee and ruler of the Jews, was having a hard time understanding this concept, *but* something prompted him to sneak out at night to meet Jesus when nobody could see him. How many folks are sitting in pews on any given Sunday asking themselves what in the world it means to be "born again"? This is a long passage, but one worth reading.

> JOHN 3:1-21 says, *Now there was a certain man among the Pharisees named Nicodemus, a ruler (member of the Sanhedrin) among the Jews, who came to Jesus at night and said to Him, "Rabbi (Teacher), we know [without any doubt] that You have come from God as a teacher; for no one can do these signs [these wonders, these attesting miracles] that You do unless God is with him." Jesus answered him, "I assure you and most solemnly say to you, unless a person is born again [reborn from above—spiritually transformed, renewed, sanctified], he cannot [ever] see and experience the kingdom of God." Nicodemus said to Him, "How can a man be born when he is old? He cannot enter his mother's womb a second time and be born, can he?" Jesus answered, "I assure you and most solemnly say to you, unless one is born of water and the Spirit he cannot [ever] enter the kingdom of God. That which is born of the flesh is flesh [the physical is merely physical], and that which is born of the Spirit is spirit. Do not be surprised that I have told you, 'You must be born again [reborn from above—spiritually transformed, renewed, sanctified].' The wind blows where it wishes and you hear its sound, but you do not know where it is coming from and where it is going; so it is with everyone who is born of the Spirit." Nicodemus said to Him, "How can these things be possible?" Jesus replied, "You are the [great and well-known] teacher of Israel, and yet you do not know nor understand these things [from Scripture]? I assure you and most solemnly say to you, we speak only of what*

we [absolutely] know and testify about what we have [actually] seen [as eyewitnesses]; and [still] you [reject our evidence and] do not accept our testimony. If I told you earthly things [that is, things that happen right here on earth] and you do not believe, how will you believe and trust Me if I tell you heavenly things? No one has gone up into heaven, but there is One who came down from heaven, the Son of Man [Himself—whose home is in heaven]. Just as Moses lifted up the [bronze] serpent in the desert [on a pole], so must the Son of Man be lifted up [on the cross], so that whoever believes will in Him have eternal life [after physical death, and will actually live forever]. For God so [greatly] loved and dearly prized the world, that He [even] gave His [One and] only begotten Son, so that whoever believes and trusts in Him [as Savior] shall not perish, but have eternal life. For God did not send the Son into the world to judge and condemn the world [that is, to initiate the final judgment of the world], but that the world might be saved through Him. Whoever believes and has decided to trust in Him [as personal Savior and Lord] is not judged [for this one, there is no judgment, no rejection, no condemnation]; but the one who does not believe [and has decided to reject Him as personal Savior and Lord] is judged already [that one has been convicted and sentenced], because he has not believed and trusted in the name of the [One and] only begotten Son of God [the One who is truly unique, the only One of His kind, the One who alone can save him]. This is the judgment [that is, the cause for indictment, the test by which people are judged, the basis for the sentence]: the Light has come into the world, and people loved the darkness rather than the Light, for their deeds were evil. For every wrongdoer hates the Light and does not come to the Light [but shrinks from it] for fear that his [sinful, worthless] activities will be exposed and condemned. But whoever practices truth [and does what is right—morally, ethically, spiritually] comes to the Light, so that his works may be plainly shown to be what they are—accomplished in God [divinely prompted, done with God's help, in dependence on Him]."

When you "believe" and have true saving faith, the Holy Spirit renews your spirit and soul, and it's like a second birth. Similar to being born the first time, you're starting from scratch by learning everything for the first time. The regeneration is evident in the fruits produced in your life. When Jesus said in John 3:5, *"I assure you and most solemnly say to you, unless one is born of water and the Spirit he cannot [ever] enter the kingdom of God,"* I believe Jesus was referencing the Old Testament priest and prophet Ezekiel who was born in 622 BC because he knew Nicodemus as a Pharisee would relate to the Old Testament Scripture concerning water and spirit. Water and spirit often refer symbolically in the Old Testament to spiritual renewal and cleansing.

EZEKIEL 37:24-27 says, *My servant David will be king over them, and they all will have one shepherd. They will also walk in My ordinances and keep My statutes and observe them. They will live in the land where your fathers lived, [the land] that I gave to My servant Jacob, and they will live there, they and their children and their children's children, forever; and My servant David will be their leader forever. I will make a covenant of peace with them; it will be an everlasting covenant with them. And I will place them and multiply them and will put My sanctuary in their midst forever. My dwelling place also will be with them; and I will be their God, and they will be My people.*

Nicodemus, being pious, an expert in the law and a ruler of the Jews, thought his good works and religious acts could get him into the Kingdom of God. Jesus made it clear that it is only by your soul and spirit being cleansed by the Word of God and producing fruit as evidence of this change that you can be re-born and enter the kingdom of Heaven.

268 | *Turning a Blind Eye*

I often think about the two criminals who were crucified next to Jesus. According to the gospel of Nicodemus (which implies he did get born again), the guy on the left who was named Gestas was hurling insults at Jesus while the second man whose name was Dimas apparently remained silent—and that man was saved while hanging on a cross next to Jesus.

> LUKE 23:39-43, *One of the criminals who had been hanged [on a cross beside Him] kept hurling abuse at Him, saying, "Are You not the Christ? Save Yourself and us [from death]!" But the other one rebuked him, saying, "Do you not even fear God, since you are under the same sentence of condemnation? We are suffering justly, because we are getting what we deserve for what we have done; but this Man has done nothing wrong." And he was saying, "Jesus, [please] remember me when You come into Your kingdom!" Jesus said to him, "I assure you and most solemnly say to you, today you will be with Me in Paradise."*

Jesus and the two thieves hung on the cross for six hours. Crucifixion is a very painful form of execution from start to finish, yet one of the two criminals gained eternal life. He was born again right before his natural death. That's too close to the edge for my taste, but it happened that way. I have to believe that as they hung there for all that time that Jesus must have shared with these men how to be born again, as hard as it must have been while slowly suffocating with his hands and feet nailed to the cross. I seriously doubt that this criminal would have known too much about God's Kingdom prior to his crucifixion since he chose to live a life of crime. I am only speculating, but something happened on that cross that changed this man's eternal destiny.

It's been said that someone discovered W. C. Fields reading a Bible on his deathbed. Since Fields did not believe in God or Jesus, this person was deeply surprised to see him with an open Bible and inquired what he was doing. Fields response was, "I am looking for a loophole."[5]

Friends, there are no loopholes when it comes to our eternal destiny. We are either born again through saving faith or deceived by the devil and destined for eternal punishment in outer darkness. It's just that simple. Let us all examine ourselves to be certain we have true saving faith.

REMOVING THE BLIND EYE

Romans 10:13 says, *For "WHOEVER CALLS ON THE NAME OF THE LORD [in prayer] WILL BE SAVED."* Though I personally believe that to be true, it's critical to look back at the preceding verses to understand the context in which it was said. Romans 10:8 says, *But what does it say? "THE WORD IS NEAR YOU, IN YOUR MOUTH AND IN YOUR HEART"— that is, the word [the message, the basis] of faith which we preach.* Calling on the name of the Lord is not like calling for a cab. Any person that desires a saving faith must receive the Word of God into their heart as they make the confession.

V ERSES 9 and 10 say, *"Because if you acknowledge and confess with your mouth that Jesus is Lord [recognizing His power, authority, and majesty as God], and believe in your heart that God raised Him from the dead, you will be saved. **For with the heart a person believes [in Christ as Savior] resulting in his justification [that is, being made righteous—being freed of the guilt of sin and made acceptable to God]; and with the mouth he acknowledges and confesses [his faith openly], resulting in and confirming [his] salvation."***

We are made righteous when the Word gets in our heart and confirms our salvation. **Faith is birthed in the heart then formed on the tongue and finally confessed through the mouth.** That's how we are born again. I think it is critically important to ask a person when they were saved and what the experience was like for them. Someone who is born again will not forget that day or the experience they had when Jesus came into their heart.

Many people *turn a blind eye* to this true saving faith by simply accepting what a person says even when they do not see the fruit of repentance that we all have if we truly surrendered to the Lord. Jesus said Himself in the parable of the sower and the four paths that one can take in Mark 4:20,

> *And those [in the last group] are the ones on whom seed was sown on the good soil; and they hear the word [of God, the good news regarding the way of salvation] and accept it and bear fruit—thirty, sixty, and a hundred times as much.*

Is it possible for someone to get right with God in a short period of time, like the criminal next to Jesus on the cross? Absolutely. That man's heart was changed during those six hours he hung on that cross.

Paul encourages all of us to examine our faith. If we are concerned about hurting people's feelings, then we are not in the right calling. Anyone could ask me about my conversion experience, and I would be happy to share it even if the question came across like a challenge. In fact, I would be grateful that someone cared enough to even ask me in the first place to ensure that I will be at the feet of Jesus after my final dying breath on earth.

Let's look at one last Scripture to drive home this point. Paul said in Philippians 2:12-13:

> *So then, my dear ones, just as you have always obeyed [my instructions with enthusiasm], not only in my presence, but now much more in my absence, **continue to work out your salvation [that is, cultivate it, bring it to full effect, actively pursue spiritual maturity]** with awe-inspired fear and trembling [using serious caution and **critical self-evaluation** to avoid anything that*

might offend God or discredit the name of Christ]. For it is [not your strength, but it is] God who is effectively at work in you, both to will and to work [that is, strengthening, energizing, and creating in you the longing and the ability to fulfill your purpose] for His good pleasure."

The takeaways for this passage are the following:

1) Continue to work out your salvation [that is, cultivate it, bring it to full effect, actively pursue spiritual maturity].

2) Do it with awe-inspired fear and trembling [using serious caution and critical self-evaluation to avoid anything that might offend God or discredit the name of Christ].

3) Realize it is [not your strength, but it is] God who is effectively at work in you.

If a person has true saving faith, then these three steps are a formula for spiritual success. If a person has not been born again or if a believer has fallen away, then don't just beat yourself up; go back to the beginning principle taught in the Bible and accept the grace and mercy God offers, not just with your lips but your entire heart.

Why did God love King David despite all his transgressions? Six words tell us why—*"a man after my own heart"* from Acts 13:22, which says the following:

And when He had removed him, He raised up David to be their king: of him He testified and said, "I HAVE FOUND DAVID the son of Jesse, A MAN AFTER MY OWN HEART [conforming to My will and purposes], who will do all My will."

If we are actively seeking after God's heart, our lives will demonstrate this truth.

I want to close this chapter with Billy Graham's declaration of saving faith.

THE Bible says that three things are necessary. First, you must be willing to turn from your sins. You must be willing to renounce sin. Second, you must commit and surrender your life to Christ. By that, I mean you give in to Christ as your only Savior. **You're not saved by joining a church. You're not saved by living a good moral life. You're saved only because of the grace of God in Christ.** And you must commit yourself to Christ as your only Savior. Are you willing to do that? Then the third thing: **You must be willing to follow Him, serve Him, confess Him and acknowledge Him.** You must be willing to go back to the factory and the home and stand up for Christ."[6] (Emphasis is mine).

CHAPTER 39

HOLY SPIRIT

Listen carefully: I am sending the Promise of My Father [the Holy Spirit] upon you; but you are to remain in the city [of Jerusalem] until you are clothed (fully equipped) with power from on high. (Luke 24:49)

HOLY SPIRIT

Greek: from *epi* and *pipto*—to embrace (with affection) or seize (with more or less violence; literally or figuratively) fall into (on, upon) lie on, press upon

Cambridge English: in the Christian church, God in the form of a spirit

Dictionary.com: the presence of God as part of a person's religious experience, Holy Ghost

Merriam-Webster: the third person of the Christian Trinity

IF YOU were raised in church, you are likely familiar with the Trinity, which represents God the Father, Jesus the Son and the Holy Spirit as the one triune God. We see all three working in harmony in Mark 1:10-11, which says,

Immediately coming up out of the water, he (John) saw the heavens torn open, and the Spirit like a dove descending on Him

(Jesus); and a voice came out of heaven saying: "You are My be-loved Son, in You I am well-pleased and delighted!"

The Father spoke, the Son emerged from the water and the Holy Spirit descended. In my mind, this is how to grasp the Holy Spirit. In the beginning there was God (Genesis 1:1) who is uncreated yet formed every created thing that we know today. God came to earth in the form of a man (John 1:14) who was with God from the very beginning of time (John 17:5). The Holy Spirit, which is the supernatural power of God, impregnated Mary to conceive Jesus and bring Him into this natural world. The reason it is important to see this in simplistic terms is because after Jesus was resurrected, that same Holy Spirit came down from Heaven to empower us to live our lives just as He empowered Mary to become pregnant while remaining a virgin.

That's what Jesus meant in Luke 24:49 when He said, *"Until you are clothed (fully equipped) with power from on high."* The purpose of the Holy Spirit is not only to help us fellowship with God but also to give us supernatural power to live victoriously in this life. He is present to help us keep our spiritual heart in good working condition. Everyone understands that God is the maker of heaven and earth and that His Son Jesus paid the price for our sin so we can live in eternity, but many overlook the Holy Spirit. Jesus said in John 15:26,

But when the Helper (Comforter, Advocate, Intercessor—Counselor, Strengthener, Standby) comes, whom I will send to you from the Father, that is the Spirit of Truth who comes from the Father, He will testify and bear witness about Me.

The Holy Spirit is our Comforter when we need peace, our advocate before God, the intercessor on our behalf, our counselor when we choose to hear, and our Strengthener!

Regardless of your position on speaking in tongues as evidenced when the Holy Spirit fell on the 120 believers in the Upper Room, our focus should be on the power He gives us to overcome our human flesh. Peter is a good example of what that power can do for a person. He is the disciple that denied Jesus three times, cut off the ear of the high priest's servant, was full of unbelief and doubt, and had an untamed tongue. Yet, when he was filled with the Holy Spirit, we never hear of these weaknesses again. Acts 3 tells us that right after he was filled with the Holy Spirit, he and John went to the temple where he healed the lame man. When he preached his first few sermons, 5,000 people were saved, and the church was birthed. What person is capable of such feats without having a power in him that is greater than himself? In the end Peter went out of this world with that same power by choosing to be crucified in Rome upside down because he felt he was not worthy to be crucified like our Lord. Positive thinking, counseling or a weekend with the boys did not change Peter. The same Holy Spirit that is in all believers is what changed this man.

Many Christians try to live in this sinful and wicked world by their own power and might end up struggling at every turn. Jesus said in John 14:18, *"I will not leave you as orphans [comfortless, bereaved, and helpless]; I will come [back] to you."* He did come back to us by sending His Holy Spirit to live within us, and we can all take that fact to the spiritual bank.

REMOVING THE BLIND EYE

We need to receive and accept the third part of the Trinity and understand His purpose for our lives. This is the same Holy Spirit that allows us to realize our need for salvation, illuminates the Bible for us so we can understand it, and will raise our mortal bodies from the grave. This same Holy Spirit can give us power to overcome strongholds in our lives and create a clean heart in us. The Holy Spirit will embrace you with affection, seize you violently in a good way, fall upon you, lie upon you or press upon you.

If you have saving faith, then that Holy Spirit is in you. Go to God in prayer and ask Him to allow the Holy Spirit to *seize* you to the point that His filling goes from being an indwelling to an overflowing powerful force within you. This is the living water John described in John 7:38, which says, *"He who believes in Me [who adheres to, trusts in, and relies on Me], as the Scripture has said, 'From his innermost being will flow continually rivers of living water.'"* Just like they did with Peter, people will see a different person when you're walking in this power. It attracts people to you because you radiate faith that is contagious. The power of the Holy Spirit will change your life and others' lives at the same time.

CHAPTER 40

HEAVEN

In My Father's house are many dwelling places. If it were not so, I would have told you, because I am going there to prepare a place for you. (John 14:2)

HEAVEN

Greek: from *ouranós*—the visible heavens: the atmosphere, the sky, the starry heavens, (b) the spiritual heavens

Cambridge English: the place where God or the gods live or where good people are believed to go after they die, sometimes thought to be in the sky

Dictionary.com: the abode of God, the angels, and the spirits of the righteous after death; the place or state of existence of the blessed after the mortal life

Merriam-Webster: the expanse of space that seems to be over the earth like a dome, the dwelling place of the Deity and the blessed dead, a spiritual state of everlasting communion with God

HUMAN NATURE causes every person to focus on his or her *"dwelling places"* here on earth. Many grow up feeling the need to own a home, or even many homes in some cases, during our temporary journey on earth. In this country, home ownership is a part of the American dream. Jesus was raised in a home by Joseph and Mary in His early life, but what many people fail to realize is that when He began His ministry, He had no permanent house according to Matthew 8:20, which says, *Jesus replied to him,* "*Foxes have holes and the birds of the air have nests, but the Son of Man has nowhere to lay His head.*" You might wonder why it is important that we not overlook that fact. The reason is that we should follow His example over 2,000 years later—Jesus was not focused on His earthly house but was instead looking toward His eternal home. He understood what was in store for Him when He chose to die for our sins.

The bottom line is that He knew His days on earth were numbered, so He looked to the future—and so should we. Paul admonished us to have that same attitude in Colossians 3:1 when he said, "*Therefore if you have been raised with Christ [to a new life, sharing in His resurrection from the dead],* **keep seeking the things that are above**, *where Christ is, seated at the right hand of God.*"

Heaven Is for Real: A Little Boy's Astounding Story of His Trip to Heaven and Back, written by Todd Burpo and Lynn Vincent, documents the near-death experience of Burpo's three-year-old son Colton. The book and subsequent movie were a national sensation. The book sold millions of copies in both ebook and printed copies and generated nearly $101 million at the box office and over $44 million in domestic sales.[1] The reason for the success of this story is because people want to believe Heaven is real and will seek out any account that can build or confirm their confidence in this truth. I read the book and watched the movie, and it blessed the socks off me.

When I was a young child and my parents would load up the Cadillac to take off for a vacation, I would always drive them crazy with one question: "Are we almost there?"

Their response was the same every time: "We will get there when we get there." I was so excited to reach our ultimate destination that I asked my parents that question about every fifty miles! That's exactly the same attitude we should have toward Heaven. We should enjoy our time on earth and do what God has called us to do while we're here, but we should also realize deep in our hearts that earth is a gas stop and Heaven is our ultimate destination. Heaven is a real place where we will have all the enjoyable experiences we have on earth but without any sickness, death or negative emotions.

Many Christians have a difficult time grasping the transition from a material body that dwells on a physical planet, to a spiritual body that dwells in God's home, which Jesus called Heaven. Surprisingly, based on a pew report conducted in 2014, 15 percent of Christians surveyed and 28 percent of all Americans do not believe in Heaven.[2] How can we be assured there is a Heaven? Jesus said there is. That's where He was before coming to earth. *"For I have come down from heaven, not to do My own will, but to do the will of Him who sent Me."* (John 6:38) This is not a secondhand account that we are supposed to accept, but firsthand knowledge from God Himself. It's my belief based on Scripture that we face the first judgment the moment we physically die and if we know Christ our soul immediately enters the presence of God in the place we call paradise or Heaven. This is where we live until the second judgment and the new heaven is ushered in upon Christ's return. Conversely, as we will discuss in the next chapter, if a person does not know Christ, their soul will go to Hades and stay in torment until the second judgment and then be thrown into the lake of fire or the permanent state we call Hell. You can think of it in these terms. When you are saved you have a "direct" flight straight to your destination of Heaven. If you're not saved, then you have one stop with a long layover in Hades until you reach your final destination of Hell.

Jesus said in John 17:5, *"Now, Father, glorify Me together with Yourself, with the glory and majesty that I had with You before the world existed."* Jesus is not telling us about Heaven because He had just heard of it; He actually lived there before the world ever existed. Peter, a man who walked with Jesus, wrote that people forget that Heaven existed long before the earth. In 2 Peter 3:5-6 he said:

> *For they willingly forget [the fact] that the heavens existed long ago by the Word of God, and the earth was formed out of water and by water, through which the world at that time was destroyed by being flooded with water.*

I can only imagine the conversations Peter and Jesus had together about Heaven that may not be recorded in the canonical Scriptures. Peter heard firsthand—just as we have through Jesus' own words in Scripture. One of the most fascinating books I have read on this subject is *Imagine Heaven, Near-Death Experiences, God's Promises, and the Exhilarating Future that Awaits You* written by John Burke. He is the Senior Pastor of Gateway Church in Austin, Texas. Burke's book recounts the near-death experiences of 1,000 people from a wide spectrum of religious faiths. He stated:

> After reading hundreds of NDE accounts, I started to see the difference between what they *reported* experiencing and the *interpretation* they might give to that experience. While interpretations vary, I found the shared core experience points to what Scripture says. In fact, the more I studied, the more I realized that the picture Scripture paints of the exhilarating life to come is the common experience that NDEers describe.[3]

Skeptics say it's just the brain communicating messages the NDEer wants to see before the brain dies. Others say it is just a figment of the imagination or their hope when they wake up and share the experience. Although that could be true for some of them, that can't be the case for 1,000 people. I am solidly in the camp that aligns with Burke. These people went through real experiences that portray what Heaven and, in some cases, Hades is like.

Another thing I find interesting about Heaven, and earth for that matter, is the outcome for both at the end. We all will live in the "new" Heaven when God's final judgment is executed. Jesus said in Matthew 24:35, *"Heaven and earth [as now known] will pass away, but My words will not pass away."* We also read this in 2 Peter 3:7-12:

> *But by His word the present heavens and earth are being re-served for fire, being kept for the day of judgment and destruc-tion of the ungodly people. Nevertheless, do not let this one fact escape your notice, beloved, that with the Lord one day is like a thousand years, and a thousand years is like one day. The Lord does not delay [as though He were unable to act] and is not slow about His promise, as some count slowness, but is [extraordi-narily] patient toward you, not wishing for any to perish but for all to come to repentance. But the day of the Lord will come like a thief, and then the heavens will vanish with a [mighty and thunderous] roar, and the [material] elements will be destroyed with intense heat, and the earth and the works that are on it will be burned up. Since all these things are to be destroyed in this way, what kind of people ought you to be [in the meantime] in holy behavior [that is, in a pattern of daily life that sets you apart as a believer] and in godliness [displaying profound rev-erence toward our awesome God], [while you earnestly] look for and await the coming of the day of God. For on this day the heavens will be destroyed by burning, and the [material] ele-ments will melt with intense heat!*

So, if Heaven and Earth in their present form are destroyed, what then do we have waiting for us? In Revelation 21:1, we have the an-swer: *"Then I saw a new heaven and a new earth; for the first heaven and the first earth passed away, and there is no longer any sea."* This is describing our eternal home using a new heaven and new earth as symbols. Many of the things we do on earth we will do in Heaven, but the main activity will be worshipping God. The Lord's prayer says,

282 | *Turning a Blind Eye*

"Thy kingdom come, thy will be done, on earth as it is in Heaven." If it can be done on Earth as it is in Heaven, then in Heaven we can do what we did on Earth!

Finally on this topic, we have to ask ourselves why, if Heaven isn't real for the non-believer or cannot be grasped by the believer, God provided the size to us in Revelation 21:15-16, which says,

> *The one who was speaking with me had a gold measuring rod to measure the city, and its gates and its wall. The city is laid out as a square, its length being the same as its width; and he measured the city with his rod—twelve thousand stadia (about 1,400 miles); its length and width and height are equal.*

That's like having a road map in your hands!

REMOVING THE BLIND EYE

We need to stop applying the limits of our finite minds to Heaven. If we have true saving faith, the question is not *if* we get there but *when* we get there. Just like when we plan a family vacation or any trip, we look forward to getting there the moment we leave the driveway, we all should live in the same expectation full of gratitude and joy as it relates to Heaven. It's a place of indescribable beauty where our senses will operate at heightened levels, the sun never sets, there is no sickness or negative emotion and—most important of all—we will worship God and the Lamb forever.

If you believe the Bible to be true, then you must believe what it says about Heaven. When we die, we are not angels, as some believe, but rather "like" angels according to Mark 12:25, which says, *"For when they rise from the dead, they do not marry nor are they given in marriage but are like angels in heaven."*

According to 1 Peter 1:4-5, we have a reservation in Heaven:

[born anew] into an inheritance which is imperishable [beyond

the reach of change] and undefiled and unfading, reserved in heaven for you, who are being protected and shielded by the power of God through your faith for salvation that is ready to be revealed [for you] in the last time.

Paul said the same in Colossians 1:4-5:

For we have heard of your faith in Christ Jesus [how you lean on Him with absolute confidence in His power, wisdom, and goodness], and of the [unselfish] love which you have for all the saints (God's people); because of the [confident] hope [of experiencing that] **which is reserved and waiting for you in heaven.** *You previously heard of this hope in the message of truth, the gospel [regarding salvation].*

We also have the full assurance that we will see those we love who have accepted Christ once we leave our earthly tents and arrive on Heaven's doorstep. 1 Thessalonians 4:13 says, "*Now we do not want you to be uninformed, believers, about those who are asleep [in death], so that you will not grieve [for them] as the others do who have no hope [beyond this present life].*" Heaven is more real than this world and once we grasp what God has in store for us there, then we will live with expectant hope instead of any fear.

CHAPTER 41

HELL

In Hades (the realm of the dead), being in torment, he looked up and saw Abraham far away and Lazarus in his bosom (paradise). And he cried out, "Father Abraham, have mercy on me, and send Lazarus so that he may dip the tip of his finger in water and cool my tongue, because I am in severe agony in this flame." (Luke 16:23-24)

HELL

Greek: from *géenna*—originally the name of a valley or cavity near Jerusalem, a place underneath the earth, a place of punishment for evil

Cambridge English: (in some religions) the place where some people are believed to go after death to be punished forever for the bad things they have done

Dictionary.com: the place or state of punishment of the wicked after death; the abode of evil and condemned spirits; Gehenna or Tartarus

Merriam-Webster: the nether realm of the devil and the demons in which condemned people suffer everlasting punishment—often used in curses

IT'S EASY to understand why any person would not want to believe in a place of damnation after death where their soul is in agony for eternity. That's not a pleasant thought for any human being to entertain, despite the fact that Scripture is very clear on this subject. According the Pew report mentioned in the previous chapter where 15 percent of Christians and 28 percent of Americans *do not* believe in Heaven, 30 percent of Christians and 42 percent of Americans *don't* believe in the existence of Hell.[1] It's concerning yet understandable in our secular society that a significant number of Americans do not believe in Heaven or Hell.

With that said, it is more troubling that the data reflects that there is less than 100 percent certainty among Christians about where we will spend eternity and especially as it relates to Hell. The entire world needs to understand the reality of Hell. As Christians, we are called to preach the good news of Jesus Christ, which allows a person to avoid the consequences of this awful existence. As a body of believers, how can we be effective in communicating eternal choices if we don't believe it ourselves or do not have the proper knowledge about Hell to share with other people? The answer to that question should be obvious—we have and will continue to struggle in this endeavor. I think there are several reasons for this, but two in particular. First, it's not a popular message to preach anymore during Sunday sermons. The world as a whole and even the church has grown tired of the "fire-and-brimstone" messages and prefer to focus on subjects that make them feel good about themselves and their fellow mankind.

Our church leaders, especially in Western cultures, need to recognize the need to preach the truth about eternal destiny and the reality of Hell. There are many different ways to communicate this uncomfortable truth without the fire and brimstone people are accustomed to from the past. When a pastor, elder, lay minister or believer is preaching the glorious plan of salvation, it's critical that we give equal time and a description of the Plan B if that message is not received. Many times it

286 | *Turning a Blind Eye*

appears that salvation gets rated like a perfect hotel with five stars yet the alternative of Hell rarely, if ever, is rated or mentioned at all. The second reason deals with the knowledge or the lack thereof, believers have through the study of Scripture about Heaven or Hell and the misconceptions in the church. It's unfair to think that any member of a church would expect to get all the information through a one-hour sermon by the pastor. The pastor should and could lay the framework though a consistent message about Hell then encourage the members to study the subject deeper through a Bible study or on their own. You can't have an upside (Heaven) without a downside (Hell), so both are equally important.

Put another way, the gospel of Jesus Christ is good news for those who accept it and bad news for those who reject it. Sad to say, many people joke more about Hell than Christians talk about how to avoid it! People throughout history, and in today's culture as well, refuse to believe that a "loving God" would send any person to Hell. In a way, they are right. God does not send any of us to Hell; we send ourselves by rejecting the grace of God for salvation through Jesus Christ His Son.

My goal for this chapter is to lay out to the best of my knowledge the existence of this horrifying fate for those who reject the gift of God in hopes it will spark a desire for all Christians to learn more about it and thereby enable a believer to communicate it more clearly. Heaven is definitely real, but so is Hell; and the only way people will understand this truth is when we stop treating the subject with kid gloves and call it by its name. At the risk of sounding like I think I'm a biblical scholar, which I am not, my extensive research on this topic has led me to the conclusion that Hell is permanent, and Hades is temporary.

Let's begin by discussing Hell. The Greek word *géenna* or *gehanna* is translated in English as "Hell." *Gehanna* originated from the Hebrew word meaning "Valley of the son of Hinnom," which is south of Jerusalem. It was the place where children were sacrificed to the false god Moloch, so it became known as being accursed and wicked. The place was later used as a garbage dump that would burn all sorts of waste from the city on a continuous basis. Jesus used the term eleven times to symbolize a place of everlasting punishment (Matthew 5:22, 29, 30; 10:28; 18:9; 23:15, 33; Mark 9:43, 45, 47; Luke 12:5), and James used it once (James 3:6). It's described as the unquenchable fire and eternal fire.

The first fact to understand about Hell and its permanency is that God did not create it for human beings. After Lucifer rebelled, prior to God's creation of man, God prepared Hell as the place where Satan and his motley crew would go. We see this in Matthew 25:41: *"Then He will say to those on His left, 'Leave Me, you cursed ones, into the eternal fire which has been prepared for the devil and his angels (demons).'"* Again, Hell wasn't created for man in the beginning, but after the fall it became the final destination for the unsaved along with the devil and his demons. The good news is that God wants all of mankind to live with Him forever in Heaven because He loves us so much.

> *The Lord does not delay [as though He were unable to act] and is not slow about His promise, as some count slowness, but is [extraordinarily] patient toward you, not wishing for any to perish but for all to come to repentance.* (2 Peter 3:9)

I believe that Hell is currently unoccupied and will be filled with the souls that are kept in the intermediate state called Hades, which I will further address. I am not talking about the concept of purgatory where all souls go to be "purged" of any remaining sin through a refining process by fire. However, there is clear evidence that it is a doctrine created by man.

Revelation 20:10 says, *"And the devil who had deceived them was hurled into **the lake of fire** and burning brimstone (sulfur), where the beast (Antichrist) and false prophet are also; and they will be tormented day and night, forever and ever."* This is referred to as the final judgment or second death, and the statement *"forever and ever"* is about as permanent as it gets.

Jesus referenced the final judgment in Matthew 13:41-42:

The Son of Man will send out His angels, and they will gather out of His kingdom all things that offend [those things by which people are led into sin], *and all who practice evil* [leading others into sin], *and will throw them into* **the furnace of fire**; *in that place there will be weeping* [over sorrow and pain] *and grinding of teeth* [over distress and anger].

So, Hades becomes Hell, and the saved will simply move over from the current paradise or Heaven to the new heaven and new earth created by God at the second coming of our Lord Jesus. It will be glorious!

Concerning Hades, the Hebrew word *Sheol* is defined the same as the Greek word *Hades*, which means "the grave, abode of the dead and a place of punishment for the wicked."[2]

I believe Hades is an intermediate state where souls that are judged by God upon physical death reside, awaiting their transfer to Hell. My belief is based on three primary Scriptures—two penned by John in Revelation and another when Jesus Himself was speaking in the book of Luke. John said in Revelation 20:14, "*Then death and* **Hades** [the realm of the dead] *were thrown into* **the lake of fire**. *This is the second death, the lake of fire* [the eternal separation from God]." What will be thrown into the lake of fire? Hades and spiritual death will be. Hades is a place of torment and the precursor to Hell. The "second death" is the closing curtain for the heavens and earth as they exist now.

REVELATION 1:17-18, *When I saw Him, I fell at His feet as though dead. And He placed His right hand on me and said,* "*Do not be afraid; I am the First and the Last* [absolute Deity, the Son of God], *and the Ever-living One* [living in and beyond all time and space]. *I died, but see, I am alive forevermore, and I have the keys of* [absolute control and victory over] *death and of Hades* (the realm of the dead)."

Going back to my illustration in the previous chapter, Hades is not a direct flight, as Heaven is for believers. The boarding pass for the lost says there will be a very long layover in Hades until the plane is ready for its final destination of Hell.

The Scripture in Luke is the only passage I could find in the New Testament that gives a clear description of what happens at death; the words were spoken by Jesus. Some say this is a parable, but I believe it was an actual conversation because a person, Lazarus, was named. Either way, it came from Jesus, so Luke 16:19-31 contains a powerful truth.

*Now there was a certain rich man who was habitually dressed in expensive purple and fine linen, and celebrated and lived joyously in splendor every day. And a poor man named Lazarus, was laid at his gate, covered with sores. He [eagerly] longed to eat the crumbs which fell from the rich man's table. Besides, even the dogs were coming and licking his sores. Now it happened that the poor man died, and his spirit was carried away by the angels to Abraham's bosom (paradise); and the rich man also died and was buried. In **Hades** (the realm of the dead), being in torment, he looked up and saw Abraham far away and Lazarus in his bosom (paradise). And he cried out, "Father Abraham, have mercy on me, and send Lazarus so that he may dip the tip of his finger in water and cool my tongue, because I am in severe agony in this flame." But Abraham said, "Son, remember that in your lifetime you received your good things [**all the comforts and delights**], and Lazarus likewise bad things [**all the discomforts and distresses**]; but now he is comforted here [**in paradise**], while you are in severe agony. And besides all this, between us and you [**people**] a great chasm has been fixed, so that those who want to come over from here to you will not be able, and none may cross over from there to us." So the rich man said, "Then, father*

[Abraham], I beg you to send Lazarus to my father's house—for I have five brothers—in order that he may solemnly warn them and witness to them, so that they too will not come to this place of torment." But Abraham said, "They have [the Scriptures given by] Moses and the [writings of the] Prophets; let them listen to them." He replied, "No, father Abraham, but if someone from the dead goes to them, they will repent [they will change their old way of thinking and seek God and His righteousness]." And he said to him, "If they do not listen to [the messages of] Moses and the Prophets, they will not be persuaded even if someone rises from the dead."

Several important takeaways from this passage can help us understand the reality of eternal choices.

1) Everyone who thinks that Heaven, Hades or Hell is either imaginary or a state of mind—or even worse, that everyone goes to Heaven regardless of their spiritual condition—is wrong.

2) We can see that once again the "rich" are the center of attention. It seems to be a common thread in the New Testament and even still today that wealth and all its earthly benefits seem to separate people from God. That's obviously not true across the board because many wealthy Christians in this world love Jesus, but it is very evident that wealth did get in the way for this rich man when it came to Lazarus. He had no concern or pity, nor did he take action to help Lazarus or try to understand his plight.

3) Hades and ultimately Hell are horrible and painful. The rich man asked Abraham to send Lazarus to dip the tip of his finger in water and cool his tongue. Why? Because he was in severe agony from the flames.

4) The thought that the soul never dies and those in Hades experience constant torment until their transfer to Hell is sobering.

5) On the flip side of the coin, Heaven is awesome, and there is no pain. Note that Lazarus was being comforted there.

6) It appears that people in Heaven are able to see people in Hades and yet have no sadness.

7) Finally, and most importantly, once death occurs, there is no second chance. Jesus said a *"a great chasm has been fixed, so that those who want to come over from here to you will not be able, and none may cross over from there to us."* (v. 26) With all of that in mind, why would anyone who doesn't know Jesus reject God's eternity-changing offer of salvation?

One might be curious to ask where Hades is located. One thing is certain: one state of existence is "above" and one is "below." The rich man said in verse 23, *"In Hades (the realm of the dead), being in torment, he looked up and saw Abraham far away and Lazarus in his bosom (paradise)."* He looked up, so obviously, Hades was below Heaven. Jesus confirmed this in John 8:22-23 (NASB) when He answered some Jewish people:

So the Jews were saying, "Surely He will not kill Himself, will He, since He says, 'Where I am going, you cannot come'?" And He was saying to them, "You are from below, I am from above; you are of this world, I am not of this world."

I think a very strong argument exists that indicates Hades is located in the center of the earth where temperatures reach 12,000°. Think of a volcano that erupts and the intensity of the lava that spills out of the earth and you will have some concept of how hot Hades must be and the agony for those who go there. This does not imply it's a geographical location because the center of the earth encompasses the entire world. Jesus said, *"In that place there will be weeping [over sorrow and pain] and grinding of teeth [over distress and anger]."* (Luke 13:28) **Just like when Moses saw the burning bush that wasn't consumed by the fire**

(Exodus 3:2)**, the soul suffers the same fate in Hades and Hell**. Hades and Hell have been described in Scripture as intensely hot, putrid and foul smelling, without life or water, a place of utter darkness, full of evil, where the soul never dies and a giant pit of fire burns and never goes out. This is not a place to which anyone would desire to be condemned for eternity.

As further evidence of Hades' being in the center of the earth, we know that, upon His death, Jesus went from being **on** earth to being **in** the earth. Matthew 12:39-40 (NASB) says,

> *But he answered and said to them, "An evil and adulterous generation craves for a sign; and yet no sign will be given to it but the sign of Jonah the prophet; for just as JONAH WAS THREE DAYS AND THREE NIGHTS IN THE BELLY OF THE SEA MONSTER, so will the Son of Man be three days and three nights in the **heart of the earth**."*

Paul also refers to those "under" the earth in Philippians 2:9-11 (NASB):

> *For this reason also, God highly exalted Him, and bestowed on Him the name which is above every name, so that at the name of Jesus EVERY KNEE WILL BOW, of those who are in heaven and on earth and **under the earth**, and that every tongue will confess that Jesus Christ is Lord, to the glory of God the Father.*

I believe Paul must have been speaking of Hades when he referred to being under the earth.

The world trivializes Hell and makes light of its seriousness. Many unbelievers and, sadly, believers alike use the term in their everyday conversations with little regard for its meaning. Why in the world would anyone ever compare the air temperature on earth to the temperature of Hell? In my opinion the worst use of the word is when one person tells another to go there. Really? That person literally has no idea what that means or he would never want his worst enemy to go there. Holly McClure wrote the foreword to *23 Minutes in Hell:*

One Man's Story About What He Saw, Heard, and Felt in that Place of Torment by Bill Wiese. Holly made an observation that rang true with me when she said,

> I MENTIONED how our culture has trivialized the subject of Hell to such an extent that we, in fact, celebrate the devil with costumes, demonic masks, and candy at Halloween, the second most commercialized holiday in America...Our culture has become desensitized and conditioned to accept various forms of demonic creatures, caricatures of Satan, and glimpses of Hell as simply "entertainment."[3]

Amen!

REMOVING THE BLIND EYE

Hades and Hell must become as much of a reality to us as Heaven is. We all need to do a better job, in spite of political correctness or the state of our culture, of discussing the topic of Hell or Hades. Some Christians choose not to think about it because they fear for friends or family members who have already died and may not have been saved. We cannot control whether a person accepts the gospel, and that includes family and friends. What we can control is whether or not we chose to share how to obtain eternal life by the blood of Christ.

I understand that it can be unsettling to think that some our loved ones and close friends may not be in Heaven when we arrive. With that said, it's only by the grace of God that we will have none of the negative emotions in Heaven that we experience here on earth. We can't be sad, angry or depressed there. It's impossible. Although it may be difficult to understand that concept, that does not make it any less true. If anything, it should motivate Christians to reach the lost with the limited time we all have on earth and give people the opportunity to choose Heaven by accepting Christ and living for Him as opposed to rejecting Him and living for self.

When you know it's going to rain, you prepare by getting out your raincoat or umbrella. We should do the same as it relates to Hell. We must be prepared to share the truth with people with whom we interact on a daily basis. We can't forget the thousands in our nation who die every single day who will face judgment before God. The question should be, "What are we doing about it?" Some say, "My faith is private and between God and me." I say those people are wrong and missed Matthew 28:19-20 that says,

> Go therefore and make disciples of all the nations *[help the people to learn of Me, believe in Me, and obey My words]*, baptizing them in the name of the Father and of the Son and of the Holy Spirit, teaching them to observe everything that I have commanded you; and lo, I am with you always *[remaining with you perpetually—regardless of circumstance, and on every occasion]*, even to the end of the age.

Failing to share the Gospel is like going to the pet store and buying a parrot that you expect to talk and having it say nothing when you get it home. What is the parrot worth if it doesn't do what you expected? And what is a Christian worth who doesn't share the gospel and the truth about Hell—as God expects us to? You don't have to be a mighty preacher or teacher. You just have to be willing to explain the choice in a loving and compassionate way. Ask God each morning to lead you to someone you can tell about Jesus and the opportunity to have eternal life. You will be pleasantly surprised when God puts that person in your path. Hades and Hell are real, and we need to treat them as such. Unfortunately, there are no second chances when it comes to eternal judgment.

CHAPTER 42

SATAN

He said to them, "I watched Satan fall from heaven like [a flash of] lightning." (Luke 10:18)

SATAN

Greek: from *satanas*—the adversary, Satan, the devil

Cambridge English: the main evil spirit; the devil (equals the origin of evil and the enemy of God)

Dictionary.com: the chief evil spirit; the great adversary of humanity; the devil

Merriam-Webster: the angel who in Jewish belief is commanded by God to tempt humans to sin, to accuse the sinners, and to carry out God's punishment, the rebellious angel who in Christian belief is the adversary of God and lord of evil

Just as God and His angels dwell in Heaven, Satan and his demons dwell in Hades. Jesus wanted to make sure we knew Satan was real when He said He saw him falling from Heaven to the earth after God dealt with Lucifer's rebellion. Revelation 12:7-9 tells us,

And war broke out in heaven, Michael [the archangel] and his angels waging war with the dragon. The dragon and his angels

*fought, but they were not strong enough and did not prevail, and there was no longer a place found for them in heaven. And the great dragon was thrown down, the age-old serpent who is called the devil and Satan, he who continually deceives and seduces the entire inhabited world; **he was thrown down to the earth, and his angels were thrown down with him**.*

Lucifer ruled as a majestic angel created by God for His purposes. He existed before Adam and Eve and was a good angel, until his heart became full of pride and arrogance. Then he rebelled against God and suffered the eternal consequences. In this chapter, we will answer some key questions about Satan: How did this enemy come into existence, what names does he go by, what is his purpose, what is his strategy and how does he operate in the physical and spiritual worlds?

How did this enemy, Satan, come into existence?

Lucifer was first mentioned as the "Star of the Morning" in Isaiah 14:12-17:

How you have fallen from heaven, O star of the morning [light-bringer], son of the dawn! You have been cut down to the ground, You who have weakened the nations [king of Babylon]! But you said in your heart, "I will ascend to heaven; I will raise my throne above the stars of God; I will sit on the mount of assembly In the remote parts of the north. I will ascend above the heights of the clouds; I will make myself like the Most High." "But [in fact] you will be brought down to Sheol, To the remote recesses of the pit (the region of the dead). Those who see you will gaze at you, They will consider you, saying, Is this the man who made the earth tremble, Who shook kingdoms, Who made the world like a wilderness And overthrew its cities, Who did not permit his prisoners to return home?"

The book, *Angels, Knowing Their Purpose, Releasing their Power*, by Charles and Annette Capps, says,

> NOTICE he is talking about Lucifer, the anointed cherub. Lucifer had a throne. He ruled over people. Evidently, his throne was on earth because he said, "I'll exalt my throne above the stars of God." The stars were already created. He said, "I'll ascend above the height of the clouds," so the clouds were already there. Lucifer had dominion. He had rule over a world, and all these precious stones were his covering. He was created to be the anointed cherub. He ruled and reigned in that world.[1]

In *Strong's Concordance*, the original Hebrew word for *Satan* means "accuser, adversary, superhuman adversary to God,"[2] and the translation given in the King James text is the Latin name for the planet Venus, *Lucifer*. This angel was created by God, he had dominion and he even was a part of the musical angelic host. Ezekiel 28:13 (KJV) says,

> *Thou hast been in Eden the garden of God; every precious stone was thy covering, the sardius, topaz, and the diamond, the beryl, the onyx, and the jasper, the sapphire, the emerald, and the carbuncle, and gold: the workmanship of thy tabrets and of thy pipes was prepared in thee in the day that thou wast created.*

The *tabret* is a musical instrument referenced in 1 Samuel 18:6. It's no wonder that young people today make life choices based on the type of music they listen to and old folks like me are taken back to certain events when we hear a particular song. Music is powerful. Satan, his body created as a musical instrument, knows that fact all too well.

What names does Satan go by?

In our church history, several other words are used to describe this fallen angel, Lucifer. The Greek for *devil* is *diabolos*, which is actually a translation of *Satan*,[3] a Hebrew word meaning "adversary or accuser."

Jesus called him **Satan** when he saw him fall from Heaven as described in Luke 10:18. He also called him the **thief** in John 10:10: *"The thief comes only in order to steal and kill and destroy. I came that they may have and enjoy life, and have it in abundance [to the full, till it over-flows]."* He was called the **devil** in John 8:44, which says,

> *You are of your father the devil, and it is your will to practice the desires [which are characteristic] of your father. He was a murderer from the beginning and does not stand in the truth because there is no truth in him. When he lies, he speaks what is natural to him, for he is a liar and the father of lies and half-truths.*

Jesus referred to Satan as the **ruler of the world** in John 14:30: *"I will not speak with you much longer, for the ruler of the world (Satan) is coming. And he has no claim on Me [no power over Me nor anything that he can use against Me]."* He called him our **enemy** in Matthew 13:39, which says, *"and the enemy who sowed them is the devil, and the harvest is the end of the age; and the reapers are angels."*

John called him the **evil one** in 1 John 2:14, which relates,

> *I have written to you, fathers, because you know Him who has existed from the beginning. I have written to you, young men, because you are strong and vigorous, and the word of God remains [always] in you, and you have been victorious over the evil one [by accepting Jesus as Savior].*

Paul called him the **tempter** in 1 Thessalonians 3:5 when he said,

> *For this reason, when I could no longer endure the suspense, I sent someone to find out about your faith [how you were holding up under pressure], for fear that somehow the tempter had tempted you and our work [among you] would prove to be ineffective.*

He is called an **angel of light** in 2 Corinthians 11:14, *"and no won-*

der, since Satan himself masquerades as an angel of light." Peter described him as a **roaring lion** in 1 Peter 5:8 when he wrote, *"Be sober [well balanced and self-disciplined], be alert and cautious at all times. That enemy of yours, the devil, prowls around like a roaring lion [fiercely hungry], seeking someone to devour."*

He is called by many names, and some seem rather frightening—but regardless of his many attributes, he is a defeated enemy to God.

What is Satan's purpose?

Jesus summed up Satan's purpose in one verse of Scripture that I have already mentioned, John 10:10. He said, *"The thief comes only in order to steal and kill and destroy. I came that they may have and enjoy life, and have it in abundance [to the full, till it overflows]."* The devil wants to steal anything he can get his hands on from you, kill your physical body and destroy your family and your life. If Satan listed his job description on his resume in short, it would be to *steal* our faith or allow others not to obtain it, *kill* as many humans as possible and to *destroy* families and the church at large. He is like the State Farm guy we see in television ads whose sole purpose is to cause mayhem. Make no mistake, he is an evil spiritual force that derives great pleasure from inflicting pain in this natural world with the hope he can deceive as many people as possible to turn away from God. And with this purpose in mind, the devil understands that he is in a race against time.

REVELATION 12:12 says, *Therefore rejoice, O heavens and you who dwell in them [in the presence of God]. Woe to the earth and the sea, because the devil has come down to you in great wrath, knowing that he has only a short time [remaining]!*

It's difficult for me to comprehend how so many people can believe in such things as conspiracy theories, aliens, secret societies and even Big Foot while refusing to acknowledge that the devil is a an angelic being created by God and that through his pride he attempted to rise up against God and suffered the consequences, which is so clearly illustrated throughout Scripture. This is why he is referred to as a *"fallen angel."* In Ephesians 2:2, Paul described Satan as the **prince of the power of the air.**

> *In which you once walked. You were following the ways of this world [influenced by this present age], in accordance with the prince of the power of the air (Satan), the spirit who is now at work in the disobedient [the unbelieving, who fight against the purposes of God].*

What does the enemy want the most besides causing mayhem on the earth? He wants the souls of God's creation. Mark 4:15-19 gives three ways the devil works to steal salvation from people. First, he takes away the Word when it is preached: *"These [in the first group] are the ones along the road where the word is sown; but when they hear, Satan immediately comes and takes away the word which has been sown in them."* (v. 15)

Secondly, Satan allows persecution to come to cause people to run from the truth.

> *In a similar way these [in the second group] are the ones on whom seed was sown on rocky ground, who, when they hear the word, immediately receive it with joy [but accept it only superficially]; and they have no real root in themselves, so they endure only for a little while; then, when trouble or persecution comes because of the word, immediately they [are offended and displeased at being associated with Me and] stumble and fall away. (v. 16-17).*

Third, Satan blinds mankind with materialism.

> *And others are the ones on whom seed was sown among the thorns; these are the ones who have heard the word, but the worries and cares of the world [the distractions of this age with its*

worldly pleasures], and the deceitfulness [and the false security or glamour] of wealth [or fame], and the passionate desires for all the other things creep in and choke out the word, and it becomes unfruitful. (v. 18-19)

Believers are not off limits to the devil. Acts 5:3 gives an account of two believers named Ananias and Sapphira who lied about the proceeds of a land sale and died instantly as a result: *But Peter said, "Ananias, why has **Satan filled your heart** to lie to the Holy Spirit and [secretly] keep back for yourself some of the proceeds [from the sale] of the land?"*

Timothy pointed out that certain widows had **turned away from the faith to actually follow Satan.** 1 Timothy 5:15 says, *"Some [widows] have already turned away [from the faith] to follow Satan."*

Then we all are very familiar with the account of Judas Iscariot who betrayed Jesus. Luke 22:3 says of this man who walked with Jesus and handled the treasury, *"Then **Satan entered Judas**, the one called Iscariot, who was one of the twelve [disciples]."* Jesus went on to say in John 6:70-71,

> *Jesus answered them, "Did I not choose you, the twelve [disciples]? And yet one of you is a **devil (ally of Satan)**." Now He was speaking of Judas, the son of Simon Iscariot; for he, one of the twelve [disciples], was about to betray Him.*

Scripture even relates a case where Paul turned over some to Satan to "teach" them not to blaspheme in 1 Timothy 1:20, which says, *"Among these are Hymenaeus and Alexander, whom I have **handed over to Satan**, so that they will be disciplined and taught not to blaspheme."* Can believers allow the devil entry into our hearts and minds? It appears so based on these Scriptures.

The devil wants to kill people that are a threat to his works, and he loves to manifest evil through others. The devil demanded to sift Peter in Luke 22:31-32:

> *Simon, Simon (Peter), listen! Satan has demanded permission to sift [all of] you like grain; but I have prayed [especially] for you [Peter], that your faith [and confidence in Me] may not fail; and you, once you have turned back again [to Me], strengthen and support your brothers [in the faith].*"

Satan targeted Peter because he was going to be Jesus' go-to guy to build the church: *"And I say to you that you are Peter, and on this rock I will build My church; and the gates of Hades (death) will not overpower it [by preventing the resurrection of the Christ]."* (Matthew 16:18)

The first step in the process of sifting wheat is to loosen the chaff from the edible grain, which is called *threshing*. The tried and true way to do this is for the farmer to spread the wheat onto a floor and then beat it with a flail. The devil wanted to beat Peter to a pulp. If he took out Peter, he believed he could take out the future of the church.

You won't find a better example of Satan's work than mass shootings, and especially those that take place in schools involving children. Many times you hear the shooters confess to hearing voices that drove them to carry out such heinous acts. One thing is certain: those voices were not from God. I believe Judas heard the same voices when he decided to betray Jesus. John 13:2 says, *"It was during supper, when the devil had already put [the thought of] betraying Jesus into the heart of Judas Iscariot, Simon's son."*

We know Satan is involved when parents kill their own children, young men slaughter kids in schools, a single individual kills masses on the streets of Las Vegas. Such actions are a result of evil, and the perpetrators are simply pawns in Satan's cruel game. The famous comedian Flip Wilson coined the phrase, "The devil made me do it"[4] as part of his comedy routine, but an unfortunate by-product was that many perceive that statement as a joke versus seeing it for the reality it is. The devil is in the killing business, and his business seems to be thriving.

The devil loves to destroy marriages so families can be splintered, which serves his purpose of disrupting the unity a family provides to communities, our nation and the church. Jesus confirmed what God said about marriage in Matthew 19:4-6:

> *He replied,* "*Have you never read that He who created them from the beginning* MADE THEM MALE AND FEMALE, *and said,* 'FOR THIS REASON A MAN SHALL LEAVE HIS FATHER AND MOTHER AND SHALL BE JOINED INSEPARABLY TO HIS WIFE, AND THE TWO SHALL BECOME ONE FLESH'? *So they are no longer two, but one flesh. Therefore, what God has joined together, let no one separate.*"

The devil took this confirmation as a personal challenge to try to separate as many married couples as possible, and he has accomplished this through several methods. Adultery and lust are at the top of his list and usually his favorite and most effective weapons. Drugs and alcohol are on his menu as well. When people abuse drugs or alcohol, they usually commit acts they regret that ultimately fracture their relationships beyond repair. Satan tops off the list by convincing society that divorce should be an acceptable norm and fighting to save a marriage denies one spouse or the other their right to happiness. With the divorce rates as high as they are among Christians and the general population, it seems like he is winning. He has also been successful in perverting God's truth about sexuality, the institution of marriage, and even gender identification, which many in the church view as a doctrine of acceptance or inclusion instead of the biblical doctrine communicated throughout the Scriptures.

What are Satan's strategies?

▶ The most common reason churches are broken apart or fail to be effective is due to accusations. Revelation 12:10 says,

> *Then I heard a loud voice in heaven, saying, "Now the salvation, and the power, and the kingdom (dominion, reign) of our*

304 | *Turning a Blind Eye*

*God, and the authority of His Christ have come; for the accuser
of our [believing] brothers and sisters has been thrown down [at
last], he who accuses them and keeps bringing charges [of sinful
behavior] against them before our God day and night."*

The devil is the master of accusations, and nothing will divide a
church faster than a false accusation against leadership or a split over
biblical doctrine. This is why Jesus said in Matthew 12:25: *Knowing their
thoughts Jesus said to them,* "*Any kingdom that is divided against itself is
being laid waste; and no city or house divided against itself will* [continue
to] *stand."* If you have been part of a local church for any length of time,
you have likely witnessed this spiritual atrocity firsthand. If a church
comes apart at the seams, the only winner is the devil.

► Just as he did with Paul, Satan will try to hinder Christians
from accomplishing something for God. 1 Thessalonians 2:18 says,
"*For we wanted to come to you—I, Paul, again and again [wanted to
come], but Satan hindered us."*

► Satan will try to fill Christians with arrogance and pride to cause
us to fail, as mentioned in 1 Timothy 3:6, which says, "*And He must
not be a new convert, so that he will not [behave stupidly and] become
conceited [by appointment to this high office] and fall into the [same]
condemnation incurred by the devil [for his arrogance and pride]."*

► Satan will bind, as he did in Luke 13:16: *"And this woman, a daughter (descendant) of Abraham whom Satan has bound for eighteen long years,
should she not have been released from this bond on the Sabbath day?"*

► Satan will try to either convince Christians of a lie or try to
make them lie. There is no such thing as a "white lie," but Satan has
convinced many otherwise. John 8:44 says,

*You are of your father the devil, and it is your will to practice the
desires [which are characteristic] of your father. He was a mur-*

derer from the beginning, and does not stand in the truth because there is no truth in him. When he lies, he speaks what is natural to him, for he is a liar and the father of lies and half-truths.

▶ Satan will set a trap for us and hope we take the bait. 2 Timothy 2:25-26 says,

He must correct those who are in opposition with courtesy and gentleness in the hope that God may grant that they will repent and be led to the knowledge of the truth [accurately understanding and welcoming it], and that they may come to their senses and escape from the trap of the devil, having been held captive by him to do his will.

▶ Satan will come at us with every type of assault he can muster, no matter how many times he has to try. 2 Timothy 4:18 says, "*The Lord will rescue me from every evil assault, and He will bring me safely into His heavenly kingdom; to Him be the glory forever and ever. Amen.*"

▶ He will always without fail try to take advantage of you or your circumstances through the schemes in his bag of tricks. 2 Corinthians 2:11 says, "*To keep Satan from taking advantage of us; for we are not ignorant of his schemes.*"

▶ If possible, Satan will try to get you to walk with a spiritual limp by sending one of his messengers to create a thorn in your side. 2 Corinthians 12:7 says,

Because of the surpassing greatness and extraordinary nature of the revelations [which I received from God], for this reason, to keep me from thinking of myself as important, a thorn in the flesh was given to me, a messenger of Satan, to torment and harass me—to keep me from exalting myself!

▶ We all need to be cognizant of the fact that Satan is always seeking a "more opportune time" to tempt us. This is exactly what he did with Jesus when he failed to tempt our Lord in the wilderness. He never gives up. He is relentless in his pursuit to destroy us. Luke 4:13 tells us, "*When the devil had finished every temptation, he [temporarily] left Him until a more opportune time.*"

▶ Satan is always the source of a spirit of error, and he will work to introduce that spirit into every situation until the end of time.

*W*e *[who teach God's word] are from God [energized by the Holy Spirit], and whoever knows God [through personal experience] listens to us [and has a deeper understanding of Him]. Whoever is not of God does not listen to us. By this we know [without any doubt] the spirit of truth [motivated by God] and the spirit of error [motivated by Satan].* (1 John 4:6)

How does Satan operate in the physical and spiritual worlds?

First of all, Satan doesn't work alone. Just as God has His angels, Lucifer has his demons. Unlike God, they are not omnipresent (everywhere all the time) or omnipotent (having unlimited power to do anything); but we must understand that the devil and his demons operate in both worlds. Fortunately, we have what we need to defeat Satan and his minions—the name of Jesus. We see this in Jude 1:9 when Michael the archangel and Satan were fighting over Moses' body in the heavenly realms: "*But even the archangel Michael, when he was disputing with the devil (Satan), and arguing about the body of Moses, did not dare bring an abusive condemnation against him, but [simply] said, 'The Lord rebuke you!'*"

Battles take place every second of every day in the spiritual world. Paul said in Ephesians 6:12,

*F*or *our struggle is not against flesh and blood [contending only with physical opponents], but against the rulers, against the powers, against the world forces of this [present] darkness, against the spiritual forces of wickedness in the heavenly (supernatural) places.*

As we will discuss in the next chapter, this is one reason we as believers are assigned guardian angels by God to protect and battle against the devil and his little demons, not just in the heavenly realm but here on earth as well.

In Job 1:7 we see an account of a conversation between God and Satan concerning Job: *The LORD said to Satan, "From where have you come?" Then Satan answered the LORD, "From roaming around on the earth and from walking around on it."* Did you catch where Satan was when God asked him where he had been? **He had been roaming around on the earth and walking around on it!** Make no mistake, Satan is alive, well and active in his duties—at least for the time being. The great news is that the ultimate dwelling place for Satan and his demons will be a place especially designed by God for them. 2 Peter 2:4 says, *"For if God did not [even] spare angels that sinned but threw them into hell and sent them to pits of gloom to be kept [there] for judgment."*

REMOVING THE BLIND EYE

I am hopeful that you by now have a firm grasp on how real the devil is and a better understanding of his methods. Once people remove this *blind eye* to the realities of Satan, both in the heavenly and physical realms, they are then prepared to learn how to battle him. It has been often said that, "You can't fight an enemy you can't see." I've changed that just a bit to say, "You can't fight an enemy you don't know."

One of the first things Christians must do is resist the devil and all of his attempts to affect our earthly life. James 4:7 says, *"So submit to [the authority of] God. Resist the devil [stand firm against him] and he will flee from you."* Did you notice the order in the remedy? Submit to God first, then you can resist Satan, and he will flee.

One way to submit to God is to submit to His Word. When you place the Word of God first in your life, you're able to develop the armor you need to fight and win a battle. That is why Ephesians 6:11 says, *"Put on the full armor of God [for His precepts are like the splendid armor of a heavily-armed soldier], so that you may be able to [successfully] stand up* against **all the schemes and the strategies and the deceits** *of the devil."*

Secondly, do not give the devil any opportunity to mount an attack. Ephesians 4:27 says, *"And do not give the devil an* **opportunity** *[to lead you into sin by holding a grudge, or nurturing anger, or harboring resentment, or cultivating bitterness]."* All sins of the flesh are a breeding ground for the opportunity to be attacked. In addition to the ones named in this verse, we can't forget lusting (which will impact your marriage), causing strife in your local church, allowing materialism to dominate your life, telling half-truths or outright lies, and other sins that would make you a prime target of opportunity for the devil.

It doesn't matter if you call him the devil, Lucifer, the enemy, Satan, the evil one, the accuser, the thief, a roaring lion, angel of light, the ruler of the world, the tempter or any other term, he is a formidable enemy—but he can be defeated if we are armed properly.

Hebrews 2:14 says, *"Therefore, since [these His] children share in flesh and blood [the physical nature of mankind], He Himself in a similar manner also shared in the same [physical nature, but without sin], so that through [experiencing] death He might make powerless (ineffective, impotent) him who had the power of death—that is, the devil."*

Jesus not only beat the devil, but he will never help him either according to Hebrews 2:16, which says, *"For, as we all know, He (Christ) does not take hold of [the fallen] angels [to give them a helping hand], but He does take hold of [the fallen] descendants of Abraham [extending to them His hand of deliverance]."* Isaiah 24:21 says, *"So it will happen in that day that the* LORD *will visit and punish the host (fallen angels) of heaven on high, And the kings of the earth on the earth."*

Satan is defeated, and the only power he has is the power we give him.

CHAPTER 43

ANGELS

Do you think that I cannot appeal to My Father, and He will immediately provide Me with more than twelve legions of angels?
(Matthew 26:53)

ANGEL

Greek: from *ággelos*—a messenger, generally a (supernatural) messenger from God, an angel, conveying news or behests from God to men

Cambridge English: in some religious traditions, a being in heaven who serves God, often represented in art as a human with wings

Dictionary.com: one of a class of spiritual beings; a celestial attendant of God, a conventional representation of such a being, in human form, with wings, usually in white robes, a messenger, especially of God, a person who performs a mission of God or acts as if sent by God

Merriam-Webster: a spiritual being superior to humans in power and intelligence, an attendant spirit or guardian

WHEN JESUS said *legions*, He meant a lot of heavenly angels. One legion can be up to 6,000 beings, so He could have called down more than 72,000 angels! Those angels would not have been sent to referee a fight; they were sent as the tip of the spear to take care of business. If we believe that Heaven, Hell and Satan are real, then we must be convinced angels are as well. The world's stereotype of an angel of God that looks like tiny doughboy characters floating around the clouds is the furthest thing from the truth. John described them in Revelation 7:1 as strong and big enough to hold back the winds from the earth, the sea and the trees: *"After this I saw four angels stationed at the four corners of the earth, holding back the four winds of the earth so that no wind would blow on the earth or on the sea or on any tree."* That description leaves little doubt that there isn't any "dough" in their DNA.

These angelic beings created by God to be ministering spirits are big, strong and bad to the bone. Hebrews 1:14 says, *"Are not all the angels ministering spirits sent out [by God] to serve (accompany, protect) those who will inherit salvation? [Of course they are!]"* Angels can be sent individually by God, as the archangel Michael was sent to Mary to inform her of her upcoming pregnancy in Luke 1:26-27:

> *N*ow in the sixth month [of Elizabeth's pregnancy] the angel Gabriel was sent from God to a city in Galilee called Nazareth, to a virgin betrothed to a man whose name was Joseph, a descendant of the house of David; and the virgin's name was Mary.

God can also send an army of angels, like He did in Luke 2:13-14 when Jesus was born: *Then suddenly there appeared with the angel a multitude of the heavenly host (angelic army) praising God and saying, "Glory to God in the highest [heaven], And on earth peace among men with whom He is well-pleased."* Angels were sent to Zacharias to announce the birth of John the Baptist, to the shepherds announcing the birth of Jesus, to Joseph to warn him to flee to Egypt because of Herod, and again in Egypt to tell him to go to Israel then to Galilee, to free the apostles from jail, and in too many other instances to list in this book.

Angels are created beings that should never be worshiped—only God should be exalted. Colossians 2:18-19 says,

Let no one defraud you of your prize [your freedom in Christ and your salvation] by insisting on mock humility and the worship of angels, going into detail about visions [he claims] he has seen [to justify his authority], puffed up [in conceit] by his unspiritual mind, and not holding fast to the head [of the body, Jesus Christ], from whom the entire body, supplied and knit together by its joints and ligaments, grows with the growth [that can come only] from God.

Jesus is superior to all angels.

Hᴇʙʀᴇᴡs 2:5, *"For this reason [that is, because of God's final revelation in His Son Jesus and because of Jesus' superiority to the angels] we must pay much closer attention than ever to the things that we have heard, so that we do not [in any way] drift away from truth."*

The following are only some of the ways angels perform on the behalf of man.

▶ Angels are messengers for God. *"Are not all the angels ministering spirits sent out [by God] to serve (accompany, protect) those who will inherit salvation? [Of course they are!]"* (Hebrews 1:14)

▶ Angels minister to us. *"Then the devil left Him; and angels came and ministered to Him [bringing Him food and serving Him]."* (Matthew 4:11)

▶ Angels protect us. *"For He will command His angels in regard to you, To protect and defend and guard you in all your ways [of obedience and service]."* (Psalm 91:11)

▶ Angels rescue us. *"The angel of the Lᴏʀᴅ encamps around those who fear Him [with awe-inspired reverence and worship Him with obedience], And He rescues [each of] them."* (Psalm 34:7)

▶ Angels will deliver us to God. "*And He will send His angels with* A LOUD TRUMPET *and* THEY WILL GATHER TOGETHER *His elect (God's chosen ones) from the four winds, from one end of the heavens to the other.*" (Matthew 24:31)

▶ Angels will help us. "*But the men (angels) reached out with their hands and pulled Lot into the house with them, and shut the door [after him].*" (Genesis 19:10)

▶ Angels will execute judgment. "*He sent upon them His burning anger, His fury and indignation and distress, A band of angels of destruction [among them].*" (Psalm 78:49)

▶ Angels are sent from God. "*Bless the* LORD, *you His angels, You mighty ones who do His commandments, Obeying the voice of His word!*" (Psalm 103:20)

The Son of Man will send out His angels, and they will gather out of His kingdom all things that offend [those things by which people are led into sin], and all who practice evil [leading others into sin], and will throw them into the furnace of fire; in that place there will be weeping [over sorrow and pain] and grinding of teeth [over distress and anger]. (Matthew 13:41-42)

▶ Angels will return with Jesus. "*For the Son of Man is going to come in the glory and majesty of His Father with His angels, and* THEN HE WILL REPAY EACH ONE IN ACCORDANCE WITH WHAT HE HAS DONE." (Matthew 16:27)

▶ Angels are present at judgment time. "*But he who denies Me before men will be denied in the presence of the angels of God.*" (Luke 12:9)

▶ Angels can be seen through visions to inform us of something that God wants us to know. "*And they did not find His body. Then they came back, saying that they had even seen a vision of angels who said that He was alive!*" (Luke 24:23)

▶ Angels obey God. *And concerning the angels He says, "WHO MAKES HIS ANGELS WINDS, AND HIS MINISTERING SERVANTS FLAMES OF FIRE [to do His bidding]."* (Hebrews 1:7)

▶ Angels receive from us.

Do not neglect to extend hospitality to strangers [especially among the family of believers—being friendly, cordial, and gracious, sharing the comforts of your home and doing your part generously], for by this some have entertained angels without knowing it. (Hebrews 13:2)

▶ Angels will lead us in worship.

Then I looked, and I heard the voice of many angels around the throne and [the voice] of the living creatures and the elders; and they numbered myriads of myriads, and thousands of thousands (innumerable), saying in a loud voice, "Worthy and deserving is the Lamb that was sacrificed to receive power and riches and wisdom and might and honor and glory and blessing." (Revelation 5:11-12)

▶ Angels give us assurance.

For this very night an angel of the God to whom I belong and whom I serve stood before me, and said, "Stop being afraid, Paul. You must stand before Caesar; and behold, God has given you [the lives of] all those who are sailing with you." (Acts 27:23-24)

▶ Angels are a rapid response team, as King Herod found out. "*And at once an angel of the Lord struck him down because he did not give God the glory [and instead permitted himself to be worshiped], and he was eaten by worms and died [five days later]."* (Acts 12:23)

▶ Angels will strengthen us. "*Now an angel appeared to Him from heaven, strengthening Him."* (Luke 22:43)

REMOVING THE BLIND EYE

It is important for anyone who wants to have the services of divine angels to believe they exist. That's not to say God would withhold dispatching them if He wanted, despite our unbelief, but believing in them gives us a beneficial weapon with different purposes if used correctly. It's the same with angels! Matthew 18:10 says,

> *See that you do not despise or think less of one of these little ones, for I say to you that their angels in heaven [are in the presence of and] continually look upon the face of My Father who is in heaven.*

We all have angels in Heaven who are intently looking into the eyes of God and waiting on His command.

I used to duck hunt a lot and had a trained Labrador Retriever named Sally who enjoyed the hunting as much as I did, even when it was freezing. She would sit in that blind on my right side staring intently at me and waiting for me to give her the command "Fetch up, Sally." She would not move an inch until that command was given, then she was off to the races to retrieve that duck. That's how I visualize these angels who are assigned to each of us. When I pray Psalm 91 prior to getting on a flight, I believe angels are literally on the wings guiding the plane. I know that to be true because it clearly says so in Psalms 91:7-13.

> *A thousand may fall at your side And ten thousand at your right hand, But danger will not come near you. You will only [be a spectator as you] look on with your eyes And witness the [divine] repayment of the wicked [as you watch safely from the shelter of the Most High]. Because you have made the LORD, [who is] my refuge, Even the Most High, your dwelling place, No evil will befall you, Nor will any plague come near your tent. For He will command His angels in regard to you, To protect and defend and*

guard you in all your ways [of obedience and service]. They will lift you up in their hands, So that you do not [even] strike your foot against a stone. You will tread upon the lion and cobra; The young lion and the serpent you will trample underfoot.

I don't have faith in the angels per se, but confidence that God will send them when I pray to do the job that only they can do.

We have to stop looking at the world's physical limitations and start seeing the world through our spiritual lens. We need to take 2 Corinthians 4:18 to heart: "*So we look not at the things which are seen, but at the things which are unseen; for the things which are visible are temporal [just brief and fleeting], but the things which are invisible are everlasting and imperishable.*" Angels are standing by, ready and waiting to be called, if we will only use them.

JESUS' OTHER SIDE

Do not think that I have come to bring peace on the earth; I have not come to bring peace, but a sword [of division between belief and unbelief]. (Matthew 10:34)

THIS IS a topic that can certainly cause considerable debate. I have discovered that most people's opinion depends on whether they are walking with God and the extent of their faith, if any. The most common description of Jesus in the world today is "nice," but that perception should perhaps change based on Matthew 10:34. People think of Jesus as nice because He performed many kind acts during His ministry—but those who believe that His only character trait is that He was nice are missing the complete Jesus who displayed many other emotions. Usually the people who believe that Jesus was "just a nice person" are the ones who need Him to be their Savior, they just don't know it or refuse to accept it. They fear that if they accept Jesus in any way other than nice, they risk shining a light on their sinful nature. That can be true for believers as well. In many cases, people are like W. C. Fields—they're "looking for a loophole."[1] Certainly a nice Jesus would let everyone come to Heaven, right? That's not only misleading, it's also wrong.

My Jesus was as tough as nails. He took a punishment that caused so much pain that we cannot even comprehend its depth. My Jesus

316

is coming on a white horse with eyes that are a flame of fire and is *"KING OF KINGS, AND LORD OF LORDS,"* as described in Revelation 19:16. My Jesus descended into the earth for three days, defeated Satan, and came out with the keys to death. Yes, one side of my Jesus was kind, compassionate, generous and loving. At the same time, my Jesus had another side that hated the devil, displayed righteous anger, grew frustrated due to unbelief, wept when His friend died, berated religious leaders and even called His main disciple Satan. But because Jesus was fully human yet divine, unlike us, He never sinned when He expressed emotions of anger, frustration or righteous indignation.

Those who claim that Jesus was simply "nice" deny the existence of His human side and His ability to feel everything that mankind feels. They also deny His deity and the necessity of the forgiveness of sins that He proclaimed in the New Testament. Philippians 2:7 says,

> *But emptied Himself [without renouncing or diminishing His deity, but only temporarily giving up the outward expression of divine equality and His rightful dignity] by assuming the form of a bond-servant, and being made in the likeness of men [He became completely human but was without sin, being fully God and fully man].*

Because He was fully man as well as fully God, Jesus knew exactly how we feel so that He could sympathize with us. Hebrews 4:15 says,

> *For we do not have a High Priest who is unable to sympathize and understand our weaknesses and temptations, but One who has been tempted [knowing exactly how it feels to be human] in every respect as we are, yet without [committing any] sin.*

Since Jesus became human while retaining His deity, He expressed some of the same emotions we do and said some of the same things we likely say. However, He did so without any of the sin that we exhibit as human beings. Hebrews 7:26 confirms He was perfect: "*It was fitting for us to have such a High Priest [perfectly adapted to our needs], holy, blameless, unstained [by sin], separated from sinners and exalted higher than the heavens.*"

Several other passages of Scripture illustrate that Jesus was more than just a nice person.

▶ Jesus was angry and grieved. *After looking around at them with anger, grieved at the hardness and arrogance of their hearts, He told the man,* "Hold out your hand." *And he held it out, and his hand was [completely] restored.* (Mark 3:5)

▶ Jesus felt righteous anger for His Father.

And Jesus entered the temple [grounds] and drove out [with force] all who were buying and selling [birds and animals for sacrifice] in the temple area, and He turned over the tables of the moneychangers [who made a profit exchanging foreign money for temple coinage] and the chairs of those who were selling doves [for sacrifice]. Jesus said to them, "It is written [in Scripture], 'MY HOUSE SHALL BE CALLED A HOUSE OF PRAYER'; but you are making it a ROBBERS' DEN." (Matthew 21:12-13)

▶ Jesus didn't mince His words. *But Jesus turned and said to Peter,* "Get behind Me, Satan! You are a stumbling block to Me; for you are not setting your mind on things of God, but on things of man." (Matthew 16:23)

▶ Jesus could be reactionary. *Seeing a lone fig tree at the roadside, He went to it and found nothing but leaves on it; and He said to it,* "Never again will fruit come from you." *And at once the fig tree withered.* (Matthew 21:19)

▶ Jesus was very challenging. *But Jesus, aware of their malice, asked,* "Why are you testing Me, you hypocrites?" (Matthew 22:18)

► Jesus could be confrontational. *"You serpents, you spawn of vipers, how can you escape the penalty of hell?"* (Matthew 23:33)

► Jesus felt sorrow.

Then Jesus came with them to a place called Gethsemane (olivepress), and He told His disciples, "Sit here while I go over there and pray." And taking with Him Peter and the two sons of Zebedee [James and John], He began to be grieved and greatly distressed. Then He said to them, "My soul is deeply grieved, so that I am almost dying of sorrow. Stay here and stay awake and keep watch with Me." (Matthew 26:36-38)

► Jesus was blunt, regardless of gender. *But Jesus, aware [of the malice] of this [remark], said to them, "Why are you bothering the woman? She has done a good thing to Me."* (Matthew 26:10)

► Jesus was very frank. *He was saying to her, "First let the children [of Israel] be fed, for it is not right to take the children's bread and throw it to the pet dogs (non-Jews)."* (Mark 7:27)

► Jesus was frustrated. *He replied, "O unbelieving (faithless) generation, how long shall I be with you? How long shall I put up with you? Bring him to Me!"* (Mark 9:19)

► Jesus was distressed.

I have come to cast fire (judgment) on the earth; and how I wish that it were already kindled! I have a baptism [of great suffering] with which to be baptized, and how [greatly] I am distressed until it is accomplished! (Luke 12:49-50)

► Jesus shed tears.

When Jesus saw her sobbing, and the Jews who had come with her also sobbing, He was deeply moved in spirit [to the point of anger at the sorrow caused by death] *and was troubled, and said,* "Where have you laid him?" *They said,* "Lord, come and see." *Jesus wept.* (John 11:33-35)

▶ Jesus was graphic.

And Jesus said to them, "I assure you and most solemnly say to you, unless you eat the flesh of the Son of Man and drink His blood *[unless you believe in Me as Savior and believe in the sav-ing power of My blood which will be shed for you],* you do not have life in yourselves. The one who eats My flesh and drinks My blood *[believes in Me, accepts Me as Savior]* has eternal life *[that is, now possesses it],* and I will raise him up *[from the dead]* on the last day. For My flesh is true *[spiritual]* food, and My blood is true *[spiritual]* drink. He who eats My flesh and drinks My blood *[believes in Me, accepts Me as Savior]* remains in Me, and I *[in the same way remain]* in him." (John 6:53-56)

▶ Jesus could be perceived as offensive. *He said these things in a synagogue while He was teaching in Capernaum. When many of His disciples heard this, they said,* "This is a difficult and harsh and offensive statement. Who can *[be expected to]* listen to it?" (John 6:59-60)

▶ Jesus' blunt honesty drove people away.

But Jesus, aware that His disciples were complaining about it, asked them, "Does this cause you to stumble and take offense? What then *[will you think]* if you see the Son of Man ascending to *[the realm]* where He was before? It is the Spirit who gives life; the flesh conveys no benefit *[it is of no account].* The words I have spoken to you are spirit and life *[providing eternal life].* But *[still]* there are some of you who do not believe and have faith." *For Jesus knew from the beginning who did not believe, and who would betray Him. And He was saying,* "This is the reason why I have told you that no one can come to Me unless it has been

granted him [that is, unless he is enabled to do so] by the Father."
As a result of this many of His disciples abandoned Him, and no
longer walked with Him. (John 6:61-66)

▶ Jesus was clever.

Jesus said to them, "I will ask you one question, and you answer
Me, and then I will tell you by what authority I do these things.
Was the baptism of John [the Baptist] from heaven [that is, or-
dained by God] or from men? Answer Me." They began discussing
it with each other, saying, "If we say, 'From heaven,' He will say,
'Then why did you not believe him?' But shall we say, 'From men?'"
—they were afraid [to answer because] of the crowd, for everyone
considered John to have been a real prophet. So they replied to Je-
sus, "We do not know." And Jesus said to them, "Neither will I tell
you by what authority I do these things." (Mark 11:29-33)

▶ Jesus was descriptive.

But whoever causes one of these little ones who believe and trust
in Me to stumble [that is, to sin or lose faith], it would be better
for him if a heavy millstone [one requiring a donkey's strength to
turn it] were hung around his neck and he were thrown into the
sea. (Mark 9:42)

▶ Jesus was very direct with His mother. *Jesus said to her, "[Dear]*
woman, what is that to you and to Me? My time [to act and to be re-
vealed] has not yet come." (John 2:4)

▶ Jesus called people liars.

"You are of your father the devil, and it is your will to practice
the desires [which are characteristic] of your father. He was a
murderer from the beginning, and does not stand in the truth
because there is no truth in him. When he lies, he speaks what

is natural to him, for he is a liar and the father of lies and half-truths." (John 8:44)

▶ Jesus called people evil. *"If you, then, being evil [that is, sinful by nature], know how to give good gifts to your children, how much more will your heavenly Father give the Holy Spirit to those who ask and continue to ask Him!"* (Luke 11:13)

▶ Jesus could be stern.

Now the day was ending, and the twelve [disciples] came and said to Him, "Send the crowd away, so that they may go into the surrounding villages and countryside and find lodging, and get provisions; because here we are in an isolated place." But He said to them, "You give them something to eat!" They said, "We have no more than five loaves and two fish—unless perhaps we go and buy food for all these people." (For there were about 5,000 men.) And He said to His disciples, "Have them sit down to eat in groups of about fifty each." They did so and had them all sit down. (Luke 9:12-15)

▶ Jesus implied that His disciples were like children in their understanding. *The disciples were amazed and bewildered by His words. But Jesus said to them again, "Children, how difficult it is [for those who place their hope and confidence in riches] to enter the kingdom of God!"* (Mark 10:24)

▶ Jesus told some shocking stories. *[The king ended by saying,] "But as for these enemies of mine who did not want me to be king over them, bring them here and kill them in my presence."* (Luke 19:27)

▶ Jesus was sometimes brash. *But He said to him, "Man, who appointed Me a judge or an arbitrator over [the two of] you?"* (Luke 12:14)

▶ Jesus had unorthodox methods.

They brought to Him a man who was deaf and had difficulty speaking, and they begged Jesus to place His hand on him. Jesus, taking him aside by himself, away from the crowd, put His fingers into the man's ears, and after spitting, He touched the man's tongue [with the saliva]. (Mark 7: 32-33)

► Jesus could be forceful. *But Jesus said, "Let her alone; why are you bothering her and causing trouble? She has done a good and beautiful thing to Me."* (Mark 14:6)

► Jesus could be hard on His disciples: *Peter asked Him, "Explain this parable [about what defiles a person] to us." And He said, "Are you still so dull [and unable to put things together]?"* (Matthew 15:15-16)

► Jesus could be perceived as being insensitive.

Now when evening had come, the boat was in the middle of the sea, and Jesus was alone on the land. Seeing the disciples straining at the oars, because the wind was against them, at about the fourth watch of the night (3:00-6:00 a.m.) He came to them, walking on the sea. And [acted as if] He intended to pass by them. (Mark 6:47-48)

► Jesus could appear to be disinterested.

And a Canaanite woman from that district came out and began to cry out [urgently], saying, "Have mercy on me, O Lord, Son of David (Messiah); my daughter is cruelly possessed by a demon." But He did not say a word in answer to her. (Matthew 15:22-23)

► Jesus could be intimidating. *But they did not understand this statement, and they were afraid to ask Him [what He meant].* (Mark 9:32)

~

My Jesus was so much more than someone to be relegated into a box labeled "nice." He experienced the same human emotions we have and responded in ways that fit those emotions, yet he did it all in love without sinning one time. When I slip up and get into the flesh, I know that my Jesus understands the feeling because He too experienced the same emotions. When I go to Him and ask for forgiveness, I know I will receive it even though my Jesus never needed to seek it Himself. My Jesus is fully God, who granted me salvation; but at the same time, my Jesus was human, allowing Him to relate to my life in the flesh.

Your perception of Jesus will determine how you frame the message of the gospel. If *your* Jesus is just meek, fragile and nice all the time, then that's how your message will be perceived when you speak. On the other hand, if your Jesus is King of kings and Lord of lords, tough as nails and powerful beyond human understanding, yet graceful, merciful and loving, that is the Jesus people will see in you.

What picture of Jesus do you want them to see?

END NOTES

INTRODUCTION

[1]Dudley, Pope, *The Great Gamble: Nelson at Copenhagen* (New York: Simon and Schuster, 1972), p. 576.

[2]"Compassion," *Lexico.com,* 2019, https://www.lexico.com/en/definition/compassion, accessed 8 August 2019.

CHAPTER 1 — RED LETTERS

[1]"How Many Pages Are There in the Bible?" *wordcounter.net,* February 21, 2016, https://wordcounter.net/blog/2016/02/21/101241_how-many-pages-are-there-in-the-bible.html, accessed 8 August 2019.

[2]"How Many Words of Jesus Christ Are in Red?" *synopticgospel.com,* https://synopticgospel.com/how_many_words_of_Jesus_Christ_are_red, accessed 8 August 2019.

[3]"Abode," *dictionary.com,* https://www.dictionary.com/browse/abode, accessed 8 August 2019.

[4]"Glorify," *Cambridge Dictionary,* https://dictionary.cambridge.org/us/dictionary/english/glorify, accessed 8 August 2019.

CHAPTER 2 — THE HEART OF MAN

[1]"Body," *Bible Hub,* https://biblehub.com/Greek/4983.htm, accessed 8 August 2019.

[2]"Soul," *Bible Hub,* https://biblehub.com/str/Greek/5590.htm, accessed 8 August 2019.

[3]"The Confession of Faith," *Westminster Confession of Faith Scriptures Proofs,* https://www.pcaac.org/wp-content/uploads/2012/11/WCF ScriptureProofs.pdf, accessed 8 August 2019.

[4]"Wind, Spirit," *Bible Hub,* https://biblehub.com/str/Greek/4151.htm, accessed 8 August 2019.

[5]"How Many Times Does a Word Appear in the Bble?" *Christian Bible Reference Site,* https://www.christianbiblereference.org/faq_Word Count.htm, accessed 8 August 2019.

[6]"Motive," *Cambridge Dictionary,* https://dictionary.cambridge.org/us/dictionary/english/motive, accessed 8 August 2019.

[7]"Enlighten," *Merriam-Webster.com,* 2019, https://www.Merriam-Webster.com/dictionary/enlighten, accessed 8 August 2019

CHAPTER 3 — THE GREATEST COMMANDMENT

[1]"All," *Dictionary.com*, 2002, https://www.dictionary.com/browse /all?s=t, accessed 8 August 2019.

[2]"The State of the Church 2016," *Barna.com*, 2016, https://www.barna.com/research/state-church-2016/, accessed 8 August 2019.

[3]"Americans Read an Average of 16.8 Minutes a Day," *Conservative.com*, June 28, 2018, https://www.4conservative.com/cnsnews.com/americans-read-an-average-of-168-minutes-per-day/, accessed 8 August 2019.

[4]How Many Pages Are There in the Bible?" *wordcounter.net,* February 21, 2016, https://wordcounter.net/blog/2016/02/21/101241_how-many-pages-are-there-in-the-bible.html, accessed 8 August 2019.

[5]Daniel John, *The Red Letter Gospel: All the Words of Jesus Christ in Red* (n.c.: Smart Publishing Ltd, 2017) iii.

[6]"How Many Words of Jesus Christ Are in Red?" *synopticgospel.com*, https://synopticgospel.com/how_many_words_of_Jesus_Christ_are_red, accessed 8 August 2019.

[7]Hawthorne Mineart, "Word Count for Famous Novels (organized), commonplacebook.com, November 22, 2011, http://common-

placebook.com/art/books/word-count-for-famous-novels/, accessed 8 August 2019.

[8]"We Listen to Music for More than 4½ Hours a Day, Nielson Says," *MarketingCharts.com,* November 13, 2017, https://www.market-ingcharts.com/industries/media-and-entertainment-81082, accessed 8 August 2019.

CHAPTER 4 — MERCY

[1]"Mercy," *Cambridge Dictionary*, https://dictionary.cambridge.org/us/dictionary/english/mercy, accessed 8 August 2019.

CHAPTER 5 — ANGER

[1]"Fool," *Merriam-Webster.com,* 2019, https://www.Merriam-Webster.com/dictionary/fool, accessed 8 August 2019.

[2]Scott A. Bonn, Ph.D., "Fear-Based Anger Is the Primary Motive for Violence," *Psychology Today,* July 17, 2017, https://www.psychologytoday.com/us/blog/wicked-deeds/201707/fear-based-anger-is-the-primary-motive-violence, accessed 8 August 2019.

CHAPTER 6 — LUST AND ADULTERY

[1]"Lust," *Cambridge Dictionary,* https://dictionary.cambridge.org/us/dictionary/english/lust, accessed 8 August 2019.

[2]"To look at," *Dictionary.com*, 2002, https://www.dictionary.com/to look at/all?s=t, accessed 9 August 2019.

[3]Glenn Stanton, "FactChecker: Divorce Rate Among Christians," *The Gospel Coalition*, September 25, 2012, https://www.thegospelcoalition.org/article/factchecker-divorce-rate-among-christians/, accessed 8 August 2019.

[4]Dr. Manny Alvarez, "Porn Addiction: Why Americans Are in More Danger than Ever," *Fox News Channel,* January 16, 2019, https://www.foxnews.com/health/porn-addiction-why-americans-are-in-more-danger-than-ever

[5]*Ibid.*

CHAPTER 7 — DIVORCE
[1]Glenn Stanton, "FactChecker: Divorce Rate Among Christians," *The Gospel Coalition*, September 25, 2012.

CHAPTER 9 — RETALIATION
[1]Walter Wink, *Engaging the Powers, Discernment and Resistance in a World of Domination* (Minneapolis: Fortress Press,1992), 175-77.
[2]*Ibid.*, 183.
[3]Erik Divietro, "Jesus' Non-Violence and Roman Law," *Unorthodox Faith*, June 16, 2018, https://unorthodoxfaith.com/2008/06/16/jesus-non-violence-and-roman-law/, accessed 8 August 2019.
[4]Dennis Bratcher, "The Needy in Jewish Tradition," *The Voice: Biblical and Theological Resources for Growing Christians,* 2018, http://www.crivoice.org/needy.html, accessed 8 August 2019.

CHAPTER 12 — PRAYER
[1]Philip Wendell Rannell, "Hallow, Hallowed," *BibleStudyTools.com,* https://www.biblestudytools.com/dictionary/hallow-hallowed/, accessed 8 August 2019.
[2]"Bar-Abba," *Wikepedia, the Free Encyclopedia*, May 24, 2010, https://en.wikipedia.org/wiki/Bar-Abba, accessed 8 August 2019.
[3]https://www.crosswalk.com/faith/prayer/12-inspiring-quotes-about-prayer-from-billy-graham.html, accessed 8 August 2019.
[4]*Ibid.*

CHAPTER 13 — FORGIVENESS
[1]"Paraptóma," *BibleHub.com*, 2004-2018, https://biblehub.com/str/Greek/3900.htm, accessed 8 August 2019.

CHAPTER 14 — FASTING
[1]"How Long Does It Take to Die From Starvation and Dehydration: Surprising Life & Death Findings," *Newbie Prepper,* https://newbieprepper.com/how-long-does-it-take-to-die-from-starvation-and-dehydration/, accessed 8 August 2019.

CHAPTER 15 — IDOLATRY

[1]"Worship," *Merriam-Webster,* https://www.Merriam-Webster.com/dictionary/worship, accessed 8 August 2019.

[2]Ariel Shanelle, "What Does the Word 'Worship' Mean in Hebrew and Greek?" *ArielShanelle.com,* December 28, 2018, https://arielshanelle.com/word-worship-hebrew-Greek/, accessed 8 August 2019.

[3]*Ibid.*

[4]Beth Felker Jones, *Practicing Christian Doctrine, An Introduction to Thinking and Living Theologically* (Grand Rapids: Baker Academic, 2014), 56.

[5]"Greed," *Dictionary.com*, 2002, https://www.dictionary.com/greed/all?s=t, accessed 9 August 2019.

[6]"Covetousness," *Vine's Expository Dictionary of New Testament Words* (St. Louis: MacDonald Publishing Co., 1989), p. 223.

[7]Beth Felker Jones, 56.

[8]*Ibid.*

[9]Stoyan Zaimov, "Billy Graham's Will and Testament Released to Public: Asks Family to Defend Gospel at Any Cost," *The Christian Post,* https://www.christianpost.com/news/billy-grahams-will-and-testament-released-to-public-asks-family-to-defend-gospel-at-any-cost.html, accessed 10 August 2019.

[10]Joy Allmond, "Billy Graham's Last Will and Testament Revealed," *Lifeway*, May 22, 2018, https://factsandtrends.net/2018/05/22/billy-graham-leaves-assets-and-parting-words-to-family-funds-to-ministry/, accessed 8 August 2019.

[11]Caleb Parke, "Singapore's Richest Man Says 'Missing Piece Was God Through Jesus,'" *FoxNews.com,* July 24, https://www.foxnews.com/faith-values/richest-man-singapore-god-jesus-wealth, accessed 8 August 2019.

CHAPTER 16 — WEALTH

[1]Anne R. Carey and Kay Worthington, "Roper Starch Worldwide for Worth," *USA Today.*

[2]"Bob Marley's Last Words to His Son Ziggy," *So True Facts,* http://www.sotruefacts.com/rule/438, accessed 8 August 2019.

[3]*National Endowment for Financial Education,* https://www.nefe.org/press-room/news/2018/research-statistic-on-financial-windfalls-and-bankruptcy.aspx, accessed 8 August 2019.

[4]Jen Doll, "A Treasury of Terribly Sad Stories of Lotto Winners," *The Atlantic,* March 30, 2012, https://www.theatlantic.com/national/archive/2012/03/terribly-sad-true-stories-lotto-winners/329903/, accessed 8 August 2019.

[5]*Ibid.*

[6]Holman Bible Editorial Staff, *Holman Concise Bible Dictionary,* *GoogleBooks.com,* https://books.google.com/books?id=eTK5AwAAQBAJ&pg=PA627&lpg=PA627&dq=physical+resources+god+gives+humans+to+control&source=bl&ots=hagHp-NRZe&sig=ACfU3U31soYbhCz5wuqgmfFZ8_ZsSFG30g&hl=en&sa=X&ved=2ahUKEwji07P_9brjAhWIQc0KHZT7B5oQ6AEwAXoECAkQAQ#v=onepage&q=physical%20resources%20god%20gives%20humans%20to%20control&f=false, accessed 8 August 2019.

CHAPTER 18 —SERVING GOD OR MAMMON

[1]"Worry," *The Oxford Pocket Dictionary of Current English, Encyclopedia.com,* https://www.encyclopedia.com, accessed 9 August 2019.

[2]"Grieve," *Dictionary.com,* 2019, https://www.Dictionary.com/browse/grieving?s=t, accessed 8 August 2019.

[3]"Greed," *Cambridge Dictionary,* https://dictionary.cambridge.org/us/dictionary/english/greed, accessed 8 August 2019.

CHAPTER 21 —THE SPIRIT OF GOD

[1]"Covetous," *Merriam-Webster.com,* 2019, https://www.Merriam-Webster.com/dictionary/covetousness?src=search-dict-hed, accessed 8 August 2019.

[2]"Power," *Merriam-Webster.com,* 2019, https://www.Merriam-Webster.com/dictionary/power, accessed 8 August 2019.

[3]Kathleen Elkins, "Here's How Much You Have to Earn to Be in the Top 1% in every US State," *CNBC.com*, July 27, 2018, https://www.cnbc.com/2018/07/27/how-much-you-have-to-earn-to-be-in-the-top-1percent-in-every-us-state.html, accessed 8 August 2019.

[4]"Haughty," *Merriam-Webster.com*, 2019, https://www.Merriam-Webster.com/dictionary/haughty, accessed 8 August 2019.

[5]"Prestige," *Merriam-Webster.com*, 2019, https://www.Merriam-Webster.com/dictionary/prestige, accessed 8 August 2019.

[6]"Influence," *Merriam-Webster.com*, 2019, https://www.Merriam-Webster.com/dictionary/influence, accessed 8 August 2019.

CHAPTER 22 — COVETOUSNESS

[1]"Epithumeó," *Bible Hub.com*, 2004-2018, https://biblehub.com/Greek/1937.htm, accessed 8 August 2019.

CHAPTER 25 — CONFESSING JESUS

[1]"Deny," *Merriam-Webster.com*, 2019, https://www.Merriam-Webster.com/dictionary/deny, accessed 8 August 2019.

[2]"Admit," *Google Dictionary*, https://www.google.com/search?q=admit+define&rlz=1C1CHBD_enUS820US820&oq=admit+define&aqs=chrome..69i57j0l5.3223j1j8&sourceid=chrome&ie=UTF-8, accessed 8 August 2019.

CHAPTER 26 — THE ULTIMATE SACRIFICE

[1]"Crucifixion: Jesus Faced a Horrible Death" *AllAboutJesusChrist.org*, 2002-2019m https://www.allaboutjesuschrist.org/crucifixion.htm, accessed 8 August 2019.

[2]"The Passion of the Christ, *Box Office Mojo*, https://www.boxofficemojo.com/movies/?id=passionofthechrist.htm, accessed 8 August 2019.

CHAPTER 27 — THE SPIRIT OF FEAR

[1]"I'm Hopeless." Billy Graham Evangelistic Association, 2017, https://billygraham.org, accessed 8 August 2019.

CHAPTER 28 — MORTALITY

[1]Melissa Gray, "Fatima Ali, 'Top Chef' Fan Favorite, Dies at 29, *CNN Entertainment,* January 26, 2019, https://www.cnn.com/2019/01/25/entertainment/fatima-ali-top-chef-dies/index.html, accessed 8 August 2019.

CHAPTER 29 — THE FEAR OF DEATH

[1]"Necrophobia," *Merriam-Webster.com,* 2019, https://www.Merriam-Webster.com/dictionary/necrophobia?src=search-dict-hed, accessed 8 August 2019.

[2]"Why You Can Believe the Bible," *EveryStudent.com,* https://www.everystudent.com/features/bible.html, accessed 8 August 2019.

[3]"Assurance," *Dictionary.com,* 2019, https://www.dictionary.com/browse/assurance, accessed 8 August 2019.

[4]"Hope," *Cambridge Dictionary,* https://dictionary.cambridge.org/us/dictionary/english/hope, accessed 8 August 2019.

[5]"Conviction," *Merriam-Webster.com,* 2019, https://www.Merriam-Webster.com/dictionary/conviction?src=search-dict-hed, accessed 8 August 2019.

CHAPTER 30 — THE FORGOTTEN

[1]Jennifer Bronson and E. Ann Carson, "Prisoners in 2017," *Bureau of Justice Statistics,* April 2019, Bulletin, https://www.bjs.gov/content/pub/pdf/p17.pdf, accessed 8 August 2019.

CHAPTER 32 — OUR PASTORS

[1]"Pastor Salaries in the United States," *Indeed.com,* August 3, 2019, https://www.indeed.com/salaries/Pastor-Salaries, accessed 8 August 2019.

[2]"Fast Facts About American Religion," *Hartford Institute for Religion Research,* 2000-2006, http://hirr.hartsem.edu/research/fastfacts/fast_facts.html, accessed 8 August 2019.

CHAPTER 37 — THE PATHWAY TO GOD

[1]"United States Deaths Clock," *IndexMundi,* 2019, https://www.index-mundi.com/clocks/indicator/deaths/united-states, accessed 8 August 2019.

[2]George Hill, "How Many People Die in a Day on Average Worldwide?" *Quora,* March 7, 2018, https://www.quora.com/How-many-people-die-in-a-day-on-average-worldwide, accessed 8 August 2019.

CHAPTER 38 — SAVING FAITH

[1]"14 Top Quotes by Billy Sunday, the Famous American Athlete and Evangelist, *The Famous People,* https://quotes.thefamouspeople.com/billy-sunday-4671.php, accessed 8 August 2019.

[2]"How Many People Have Died in the World Since the Beginning of Time?" *Quora,* June 25, 2018, https://www.quora.com/How-many-people-have-died-in-the-world-since-the-beginning-of-time, accessed 8 August 2019.

[3]*Billy Graham: An Extraordinary Journey,* Film, Directed by Daniel Camenisch and Vonda Harrell, Charlotte, Billy Graham Evangelistic Films, 4 March 2018.

[4]Craig L. Blomberg, *The New American Commentary: Matthew* (Nashville: B & H Publishing Group, 1992).

[5]Neil Sherman, "What Did W. C. Fields Do and Say on His Death Bed?" *Quora,* October 12, 2019, https://www.quora.com/What-did-W-C-Fields-do-and-say-on-his-death-bed, accessed 8 August 2019.

[6]Billy Graham, "Spiritual Heart Disease," Billy Graham Evangelistic Association, February 6, 2018, https://billygraham.org/decision-magazine/february-2018/spiritual-heart-disease, accessed 8 August 2019.

CHAPTER 40 — HEAVEN

[1]"Heaven Is for Real" (Film), Nash Information Services, LLC, 1997-2019, *The-Numbers.com,* https://www.the-numbers.com/movie/Heaven-is-for-Real#tab=summary, accessed 11 August 2019.

[2]Caryle Murphy, "Most Americans Believe in Heaven...and Hell," *PewResearchCenter.org,* November 10, 2015, https://www.pewre-

search.org/fact-tank/2015/11/10/most-americans-believe-in-heaven-and-hell/, accessed 8 August 2019.

[3]John Burke, *Imagine Heaven: Near-Death Experiences, God's Promises, and the Exhilarating Future That Awaits You* (Grand Rapids: Baker Books, 2015).

CHAPTER 41 — HELL

[1]Caryle Murphy, "Most Americans Believe in Heaven…and Hell," *PewResearchCenter.org*, November 10, 2015, https://www.pewresearch.org/fact-tank/2015/11/10/most-americans-believe-in-heaven-and-hell/, accessed 8 August 2019.

[2]Orr, James, M.A., D.D., General Editor, "Entry for *Hades*," *International Standard Bible Encyclopedia*, 1915, *Bible Study Tools.com*, https://www.biblestudytools.com/dictionary/hades/, accessed 10 August 2019.

[3]Bill Wiese, *23 Minutes in Hell: One Man's Story About What He Saw, Heard, and Felt in that Place of Torment* (Lake Mary, Fla: Charisma House, 2006).

CHAPTER 42 — SATAN

[1]Charles Capps and Annette Capps, *Angels: Knowing Their Purpose, Releasing Their Power* (Broken Arrow, Okla.: Capps Publishing, 1984).

[2]"Satan," *BibleHub.com*, 2014-2018, https://biblehub.com/hebrew/7854.htm, accessed 8 August 2019.

[3]"Diabolos," *BibleHub.com*, 2014-2018, https://biblehub.com/str/Greek/1228.htm, accessed 8 August 2019.

[4]"Famous Quotes by Flip Wilson, *Quotes.net: The Web's Largest Resource for Famous Quotes and Sayings*, August 8, 2019, https://www.quotes.net/authors/Flip+Wilson, accessed 8 August 2019.

CONCLUSION — JESUS' OTHER SIDE

[1]W. C. Fields as quoted by Vernon Grounds. "Looking for Loopholes." *Our Daily Bread*. October 5, https://odb.org/2002/10/05/looking-for-loopholes/, accessed 8 August 2019.

BIBLIOGRAPHY

Blomberg, Craig. *The New American Commentary: Matthew.* Nashville: B & H Publishing Group, 1992.

Burke, John. *Imagine Heaven: Near-Death Experiences, God's Promises, and the Exhilarating Future That Awaits You.* Grand Rapids: Baker Books, 2015.

Cambridge University Press. *Cambridge Online Dictionary, Cambridge Dictionary* online. Retrieved August 8, 2019, from the website temoa: Open Educational Resources (OER) Portal at http://temoa.tec.mx/node/324.

Capps, Charles and Annette Capps. *Angels: Knowing Their Purpose, Releasing Their Power.* Broken Arrow, Okla.: Capps Publishing, 1984.

Dictionary.com.

"Flip Wilson Quotes." Quotes.net. STANDS4 LLC, 2019. Web. 8 Aug. 2019. <https://www.quotes.net/authors/Flip+Wilson+Quotes>.

"Heaven Is for Real (Film)," *Wikepedia, the Free Encyclopedia,* July 20, 2019, https://en.wikipedia.org/wiki/Heaven_Is_for_Real_(film)

Holman Bible Editorial Staff. *Holman Concise Bible Dictionary. Google Books.com.* https://books.google.com/books?id=eTK5AwAAQBAJ&pg=PA627&lpg=PA627&dq=physical+resources+god+gives+hu

mans+to+control&source=bl&ots=hagHp-NRZe&sig=ACfU3U3
1soYbhCz5wuqgmfFZ8_ZsSFG30g&hl=en&sa=X&ved=2ahUKE
wji07P_9brjAhWIQc0KHZT7B5oQ6AEwAXoECAkQAQ#v=one
page&q=physical%20resources%20god%20gives%20humans%20
to%20control&f=false, accessed 8 August 2019.

John, Daniel. *The Red Letter Gospel: All the Words of Jesus Christ in Red*. n.c.: Smart Publishing Ltd, 2017.

Jones, Beth Felker. *Practicing Christian Doctrine, An Introduction to Thinking and Living Theologically*. Grand Rapids: Baker Academic, 2014.

Merriam, George and Charles Merriam. *Merriam-Webster's Collegiate Dictionary*, 1999.

Murray, James, Ed., *Oxford Dictionaries*, 1884.

The Oxford Pocket Dictionary of Current English. Encyclopedia.com. https://www.encyclopedia.com.

Piper, Don and Cecil Murphey. *90 Minutes in Heaven, A True Story of Death and Life*. Grand Rapids: Revell, 2015.

Strong, James. *Strong's Exhaustive Concordance of the Bible*, 1890.

Vine, W. E. *Vine's Expository Dictionary of New Testament Words*. St. Louis: MacDonald Publishing Co., 1989.

Wiese, Bill. *23 Minutes in Hell: One Man's Story About What He Saw, Heard, and Felt in that Place of Torment*. Lake Mary, Fla: Charisma House, 2006.

Wink, Walter. *Engaging the Powers, Discernment and Resistance in a World of Domination*. Minneapolis: Fortress Press, 1992.

ACKNOWLEDGMENTS

WRITING THIS book was a much bigger project then I ever anticipated. The hundreds of hours invested in it was truly a labor of love that was motivated by an act of obedience on my part. I have no idea what it feels like to have labor pains, but completing a book would seem to cause similar pain on the one hand but tremendous joy on the other hand when it's done. That's my story, and I am sticking to it!

I want to thank the love of my life, my wife Kelley, for her patience and understanding of the enormous time commitment to finish this project. *Thank you for the grace and support you gave me on the countless nights you went to bed without me by your side as I worked into the late hours throughout this journey.*

Gregory, Kristen, Joshua, Hannah and Caleb, *thank you all for the support you gave me to make this book a reality.* You never waivered that I would see this to the end. *Love you all so much.*

Thank you to my dad, Dr. Joe Feste, for always checking in to see how the progress of the book was going. *You have always been in my corner and your encouragement never failed to motivate me just at the right moment.*

A special thanks to my business partners and dear friends, Jed Seneca and Raymond Boyd. *In spite of all the work required to build recording labels together, you always supported me, the message and the vision for this book.*

Thank you to the entire Blind Eye Worship team of Kevin Single-ton, Shauna Chanda Zimbelman, Shelley Rusk, Claire Seneca and Kev-in Click for your unwavering support and encouragement throughout the process.

Thank you, Pastors Dave Jamerson and John Blue, for your prayers and counsel that were invaluable and made all the difference in the world.

Thanks to my close friends, Richard Steffan, Allen Skinn and Larry Zimbelman, for constantly cheering me on and offering me encourag-ing words which strengthened my resolve.

As a new author, this book would not have been possible without the guidance of Angie Zachary and Linda Stubblefield of Affordable Christian Editing. Angie, as my sole editor from day one, used her un-paralleled skills to make my words flow like a river. Linda who format-ted the manuscript to come to life in as a book surpassed my wildest expectations. *Thank you both for your patience and grace and know that I am eternally grateful for your efforts and sacrifices.*

At the risk of sounding like a canned response you would hear at an awards ceremony, I am going to say it anyway but with total sincer-ity and a joyful heart. *Thank You, Jesus, for allowing a flawed human being such as myself to write about You. My love, gratitude and knowl-edge for You grew by leaps and bounds as I poured over all the words You spoke for these many months. Thank You, God, for Jesus, who is not only my Savior but the best friend I could ever have. Finally, thank You, Holy Spirit, for the revelation and strength to complete this book. Without Your presence, it would have been a labor of the mind instead of what is was—a labor of love through my heart.*